Olaf Metzel at Ein Harod

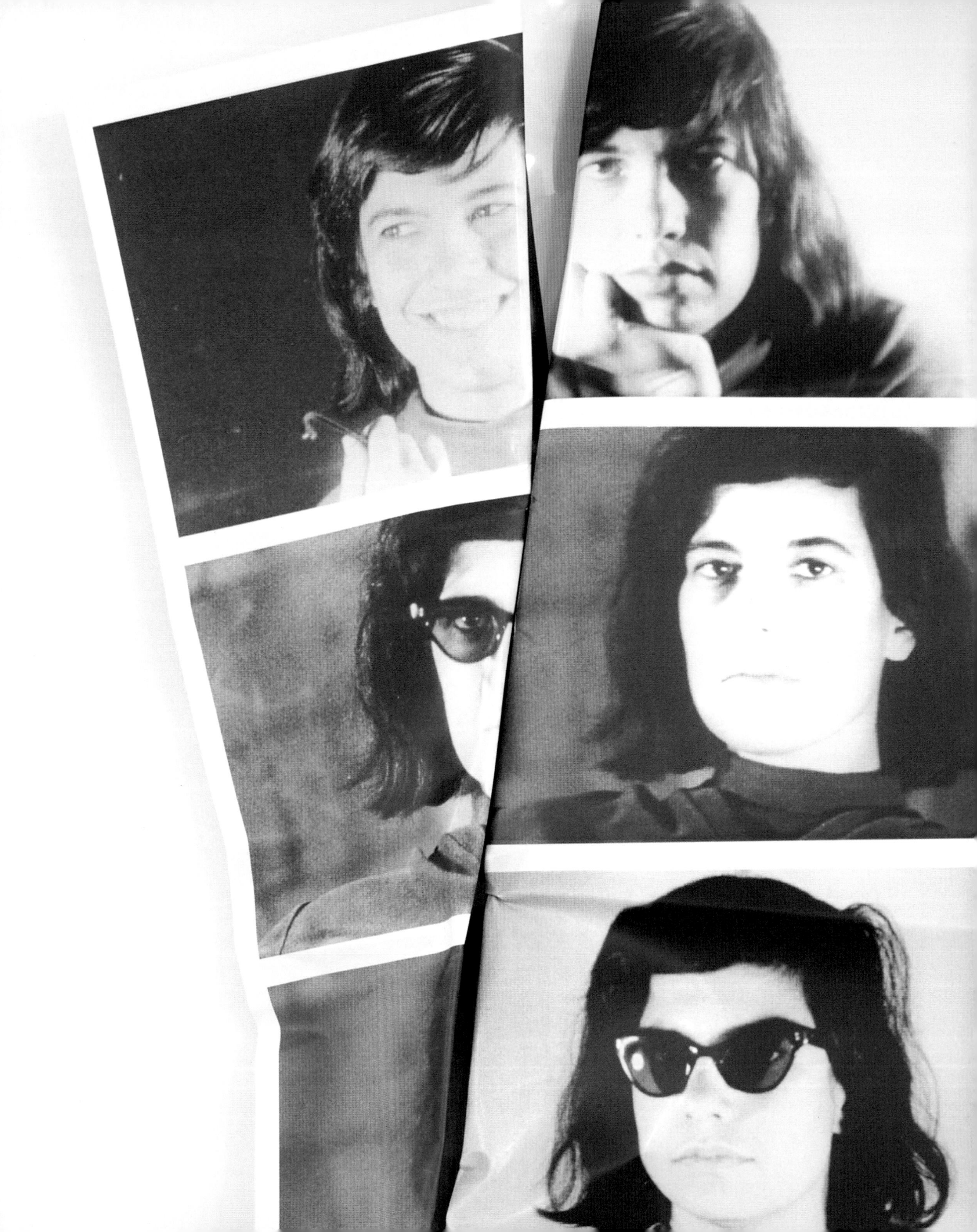

Olaf Metzel at Ein Harod

Mishkan Museum of Art, Ein Harod   March 24 to July 14, 2018

DISTANZ

Dedicated to Elisabeth Hensel

This catalogue is published
on the occasion of the exhibition
Olaf Metzel at Ein Harod
Mishkan Museum of Art, Ein Harod
March 24 to July 14, 2018

Curators: Matthias Winzen and Galia Bar Or

Editor: Matthias Winzen
Editorial work: Nina Holm
Hebrew copyediting: Ami Asher
Hebrew translation: Talya Halkin
English translation: Pauline Cumbers
English proofreading: Sarah Trenker
Design: wigel, Petra Lüer
Lithography: Reproline Genceller, Munich
Printing & binding: Druckerei Vogl, Munich
Printed in Germany

Cover: *Hannah Arendt*, 2017 (detail),
We Refugees, 2018 (detail)

Bibliographic information published
by the Deutsche Nationalbibliothek.
The Deutsche Nationalbibliothek lists this
publication in the Deutsche Nationalbibliografie;
detailed bibliographic data is available on the
Internet at http://www.dnb.de

Distribution
Edel Germany GmbH
www.edel.com
distanz@edel.com

ISBN 978-3-95476-244-6
Printed in Germany

Published by
DISTANZ Verlag
www.distanz.de

Mishkan Museum of Art, Ein Harod
Director and Chief Curator: Yaniv Shapira
Co-Director: Ayala Oppenheimer
Administration: Ayala Bessor, Nili Heller, Aya Bessor
Registration: Judith Bejerano
Conservation: Mor Tabenkin, Ion Nanu
Public Relations: Lilach Smilansky, Ofri Gardi
Technical assistance: Eyal Cohen

Thanks to

Galia Bar Or
Hans Belting
Christoph Heinrich
Yaniv Shapira
Matthias Winzen

Yuval Barel
Yaacov Chefetz
Zohar Doron
Fred Feuerstein
Matthias Glas
Boris Hoelter
Nina Holm
Wolf Iro
Galerie Parisa Kind, Frankfurt a. M.
Galerie Klüser, Munich
Claudia Kohlhoff
Petra Lüer
Constanze Metzel
Andreas Peiffer
Produzentengalerie Hamburg
Catherine Rennert
Bernd Schöppner
Galerie Florian Sundheimer, Munich
Florian Waldvogel
Wentrup Gallery, Berlin
Penny Hes Yassour
The staff of the Mishkan, Museum of Art
and the Kibbutz Ein Harod for the warm welcome

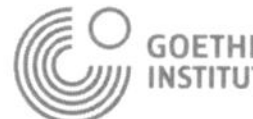

משכן לאמנות עין חרוד, ע״ש חיים אתר בע״מ (חל״צ)
Mishkan Museum of Art, Ein Harod

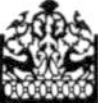

Foreword
Yaniv Shapira

The aim of our exhibition *Olaf Metzel at Ein Harod* and the accompanying catalogue is to enable the Israeli audience to become better acquainted with the breadth and depth of the oeuvre of Olaf Metzel.

Metzel is one of the most prominent German artists active today. His works include large-scale sculptural installations in urban public space, digital prints on thin metal sheets and intensely expressive drawings—all largely shaped by the circumstances of both a personal and a national biography.

The artist was born in East Berlin in the early fifties, and as a nine-year-old experienced the building of the Berlin Wall, which bisected his childhood memories overnight, erecting a barrier between childhood friends, between East and West, between what was permitted and what was forbidden. This foundational experience continues to shape his recurring preoccupation with motifs of fences and barriers, with sociopolitical discourse, with national identities and with "parallel cultures," as is articulated in his book *The Good Neighbor*, an excerpt of which is included in this catalogue:

"There was always something self-evident about the way we and the Turkish girls and boys got along, due also to the typical secrecies we shared. No one invited you to their homes—people kept to themselves at home and tended to close themselves off.... For all the liberality there was something hermetic about it, what one refers to today as parallel cultures."

It is not surprising, then, that an essential component of Metzel's work is the creation of social and cultural bridges, together with an understanding of the power of the artistic image and its ability to impact the human spirit.

This exhibition at the Mishkan Museum of Art, Ein Harod, brings together known works as well as works especially created for this occasion, following Metzel's visit to Israel in the fall of 2016. He wandered through the streets of Tel Aviv and Jerusalem, visited Ein Harod, where he participated in the exhibition *Contemporary Art from Germany*, and gathered images from Israeli public space—from Rothschild Boulevard in Tel Aviv and from the Shrine of the Book in Jerusalem. These are complemented by his fascination with the figures and thoughts of Hannah Arendt and Susan Sontag, the installation *Any More Questions?*—adjusted to the dimensions of the central hall of the museum—and *Turkish Delight*, a piece that gains additional significance in the present context. The specificity of this exhibition also stems from Metzel's sense of affinity with the Mishkan Museum of Art, Ein Harod, as a representation of human and universal values that he relates to childhood memories. According to his description of his first visit to the site, he felt that the museum and the particular atmosphere it evokes match a deep and identifiable internal cultural code: "I understood it all immediately, as if I had known it for a long time, although I had just arrived."

I would like to extend my heartfelt thanks to Olaf Metzel for our productive collaboration and open dialogue, as well as for an inspiring exhibition so rich in meanings. Special thanks to Matthias Winzen for initiating this project and serving as the curator of the exhibition, as well as for his insightful interview with Metzel, which is included in this catalogue. Many thanks to Galia Bar Or, who was an active partner in realizing this exhibition and for her text that sheds light on Metzel's oeuvre in a local and contemporary context. Thanks to the other writers, Christoph Heinrich and Hans Belting, whose articles contribute to expanding our understanding of Metzel's work. Thanks to Petra Lüer/wigel for the fine catalogue design, to Pauline Cumbers for the English translation, to Sarah Trenker for the English editing, and to Talya Halkin and Ami Asher for the Hebrew translation and editing. I thank Yuval Barel and Zohar Doron for their help in setting up the exhibition. Finally, heartfelt thanks go to my partners on the staff of the Mishkan Museum of Art, Ein Harod, for dedicating their energy and passion for art to making this important exhibition a reality.

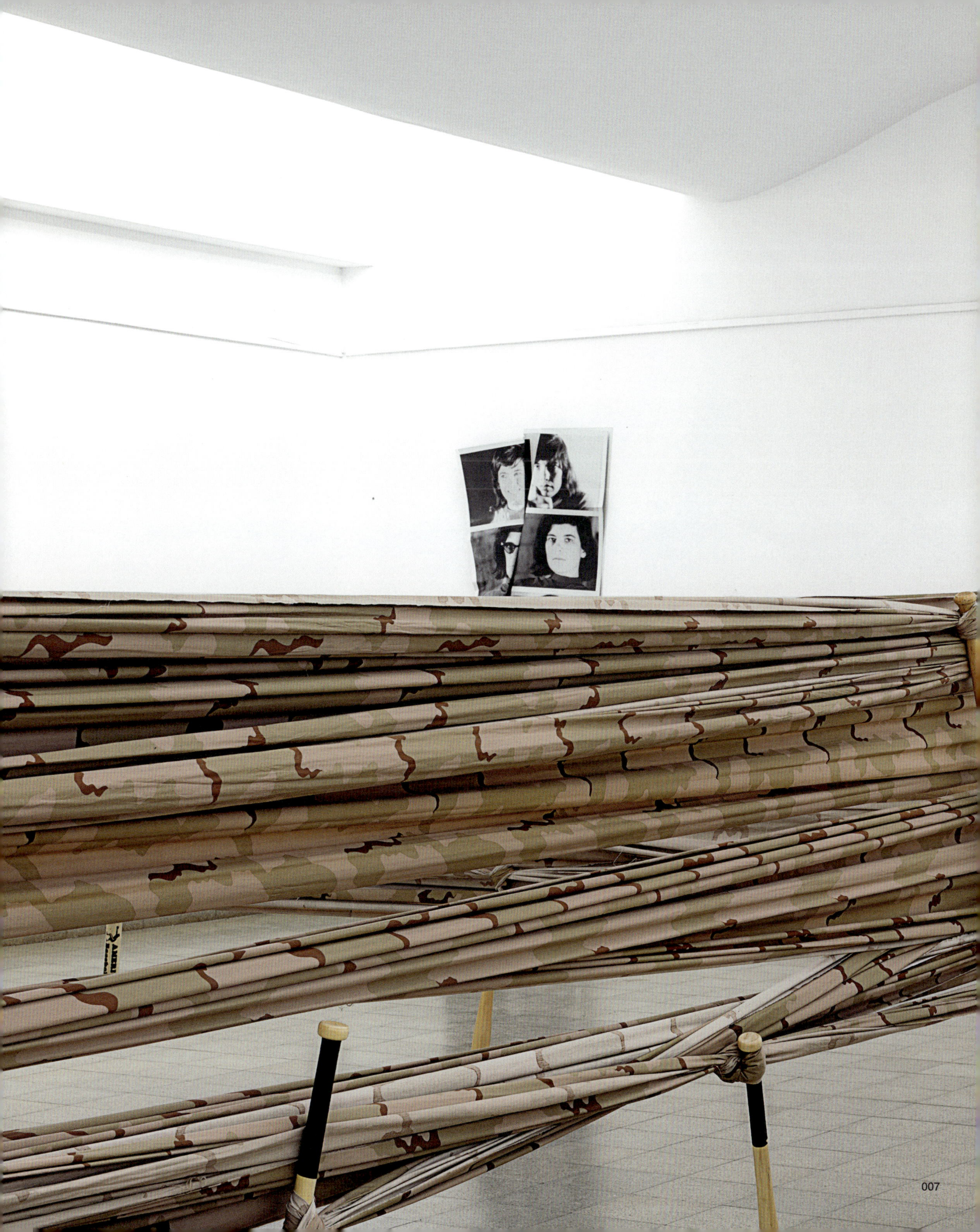

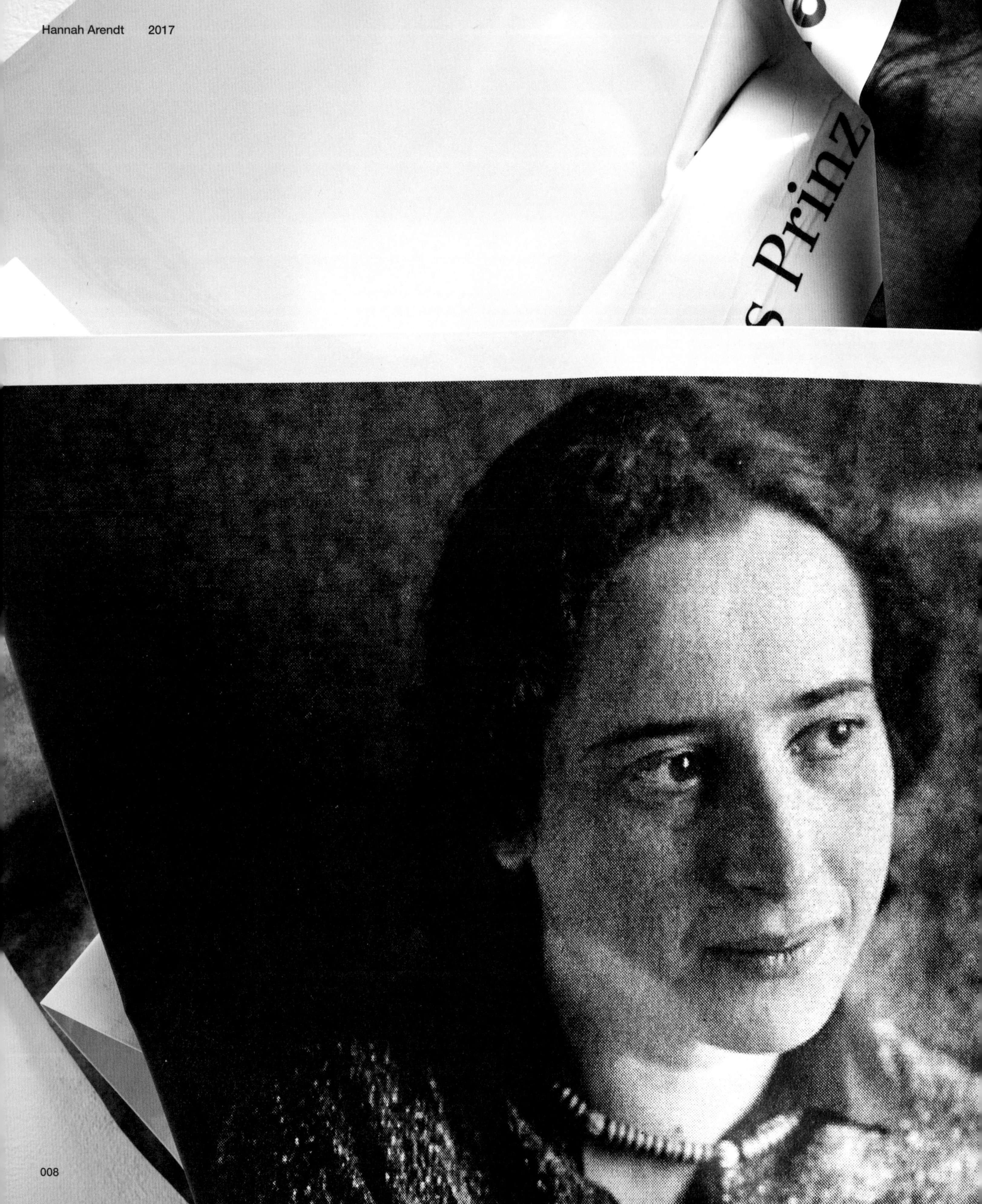
s Prinz

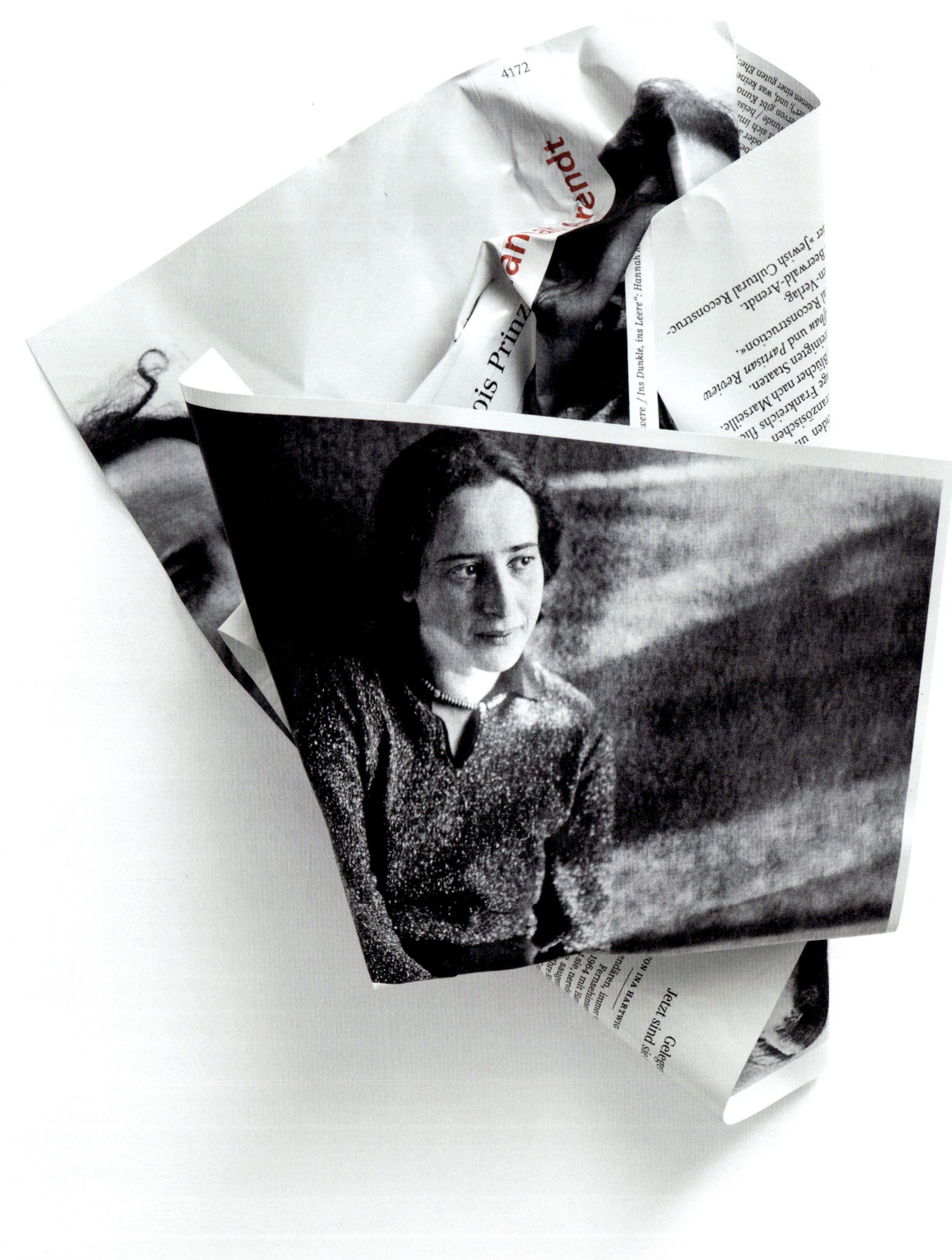

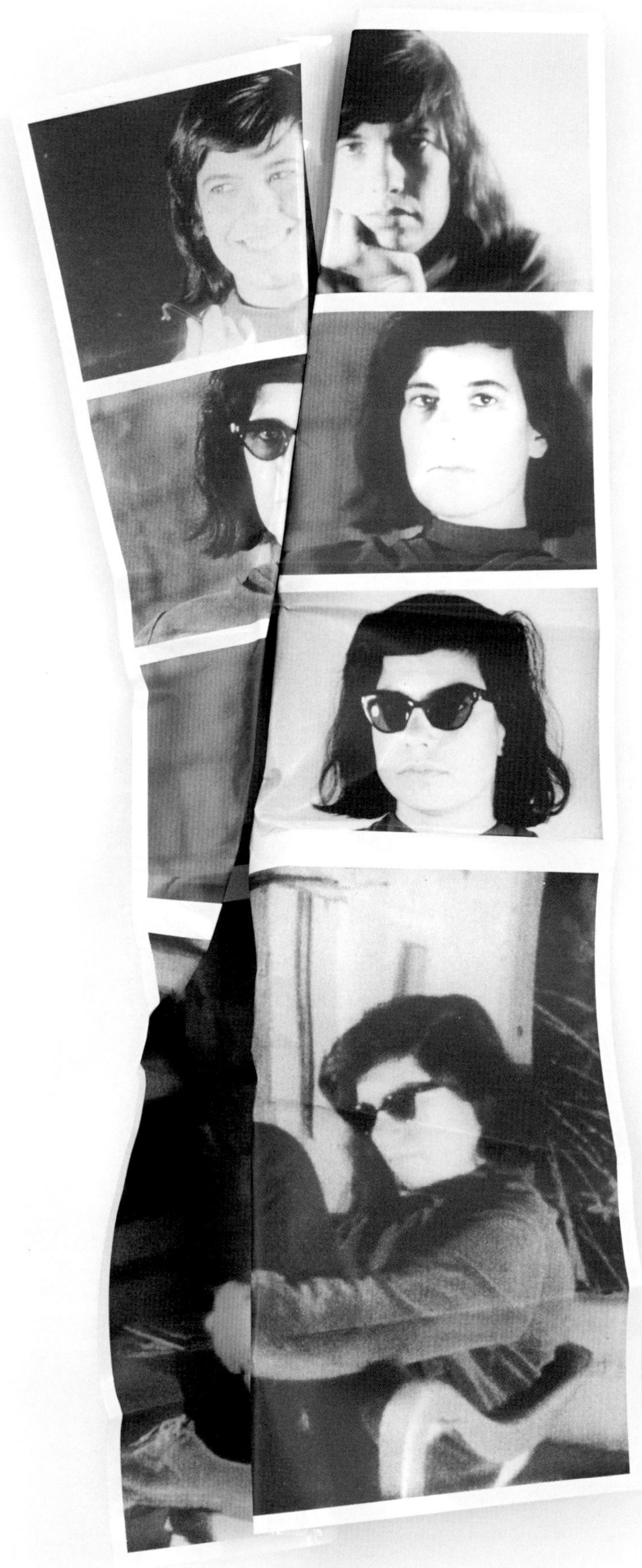

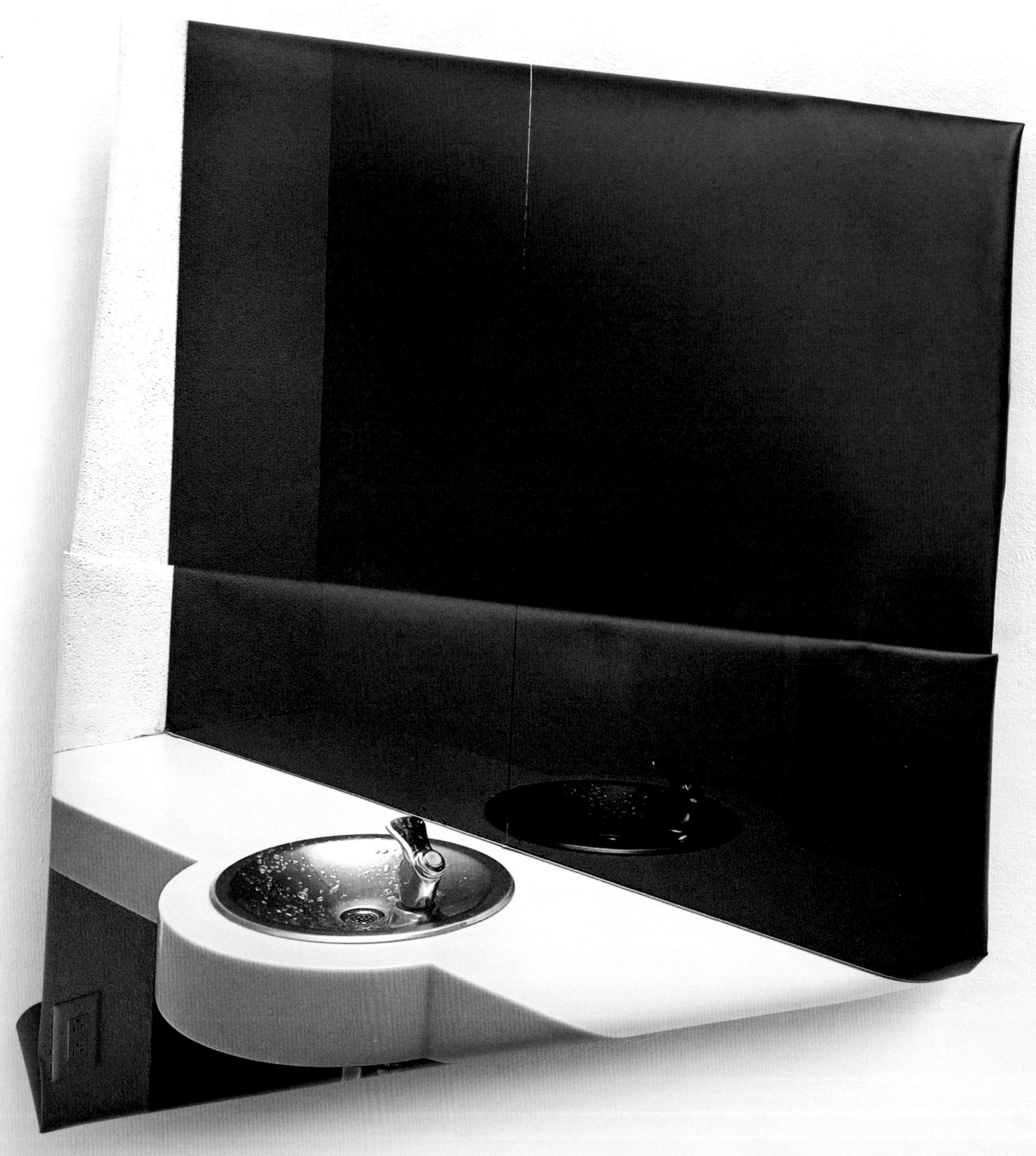

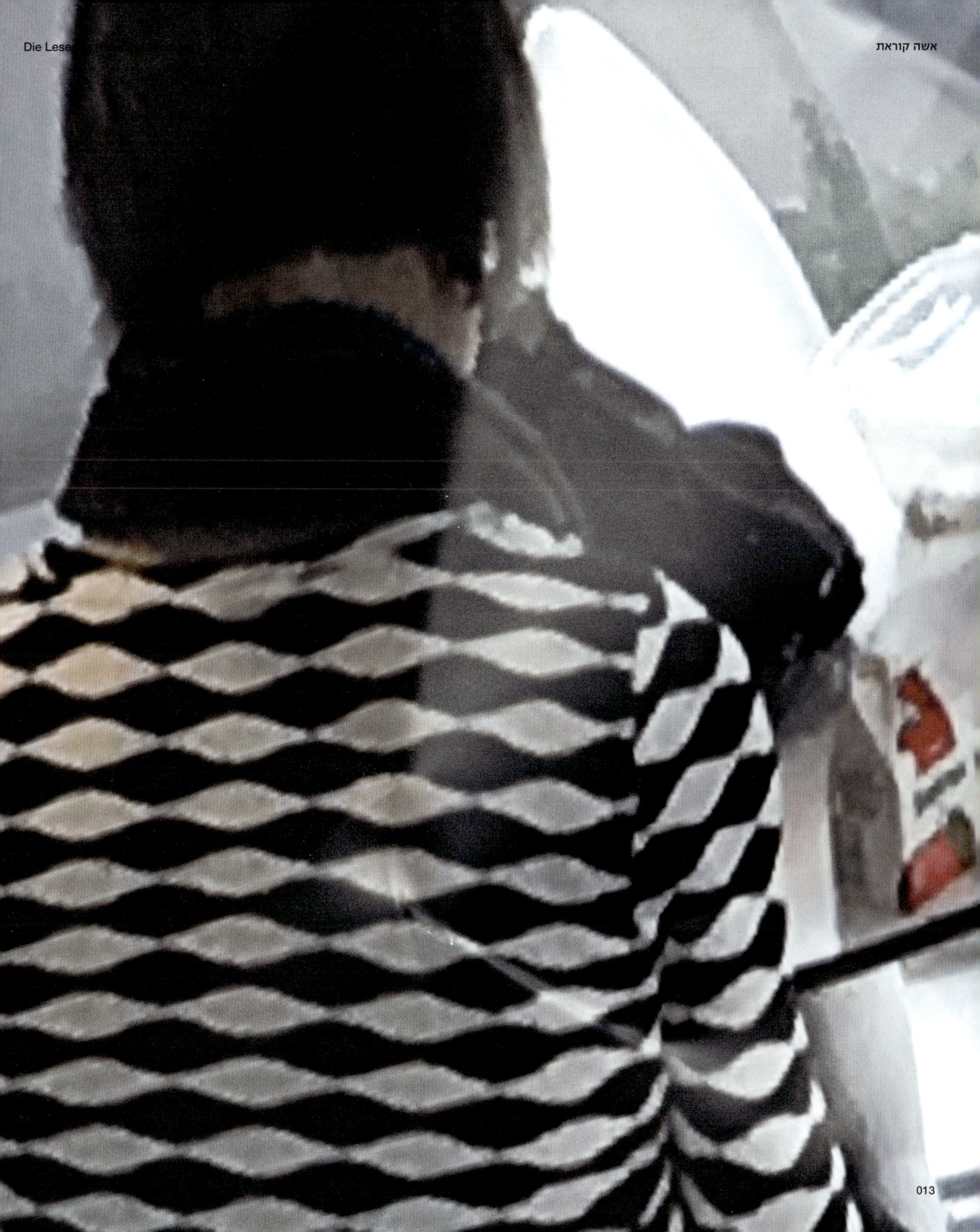

Wir Flüchtlinge (We Refugees) 2018

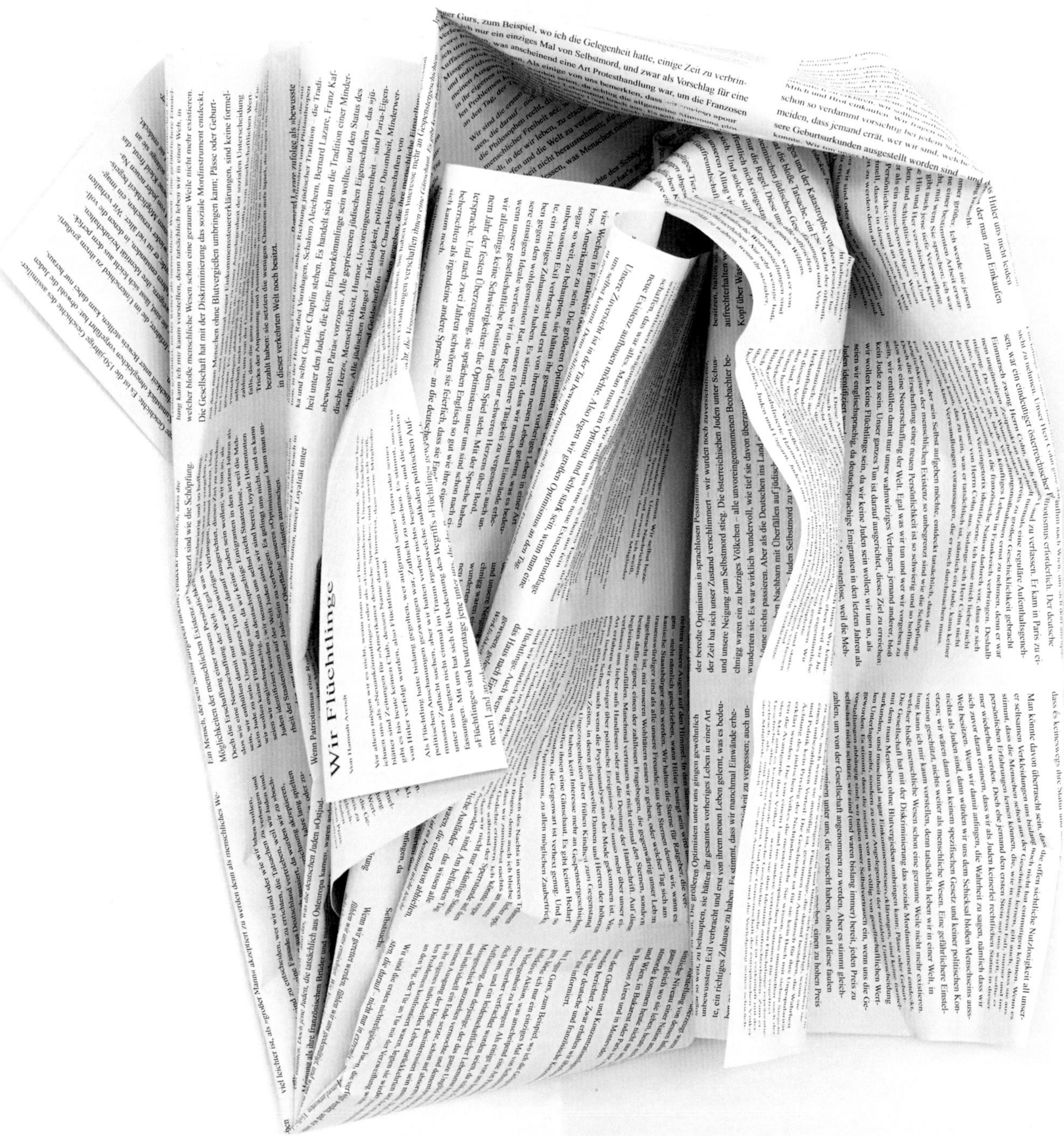

Wir Flüchtlinge

Von Hannah Arendt

Vor allem mögen wir es nicht, wenn man uns »Flüchtlinge« nennt. Wir selbst bezeichnen uns als »Neuankömmlinge« oder als »Einwanderer«. Unsere Nachrichtenblätter sind Zeitungen für »Amerikaner deutscher Sprache«; und soweit ich weiß, gibt es bis heute keinen Club, dessen Name darauf hinweist, dass seine Mitglieder von Hitler verfolgt wurden, also Flüchtlinge sind.

Als Flüchtling hatte bislang gegolten, wer aufgrund seiner Taten oder seiner politischen Anschauungen gezwungen war, Zuflucht zu suchen. Es stimmt, auch wir mussten Zuflucht suchen, aber wir hatten vorher nichts begangen, und die meisten unter uns hegten nicht einmal im Traum irgendwelche radikalen politischen Auffassungen. Mit uns hat sich die Bedeutung des Begriffs »Flüchtling« [...] »Flüchtlinge« sind heutzutage jene [...]

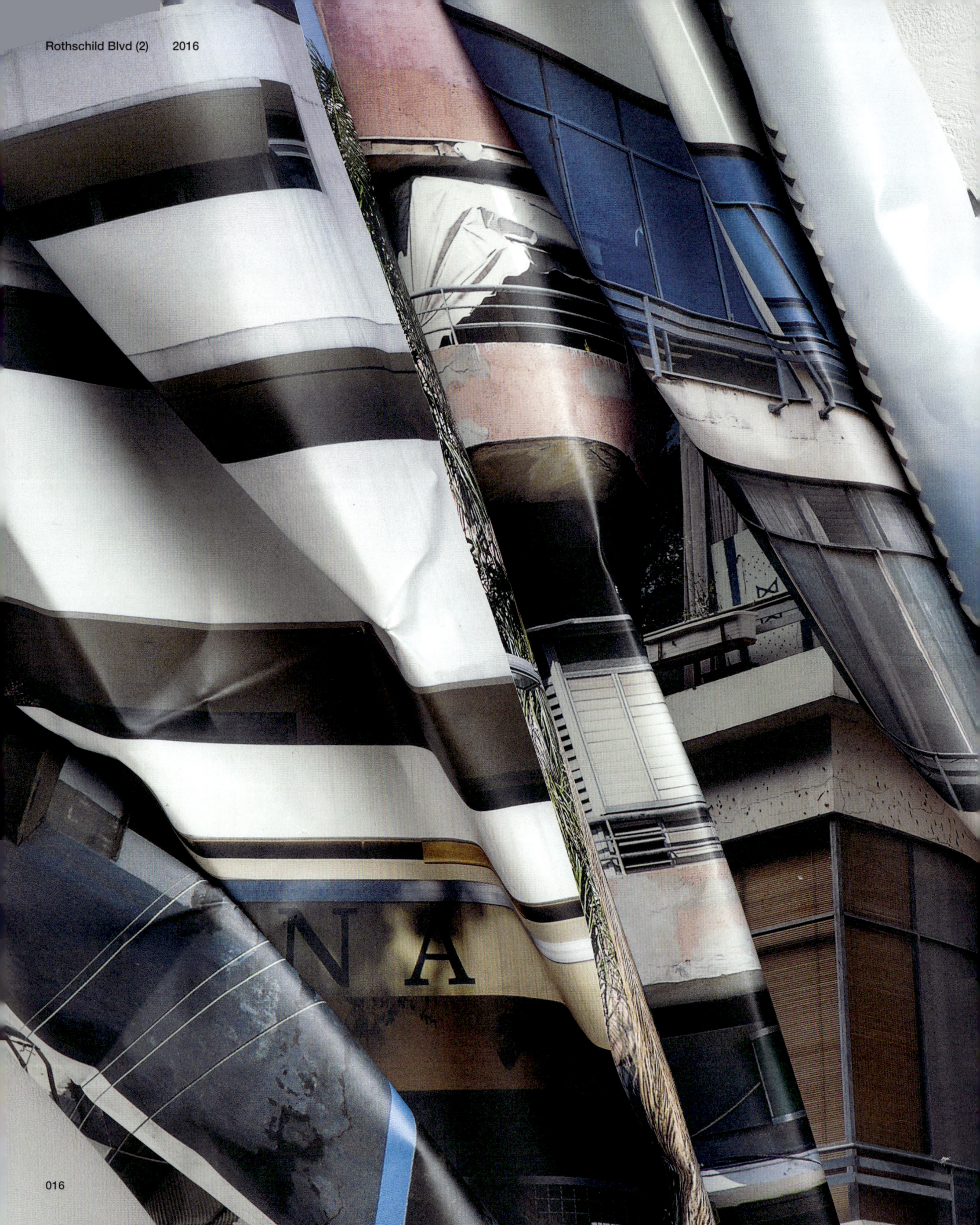
N A

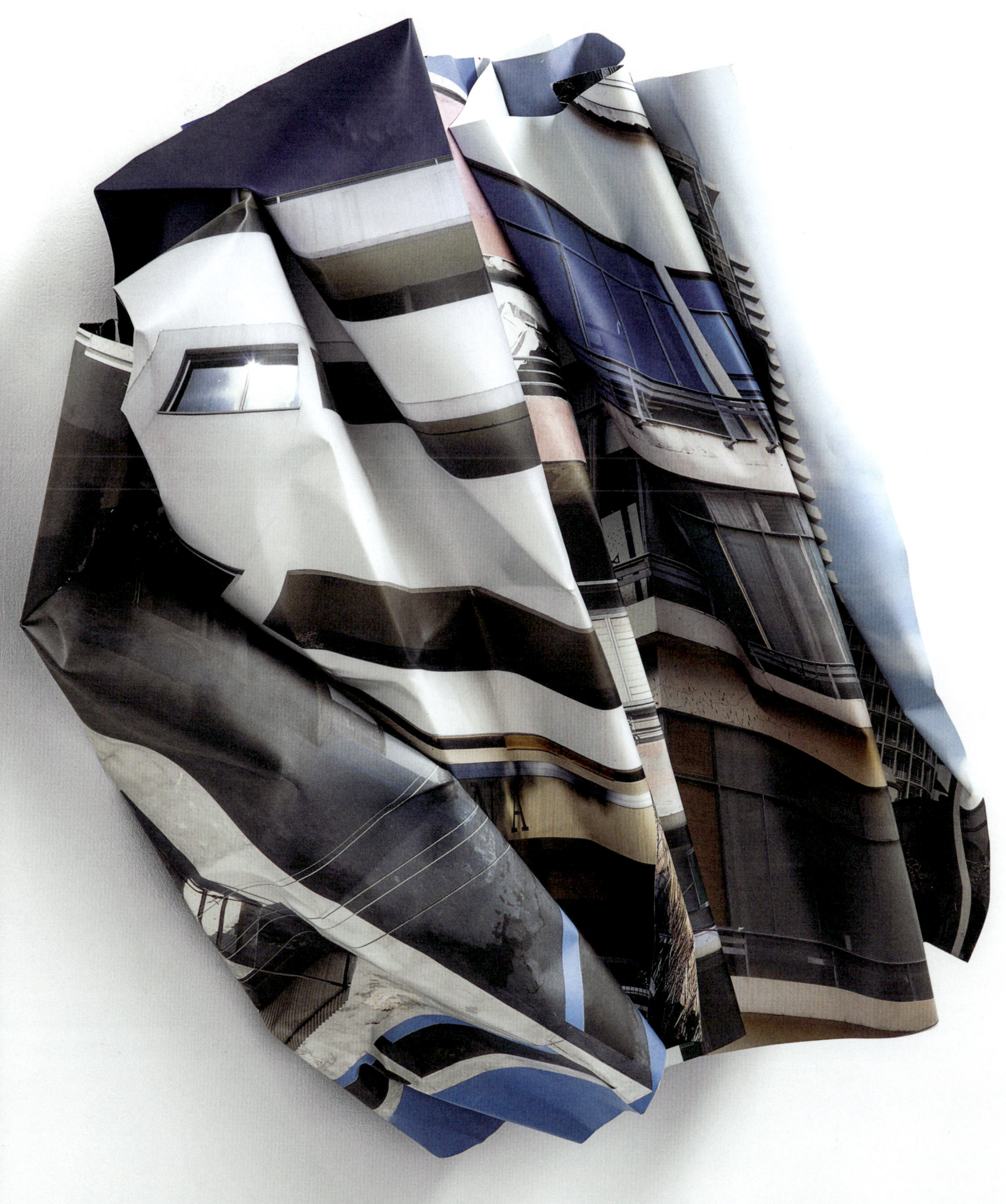

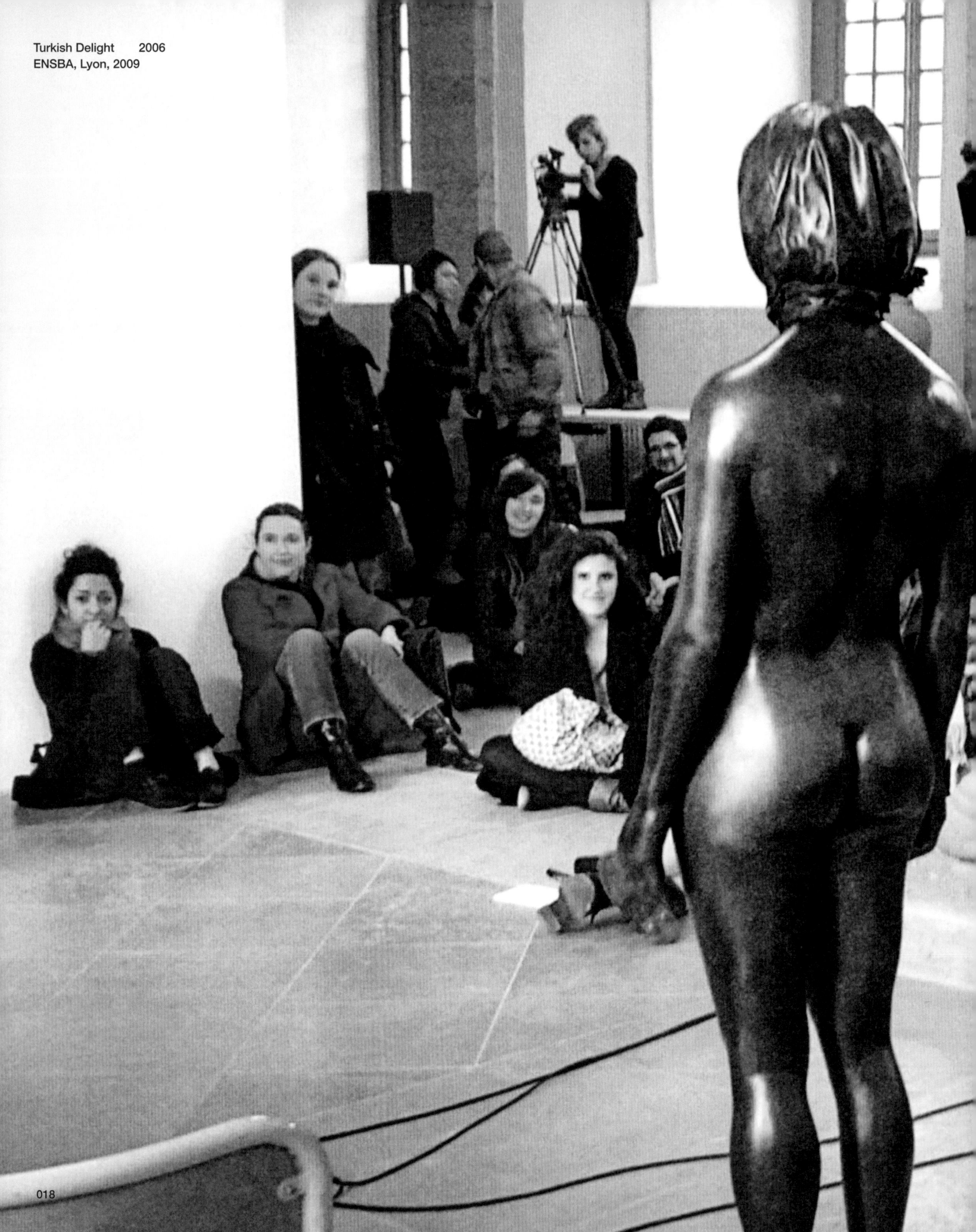

Turkish Delight 2006
ENSBA, Lyon, 2009

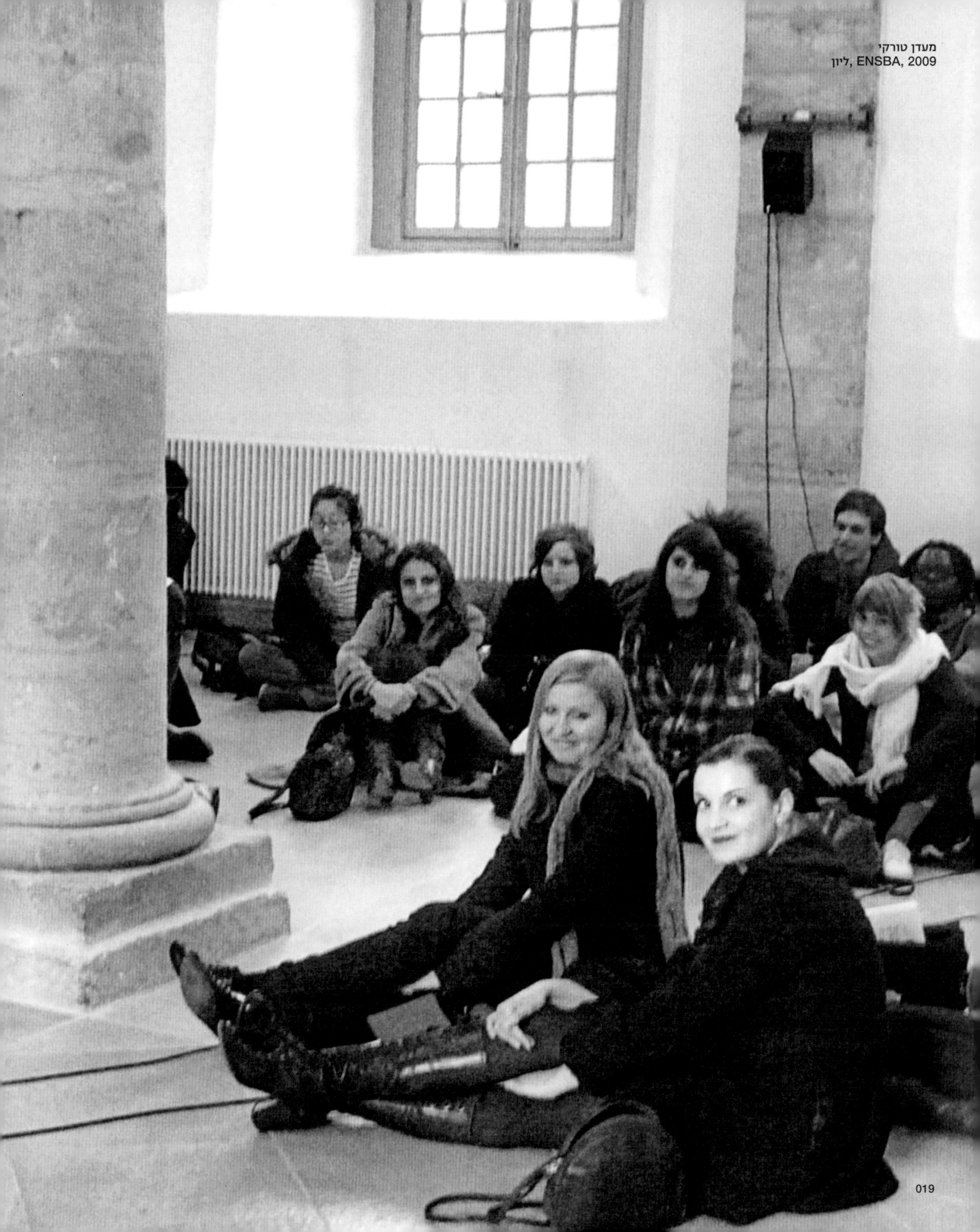

מעדן טורקי
ליון, ENSBA, 2009

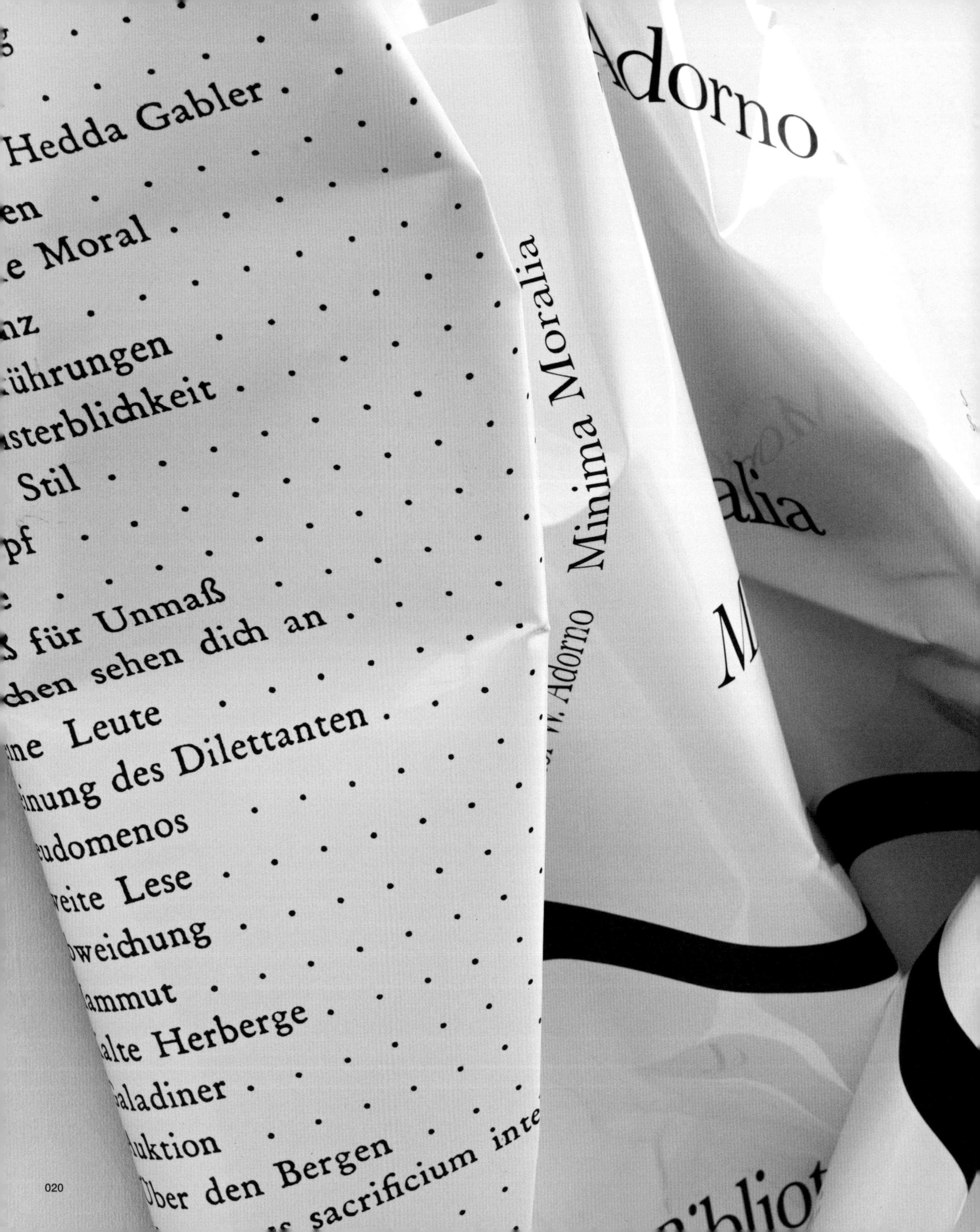

g
Hedda Gabler
en
e Moral
nz
ührungen
sterblichkeit
Stil
pf
e
für Unmaß
chen sehen dich an
ne Leute
inung des Dilettanten
eudomenos
weite Lese
oweichung
Mammut
Kalte Herberge
Galadiner
uktion
Über den Bergen
s sacrificium inte

Adorno

Minima Moralia

Th. W. Adorno

alia

M

Biblio

List of Works

Cover / pp. 008–009 / 010 / 051
Hannah Arendt
2017
Aluminum, stainless steel, digital print
165 × 128 × 40 cm

Frontispiece / 011 / 050
Susan Sontag
2017
Aluminum, stainless steel, digital print
250 × 145 × 35 cm

013 / 051 / 131
Die Lesende (Reading Woman)
2017
Aluminum, stainless steel, digital print
95 × 80 × 25 cm

014–015 / 099
Wir Flüchtlinge (We Refugees)
2018
Aluminum, stainless steel, digital print
135 × 100 × 87 cm

016 / 017, 134–135
Rothschild Blvd (2)
2016
Aluminum, stainless steel, digital print
133 × 140 × 39 cm

142 / 143
Shrine of the Book (Frederick Kiesler)
2017
Aluminum, stainless steel, digital print
165 × 145 × 35 cm

044–047 / 049 / 052 / 100–107 / 132–133 / 144
Noch Fragen? (Any More Questions?)
1998
Fabric, baseball bats
Variable sizes

018–019 / 048–049 / 144
Turkish Delight
2006
Bronze, diabase
171 × 44 × 30 cm

012 / 137
Mirror
2017
Aluminum, stainless steel, digital print
118 × 103 × 17 cm

Back Cover, 139, 140–141
We Refugees
2018
Aluminum, stainless steel, digital print
127 × 145 × 25 cm

020 / 136
Minima Moralia (Theodor Adorno)
2017
Aluminum, stainless steel, digital print
128 × 150 x 42 cm
(not in the exhibition)

148
Rothschild Blvd
2016
Marble, aluminum, stainless steel, digital print
133 × 140 × 39 cm
(not in the exhibition)

רשימת עבודות

כריכה / עמ' 008–009 / 010 / 051
חנה ארנדט
2017
אלומיניום, פלדת אלחלד, הדפסה דיגיטלית
165 × 128 × 40 ס"מ

איור שער / 011 / 050
סוזן זונטג
2017
אלומיניום, פלדת אלחלד, הדפסה דיגיטלית
250× 145 × 35 ס"מ

013 / 051 / 131
אשה קוראת
2017
אלומיניום, פלדת אלחלד, הדפסה דיגיטלית
95 × 80 × 25 ס"מ

014–015 / 099
אנו הפליטים
2018
אלומיניום, פלדת אלחלד, הדפסה דיגיטלית
135 × 100 × 87 ס"מ

016 / 017 / 134–135
שד' רוטשילד 2
2016
אלומיניום, פלדת אלחלד, הדפסה דיגיטלית
133 × 140 × 39 ס"מ

142 / 143
היכל הספר (פרדריק קיסלר וארמן ברטוס)
2017
אלומיניום, פלדת אלחלד, הדפסה דיגיטלית
165 × 145 × 35 ס"מ

044–047 / 049 / 052 / 100–107 / 132–133/ 144
יש עוד שאלות?
1998
בד, מחבטי בייסבול
ממדים משתנים

018–019 / 048–049 / 144
מעדן טורקי
2006
ברונזה, סלע דיאבז
171 × 44 × 30 ס"מ

012 / 137
מראה
2017
אלומיניום, פלדת אלחלד, הדפסה דיגיטלית
118 × 103 × 17 ס"מ

כריכה אחורית / 139 / 140–141
אנו הפליטים
2018
אלומיניום, פלדת אלחלד, הדפסה דיגיטלית
127 × 145 × 25 ס"מ

020 / 136
מינימה מורליה (תיאודור אדורנו)
2017
אלומיניום, פלדת אלחלד, הדפסה דיגיטלית
128 × 150 × 42 ס"מ
(לא מוצגת בתערוכה)

148
שד' רוטשילד
2016
שיש, אלומיניום, פלדת אל-חלד, הדפס דיגיטלי
ס"מ 133 × 140 × 39

"Stop, leave it just like that!" A Conversation between Olaf Metzel and Matthias Winzen

Matthias Winzen
Do you enjoy being provocative?

Olaf Metzel
No. Why? Should I? Anyone who feels provoked hasn't understood or doesn't want to understand. Besides, you cannot plan something like that. While I'm working I don't constantly consider who I might annoy. I try to narrow down themes and out of that develop works which, for me, are new and different. If you do that consistently, then the result can often be seen as radical or provocative.

MW
But, for example, when you placed the bronze sculpture *Turkish Delight,* of a naked women with a headscarf, on Karlsplatz in Vienna in 2007, some people were so enraged that one night they knocked the sculpture down. This even had damaging implications for Viennese-Turkish relations. That wasn't a surprise, was it?

OM
But I was surprised, nevertheless. We had actually considered all aspects in advance and organized a panel discussion in Vienna. I had pointed out the historical controversy, and the depiction of women, by Delacroix, for example, in Ingres's famous painting *The Turkish Bath*. In the nineteenth century those exotic fashions were sometimes almost lewd. I combined those historical aspects with what is to be seen today in everyday life. Veiled women have to walk a few steps behind their men and do not have much of a say in public. In former times, when women in Berlin Kreuzberg used to wear headscarves, it was because they had wet hair after swimming. What is more, I was attracted to the classical motif in sculpture of the standing female nude. I tried to condense all that into one image. Women think the work is great, it is only the old machos who complain.

MW
You worked on the figure in you studio, with a model, in a relatively classical way, whereby the young women looks quite natural rather than sublime.

OM
When you work with a living model you notice that, after a certain time, the model alters her pose and her gaze becomes very distant. And to avoid monumentality, the figure should not be as large as life and not idealized. As a result, the impact was not one of perfection—Hellenist, classical, classicist, or whatever—but just ordinary. Then there were the numerous headscarf studies; there are many types of headscarf and they can be worn in very different ways.

MW
Which way of working comes easiest to you? Bending metals or other materials, or modeling portraits in clay, or drawing? You have made larger groups of works using all these techniques.

OM
Nothing comes easy to me. First you move the work in your mind from right to left, then up and back, and then you get annoyed when it doesn't work. Although I've been doing this now for decades, each time is a new beginning. Of course I have assistants, but it is important for me to have a hand in it all. It doesn't matter which medium—wood, steel, concrete, aluminum or digital techniques—I choose the appropriate material in keeping with the theme. That's it really. I always hope that in the end it looks easy to the viewer.

MW
When you say something doesn't work, what is your criterion?

OM
When you become involved in a new project it's always a journey into the unknown. You are torn between aspiration and implementation. Usually things turn out differently to what you planned. The free scope you attain while realizing the work is exciting because you just don't know where the path is leading and where it will end up.

MW
And during that working process, what is your criterion for "interesting," or above all for "unsuccessful"? Too easily recognizable, too much artistic intentionality?

OM
This is where drawing comes into play. I begin with that. I try to circle round the theme associatively, to grasp an idea, a formal solution. I also do this so as not to lose track of the project and come to an impasse.

MW
But what exactly is your criterion, or the trigger to reconsider?

OM
It simply looks awful. This has to do with the experiences you have had and repeatedly have. Meantime, I see what works and what doesn't right away. Sometimes, with certain forms or combinations, you see something that you yourself cannot really outline yet. Then you say to yourself: So, let's put that away, in a far corner, cover it up. After six months you take it out again and suddenly see how it can be continued, and possibly you combine the half-finished work with another work on which you had also made no progress. Often, one and one then make three. And then you are somewhere you didn't believe you would ever get to.

MW
At first glance, your works can give the impression that they were randomly dropped there, that they have burst through

from somewhere else, or just happened to turn out that way. On closer examination, however, their very precisely calculated composition and proportions become visible. The "Newspaper Works" often have the compositional mobility of Italian Baroque painting. The tilted diagonals of *112:104* recall Caspar David Friedrich's *Failed Hope*.

OM
That a work is just right, that the impression is powerful, but that the whole thing looks unconstrained and not too deliberate, is something you only succeed in achieving when you manage to say: "Stop, leave it just like that!" at the right moment. In my case, this way of working is like being in a palazzo and going from one door to the next. One double door opens after the other until everything is dark. There is another door there or there is none. And at some point you go through the last door and the work is finished. My assistants know this. When will he stop? How and where will he stop? Or will he go on? Of course you can always make a mess of things—that happens.

MW
What is the main thing about the "Newspaper Works" in your view, crumpling the paper, distorting the article, the effect of force, the moment of destruction? Or is it the arrangement, or the composition? Often the smashed works have a rhythm and an elegance of their very own.

OM
Just for the record, I don't only use newspapers as material, but also photographs and collages. You have to think of them as a visual diary. Now to your question: you shouldn't work around the nicest bits. They need to be squashed first. That is the only way to make progress. The moment it looks finished is when I really start. I am interested in the possibilities of sculpture. For me personally, sculpture is the medium that enables me to make a strong impact through its spatial presence, unlike painting. When something is bent or cut then, in itself, it refers to aggression and force, even if that is only the technical working of the material. The materiality become increasingly clearer. For example, when I bend a piece of aluminum that is already folded. If it is folded like a piece of paper. You can do that twice. The third time it becomes more solid and sturdy. If you then turn it in on itself, it becomes really heavy and also dicey. You can only do that by hand, not by machine. And so of course you automatically develop a very different motoric skill. The motif is distorted or disappears, or else a view of the back a of printed aluminum plate which was not visible until then is turned to the fore and suddenly plays along. Technically working the thing then results in a new composition. Sometimes, but sometimes not.

MW
If you bend it once too often, you can throw it away?

OM
One of my works is called *Only the Waste Bin is Thrown Away.* When something doesn't work it preys on you. I have to go on trying, turning it differently, folding it this way and that, bending, or else smashing it up. In New York I photographed a waste bin at the side of the road with a few crumpled bits of newspaper in it and then used the photograph as the starting point for a work: crumpled newspaper as an image of printed aluminum plates that themselves look like crumpled newspaper. What is real, what is illusion? Some people thought I had photographed a work of my own and made the next work out of it. In fact at first sight the waste bin in New York looked as if someone had skilfully copied a work by me using real newspaper. Maybe that is why I noticed it in the first place. In the case of such works the question quickly arises as to whether they are "genuine or illusionistic," like facts or fake news on the news market.

MW
You are regarded as a "political artist." Do you think that designation describes you properly?

OM
No. I'm tired of hearing about this moral domination/patronizing of art, this political leveling, when art is used for particular aims. When I'm asked about the political aspect of my art, all I can do is ask back: What on earth is "political art"? I prefer the black square to the red flag.

MW
So there are no social references at all in Olaf Metzel's work?

OM
On the contrary, there are many, but not as politically correct guidelines for the viewer. A work must always go beyond one's own experience: on the one hand there is the experience of the viewer in front of a multifaceted and ambiguous work of art that challenges him to think himself, and on the other there are my experiences in the society in which I live. Some of the critics writing about my most recent works believed that the large reliefs of crumpled newspaper turned up at precisely the same point in time as the news business migrated to the Internet. The irony here is that those works can only be made using digital technology.

MW
The acceleration in the Internet causes constant pressure that taxes man's capacity to perceive. That pressure is further increased by the fact that the news and the information are accompanied by images that are in turn being constantly replaced by new images, or else are films in the first place. A while back that was called a flood of images, but that designation seems to me to be almost too harmless for this permanent mental overload.

OM
I experience the daily inundation of news and images as if I were traveling on a train. It gets faster and faster and at some point I feel the need to pull the emergency brake. And the train stops abruptly. Then it starts again. But what really interests me is that moment when everything stops, that "still." And a "still" an artist took in 1984 is different from a "still" taken in 1994, 2004 or 2018.

MW
A work by you, that is to say, an individual work of art, is a "still"?

OM
Yes, a frozen moment. I try to capture that moment. And it also contains all the backgrounds, meaning a certain mood of the time, certain social problems, as in *Turkish Delight* or *Noch Fragen?* The social and the political are allusions, but for me the realization of the sculpture or installation is always in the foreground. I am delighted if it still works and interests people thirty years later. That became clear to me again recently when I showed *112:104*, the shattered basketball field. It is not a really basketball field. It is pure sculpture, as it were, the artificiality of art. I made a new sports gym floor and cut it up according to a precise plan, altering and distorting the measurements. It consists of large heavy planks which four people can scarcely lift. Needless to say, the construction should never collapse, even if it looks as if it might. On the one hand, I was thinking of Caspar David Friedrich's *Failed Hope* in the Hamburger Kunsthalle, and on the other the situation during the game, the aggression when not ice floes but two teams clash. And that strange ambiguity when teams are spurred on by fans and physically charge at one another, and those aggressions often still prevail even after the game is over.

MW
You have exhibited a lot abroad and often developed the works in the respective country, be it France, Italy, Austria or Turkey. In 1995 in Istanbul you worked together with the football club Besiktas for an installation. What does the society of the host country mean for your art? Is it a kind of resonance chamber, like a guitar, and is the work of art a string? Let's see how it vibrates!

OM
When you arrive in a country as a foreigner, you see it differently. You would like to observe and understand as much as possible. A long time ago I had an argument with Hans Haacke, who for forty years has been Germany's artistic-moral conscience from his base in New York. I said to him: Hans, you can't sit in New York and pick out topics from the *Spiegel* which you then illustrate and exhibit in Germany. The behavior patterns, the tensions, the humor in a country are something you grasp on the street, in the pub, in everyday life. How do people treat one another? Who's in charge? What do the ads look like? Without a grasp of this, everything about the art quickly becomes sterile.

When I am a guest somewhere I like to engage with the respective art history of the location. In the Sadberk Hanim Museum in Istanbul, for example, I looked at Ottoman tiles, pots, vases, patterns and structures. Recently in Naples I stood for a whole hour in front of a painting by Caravaggio—how he got the subtle tensions into his painting, how he created such spatial depth with apparent ease, adding some light here and some darkness there. You can't figure that out quickly. In Jerusalem I was overwhelmed by the Shrine of the Book by Friedrich Kiesler and Armand Bartos. How do you achieve such a link between sculpture and architecture?

MW
On your advance trip to the exhibition in Ein Harod you also visited the old town of Jerusalem and Tel Aviv.

OM
In Tel Aviv I found that the Bauhaus idea of a city layout has been implemented more comprehensively than anywhere else. The Rothschild Boulevard with the row of trees down the middle strip, the partly dilapidated classical modern facades with their melancholic grandeur, beside well-restored buildings, the life, the kiosks—all of it engendering a Mediterranean metropolis, quite apart from the fact that Tel Aviv is a really thriving large city. When you go for a meal you become aware of the mix, kosher and oriental cuisine, Mediterranean and Russian, even German. I was very impressed by that. Rothschild Boulevard was the starting point for some new works of mine.

MW
The architect and urban planner Genia Averbuch was one of those strong women who shaped the newly emerging district in the nineteen-thirties and forties. You have dedicated one of your works to another famous woman who engaged with the murderous guilt of the Germans as dealt with in front of the district court in Jerusalem in 1961: Hannah Arendt.

OM
I discovered Hannah Arendt through Heidegger. I was interested not in their special relationship but in her texts. *We Refugees*, a slim Reclam volume, is still of major relevance. Then there is the interview between her and Günther Gaus on German television in 1964. You may know it—the two of them almost blotted one another out with cigarette smoke.

The starting point for the three-part work was a portrait photograph of Arendt. I complemented that with photographs I took in New York. A woman sitting in a café reading—you can still see the used plastic dishes. It's not clear whether she is reading a book or a magazine or busy with her iPhone. To the left is the motif of a mirror from the toilet of the Guggenheim Museum. It is black, and the square becomes a trapezium as a result of the view from the side.

For me, Susan Sontag is as fascinating as Hannah Arendt. Her essays on photography are classics and you simply cannot avoid engaging with them again and again. In the past there were machines, usually near railway stations, where you could have passport photos taken and often people performed for fun behind the curtain. Then the machine spat out a narrow strip with the portraits and sometimes the funny faces as well.

MW
On that same trip you got involved quickly in topical art political debates in Israel.

OM
I was invited to lectures and the subsequent discussions were always quite emotional. I liked that. Then I looked at the old city of Jerusalem, the Armenian, Jewish, Muslim and Christian quarters. The Temple of the Mount was not accessible. The tension there—it is oppressive and it is very hard to understand why it worked once in the past and why it no longer works today.

MW
You were born in Berlin so you are familiar with everyday life with demarcation lines.

OM
Divided once and then divided again. The Berlin Wall ran right through the city. I was a child when it was built—how old was I, nine? And the playground—in those days it was called a pioneer park—was in the East, where many of my friends lived. I could see from our kitchen window that the wall had been built over night. I couldn't understand it at all. My friend lived on the other side of the street. He was in the East. I never saw him again.

MW
That was surely an experience ...

OM
... that you can never forget. Then, after decades, when the Wall was gone, everything was open again—that was also really something. At the time I was in Canada and had an exhibition in the power plant in Toronto. Prior to the opening I was back in the hotel changing and the television was running, and I thought: Oh, I would never have thought that Hollywood could get that across so convincingly. I had been on the road for quite some time and had not really followed the story of the end of the division. When you look at television in the United States, ads, film and news run seamlessly into one another. But that evening, during the opening, everyone was asking: Have you heard? I had actually seen it, but I didn't believe it!

MW
What were your first impressions of Ein Harod?

OM
After traveling by car from the airport I was suddenly in front of the Mishkan Museum, that wonderful building by Samuel Bickels. I was so impressed by the serene authority and elegance of the building. It was accessible, practical—pure modernism and not prettified later through strange overhauls. Library, café, museum rooms with incredibly subtle and unobtrusive natural lighting. Books. Works of art, reading, looking, thinking—all under one roof. That's the kind of culture I like. I had in no way expected to arrive in this way after the long journey. It was a very powerful impression. Whereby the building does not have an overwhelming style, but rather a finely tuned easy combination of inside and out, peace and openness.

MW
You would scarcely expect to find a building like that in a kibbutz.

OM
No. Although the museum does somehow fit into the archaic landscape around Ein Harod. But of course the other sight I also remember is the barrier with the guards at the entrance to the kibbutz, a strange reminder of my hometown Berlin during my childhood, wall, barbed wire, armed guards, etc. As a Berliner, I lived long enough with that sort of thing: show your ID, check, harassment or not, barrier raised. It was somehow unreal to be reminded so unexpectedly of such a repressed routine. In my view the Mishkan Museum stands for authentic modernism and its ideals. You could see individual buildings like that in the destroyed and divided Berlin of my childhood. And there was also the grey everyday with barriers and checks. This double flashback on arriving in Ein Harod unleashed in me something like in *À la recherche du temps perdu.*

MW
Like Marcel Proust and the little cake that suddenly reminded him of his childhood.

OM
In a very different form of course. But those first impressions were strongly linked with memories of childhood and adolescence. I had the feeling that the museum and its particular atmosphere, the place, the kind of culture—that I understood it all immediately, as if I had known it for a long time, although I had just arrived. As a child I was brought up not only by my mother—who was very ill unfortunately—but also by her best friend, who, as a Jew had flown to the United States, but who came back to help her.

MW
You were brought up by a Jewish women who had escaped being murdered in Berlin two decades previously.

OM
You could say that. Her subtle way of putting something, her quiet humor, her thoughts about Israel, which she never visited, I remember all that. And the many cigarettes she smoked. Only later did I realize that I just had to go to Israel at some point and engage with that country. For me Ein Harod is a very special place.

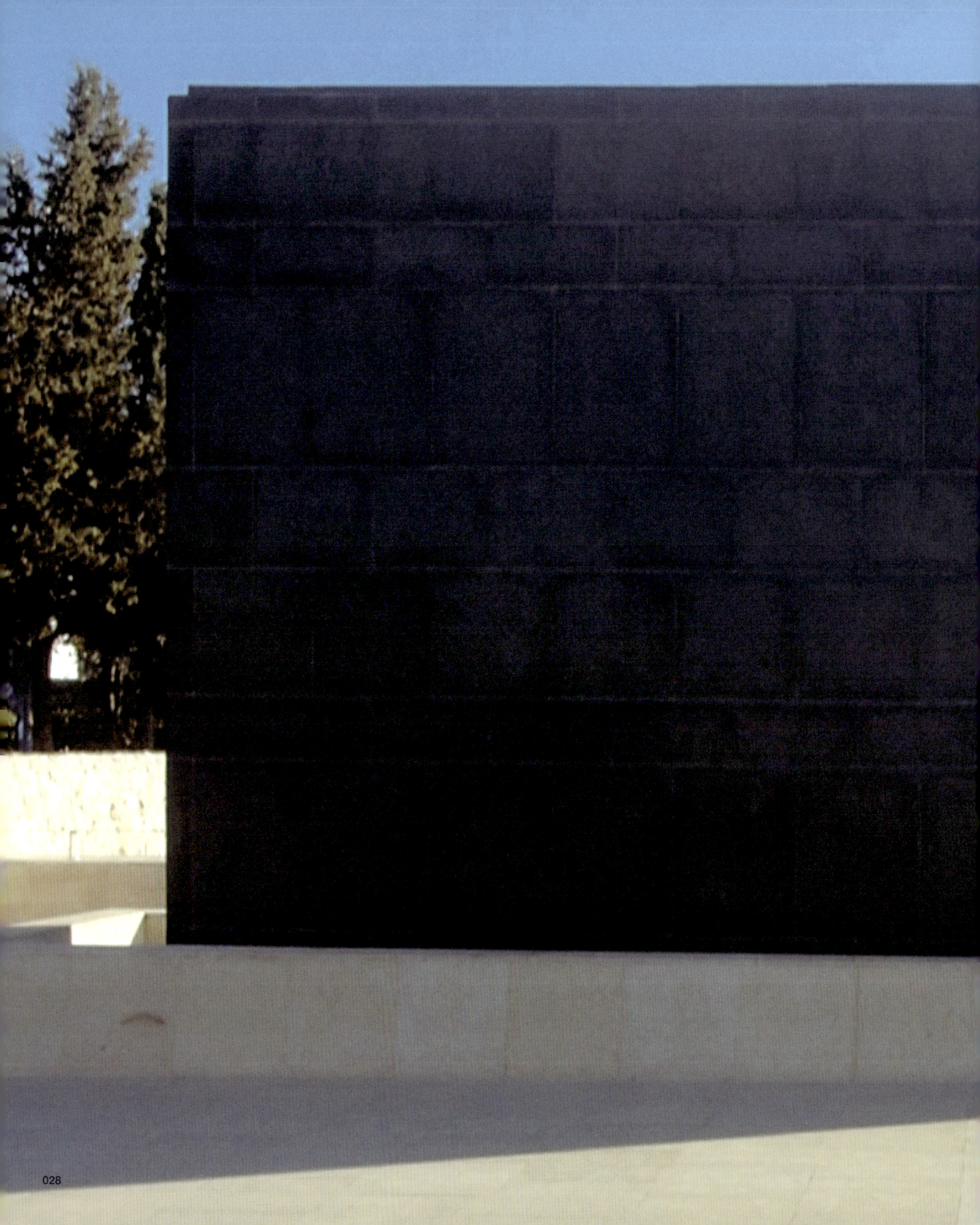

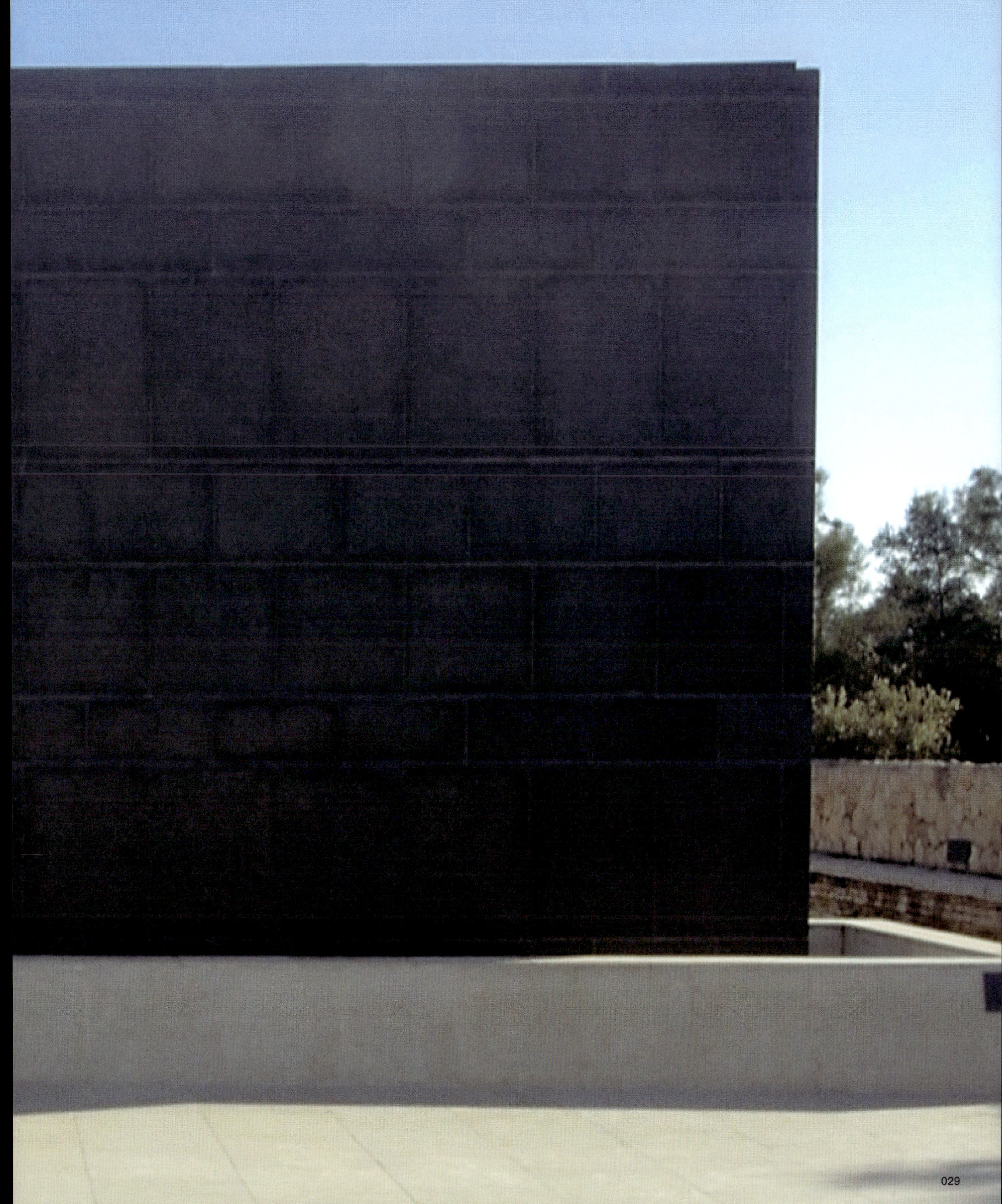

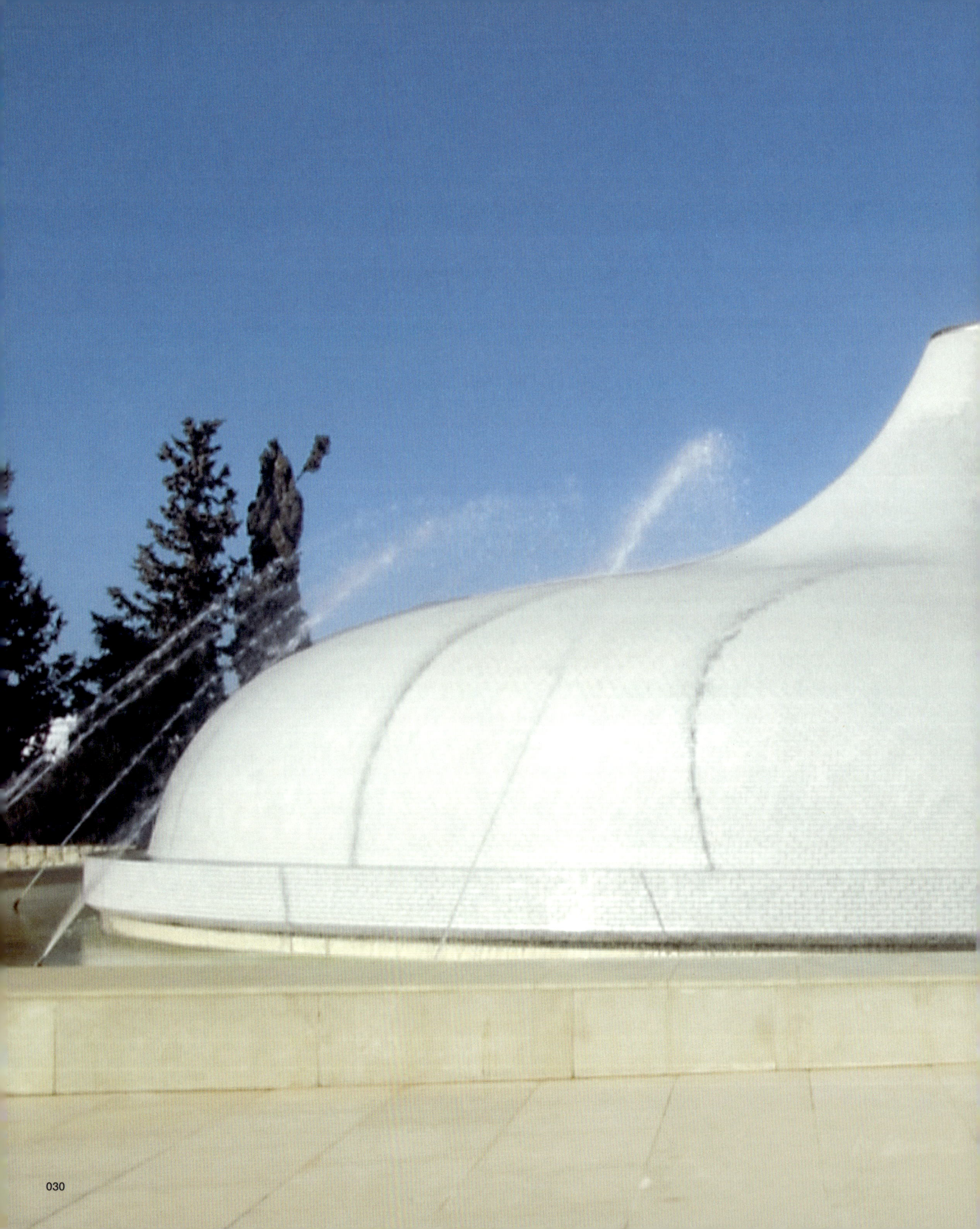

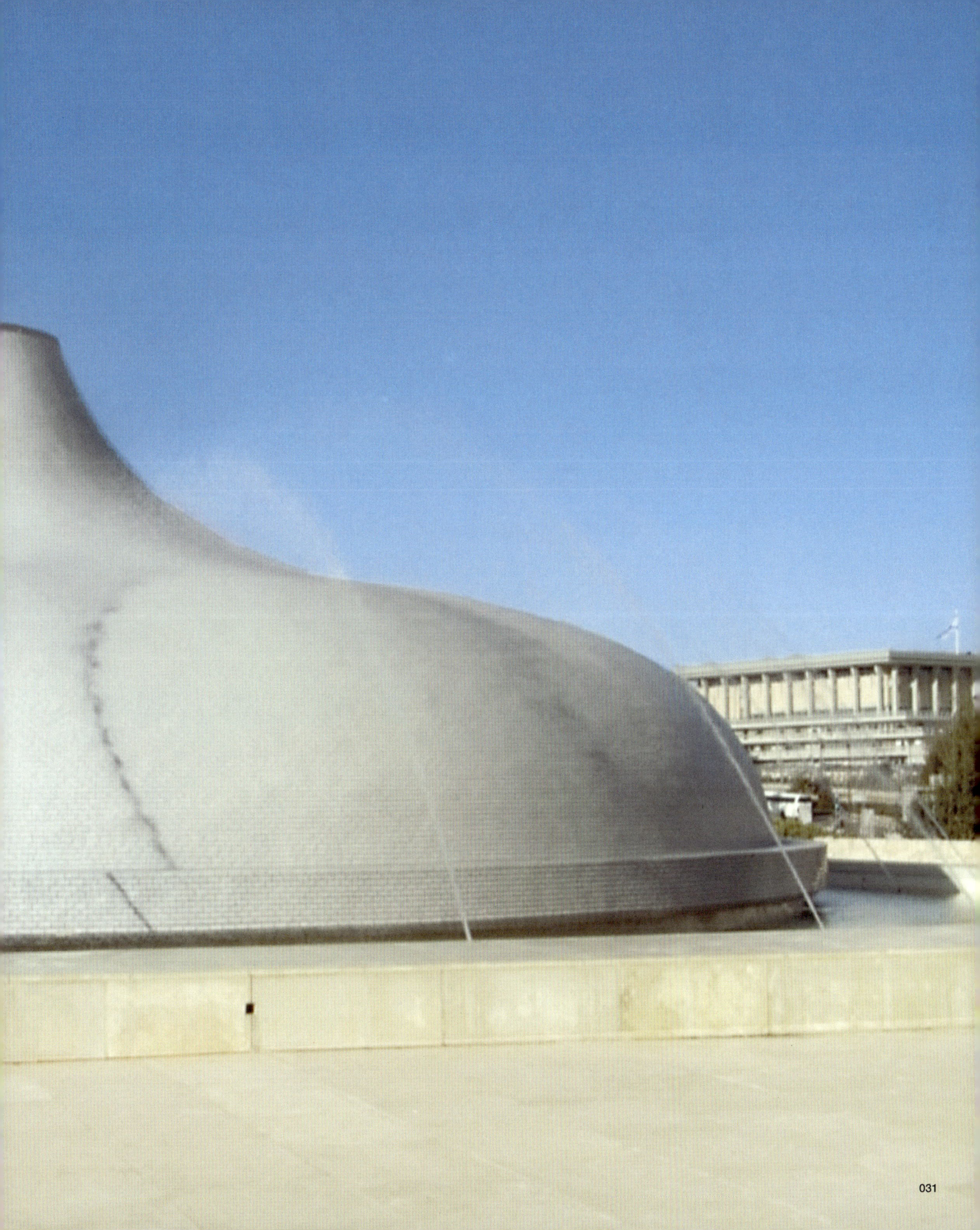

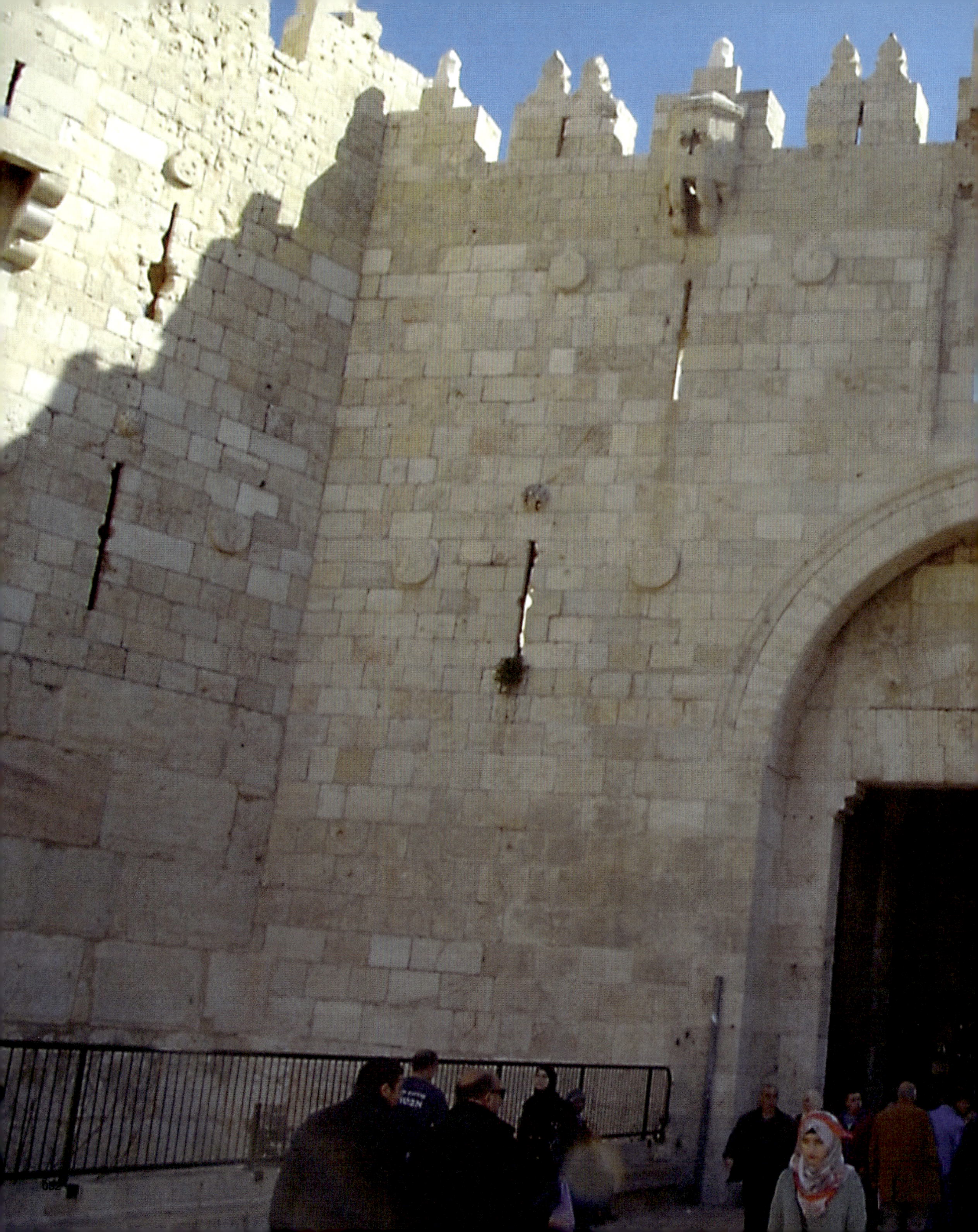

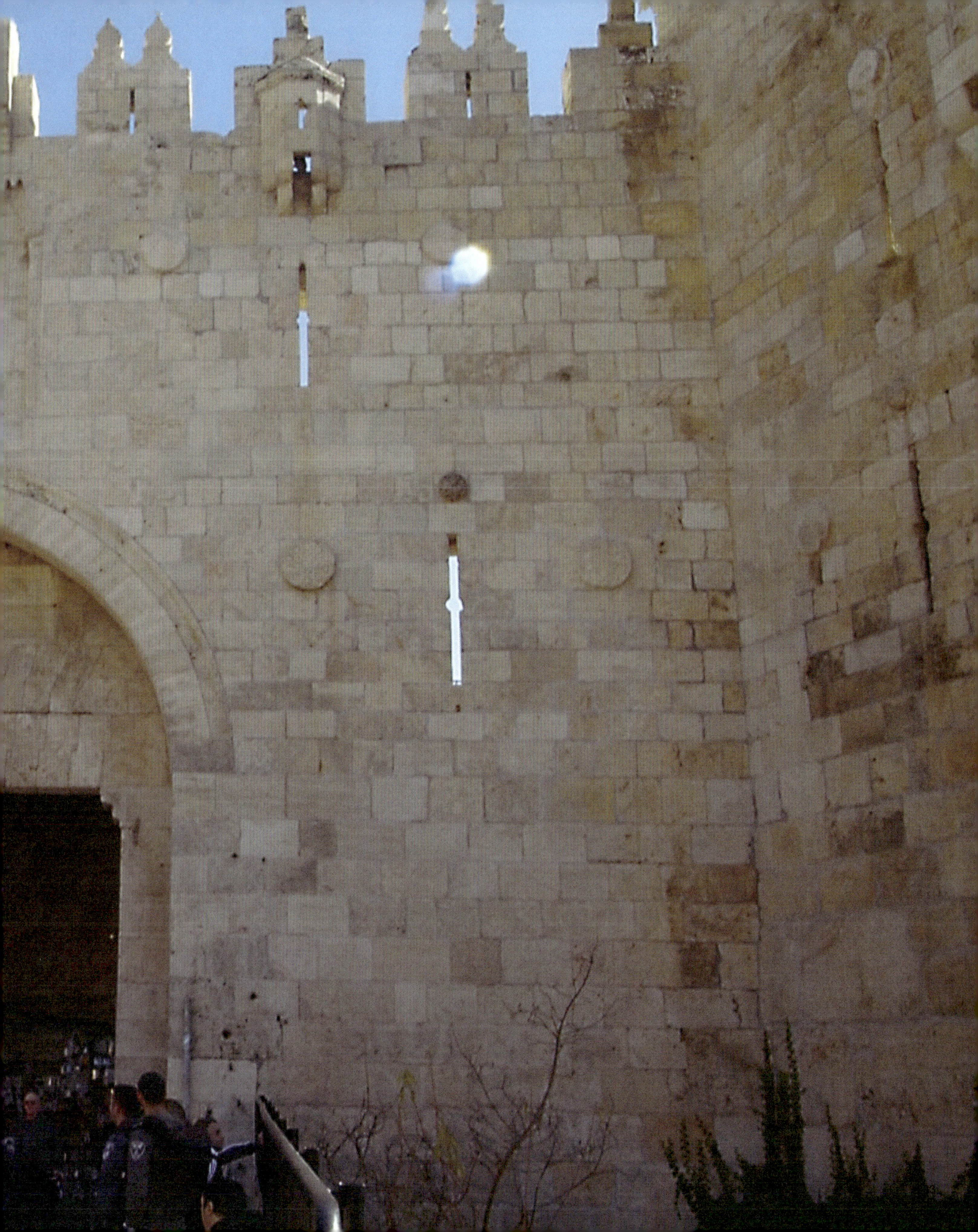

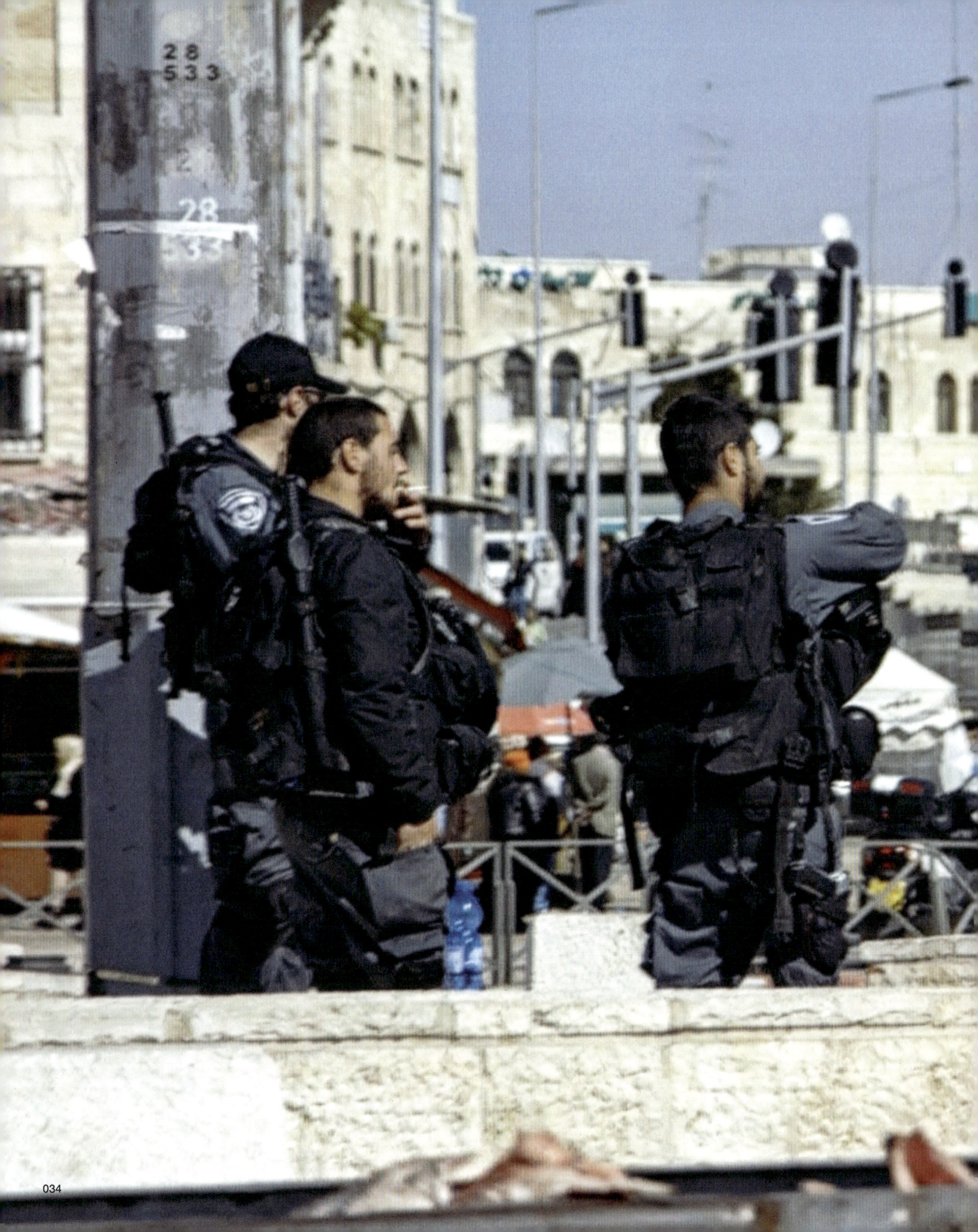
28
533
28
533

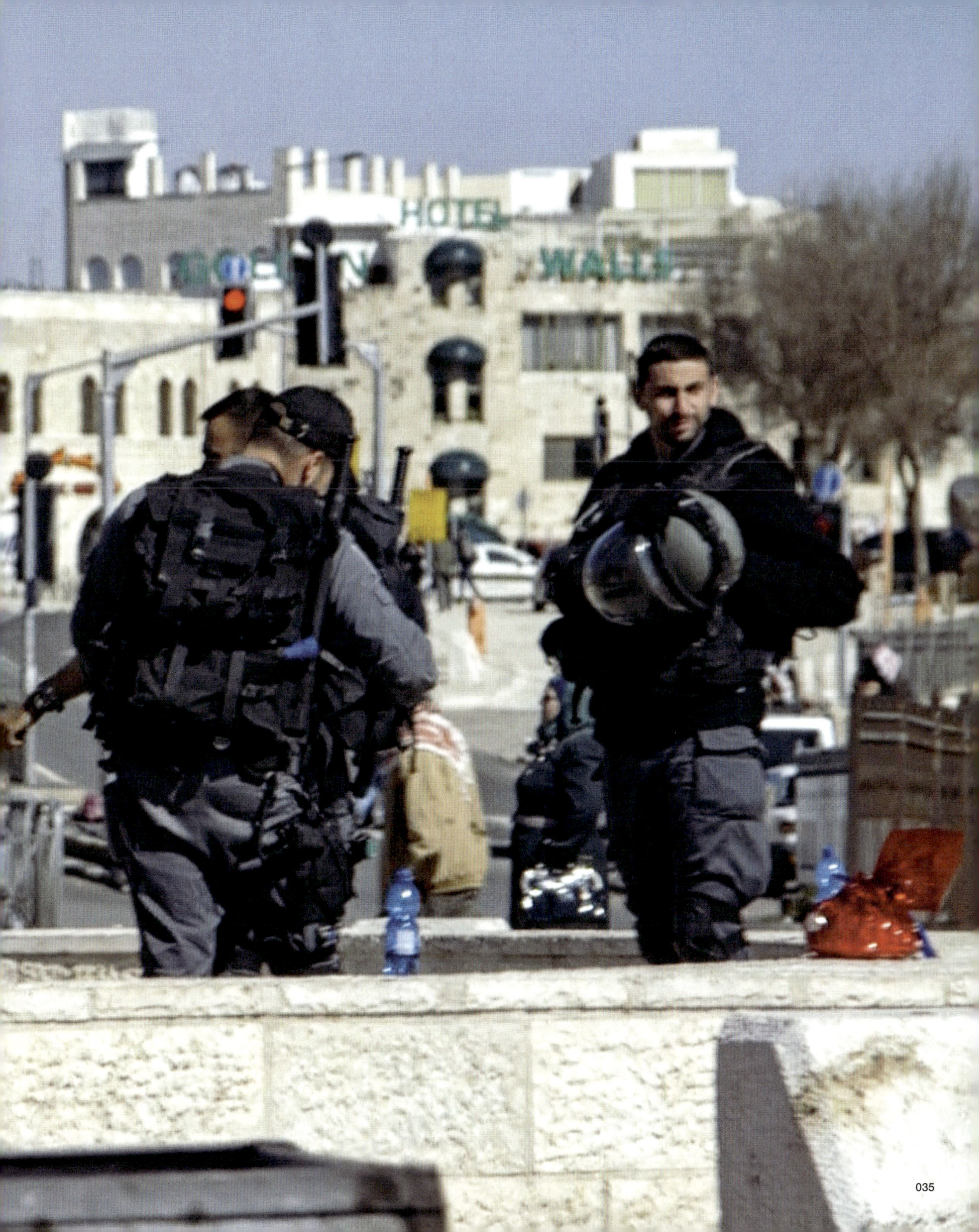
HOTEL
WALLS

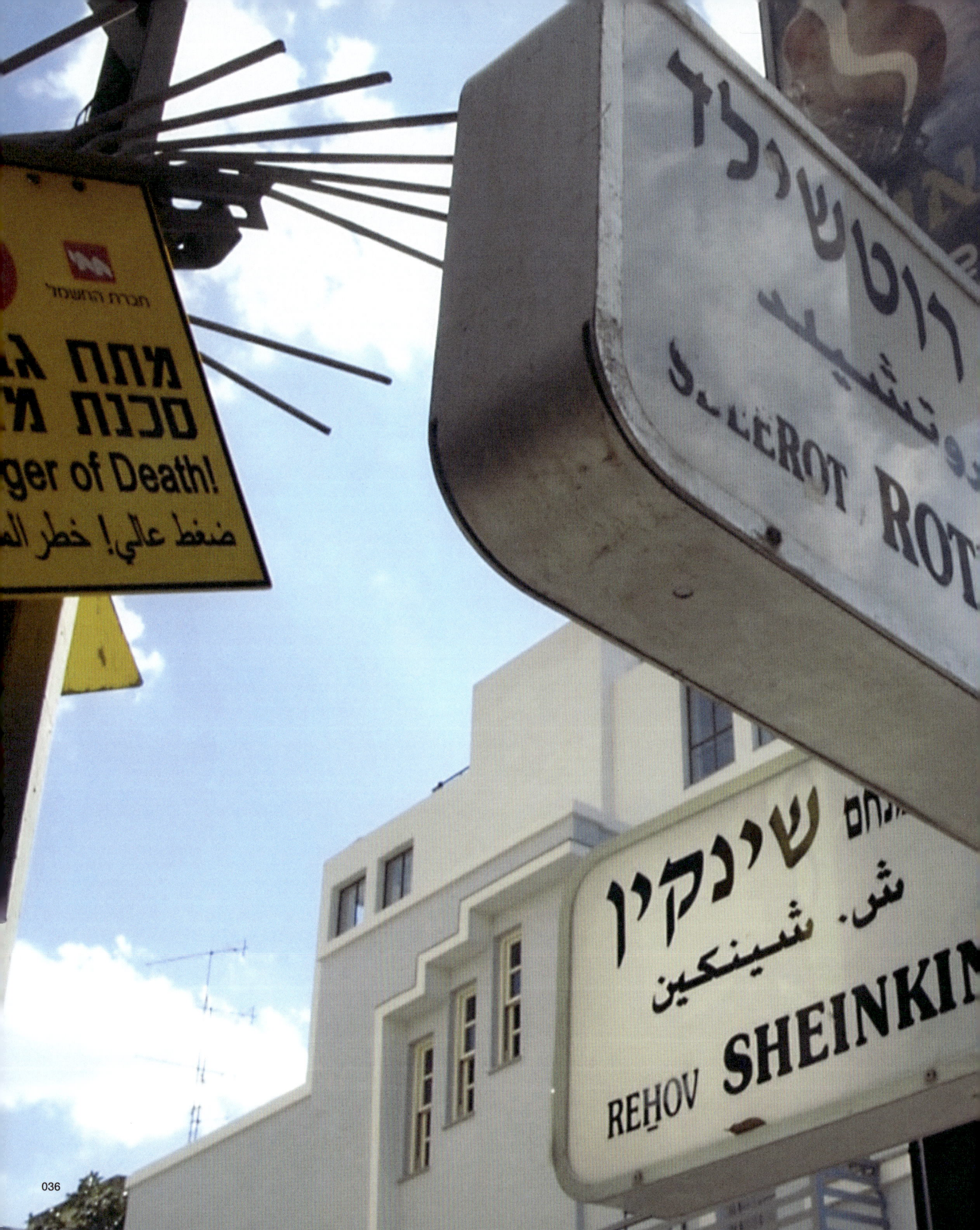

ger of Death!
שינקין
ש. شينكين
REHOV SHEINKIN

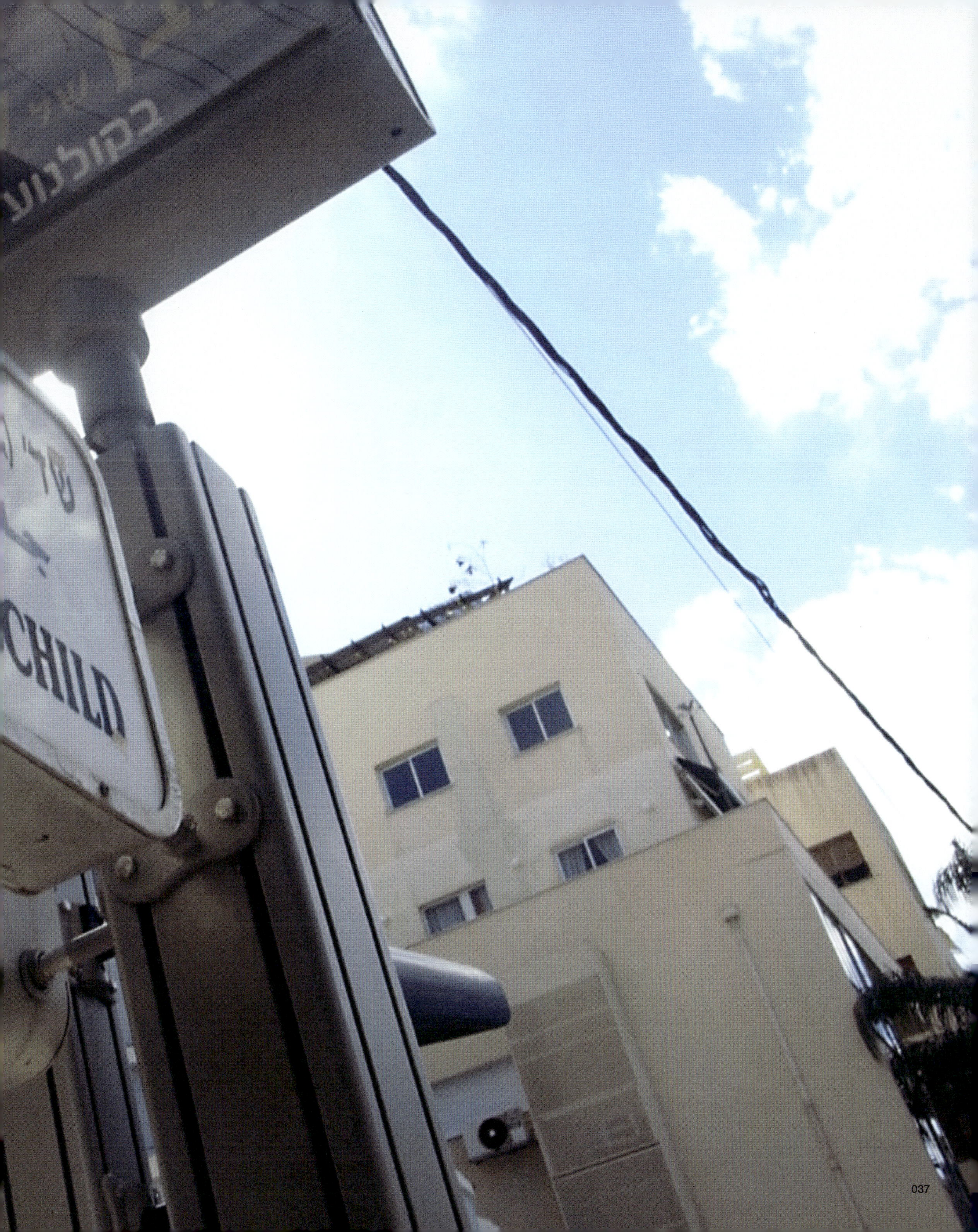
בקולנוע
CHILD

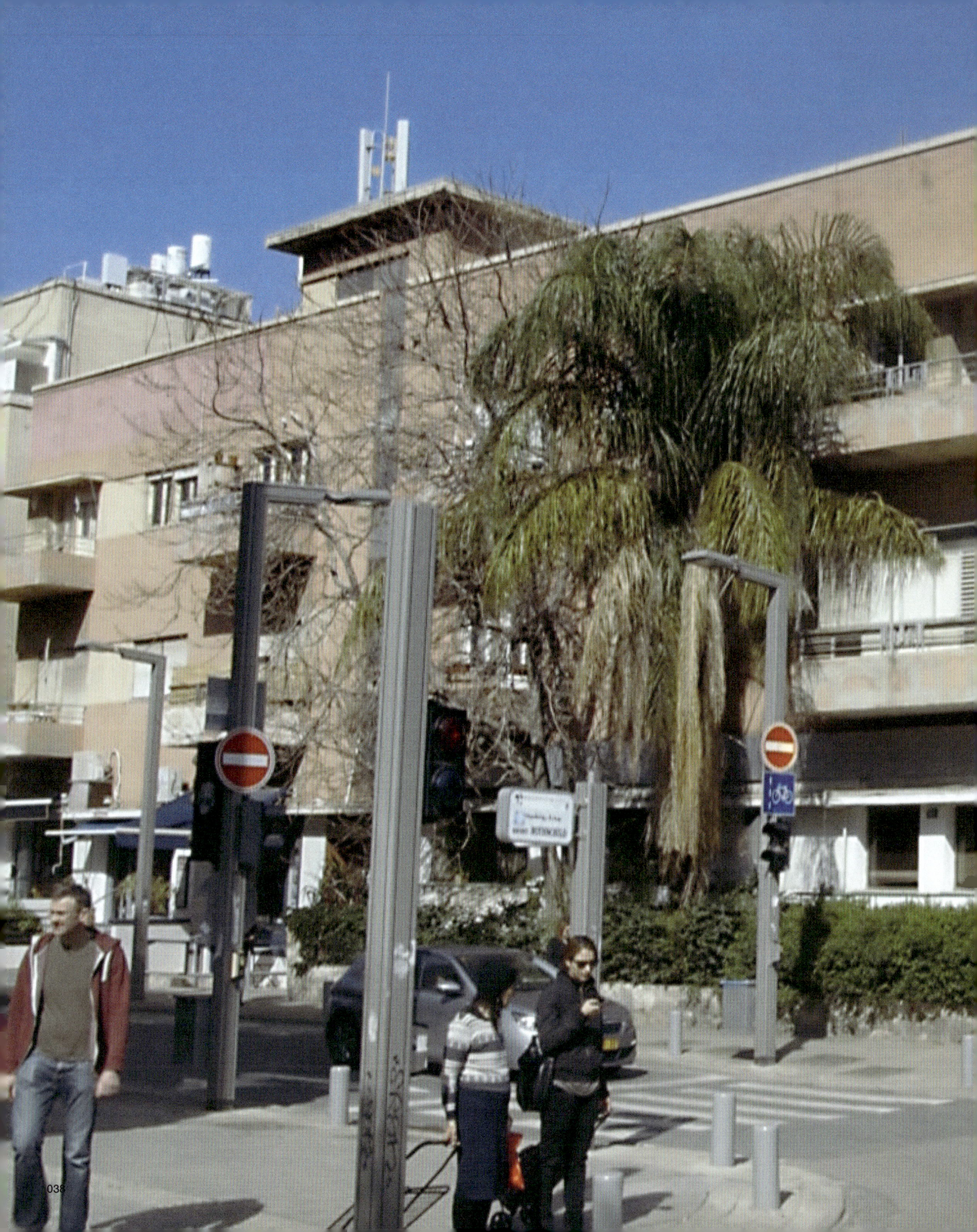

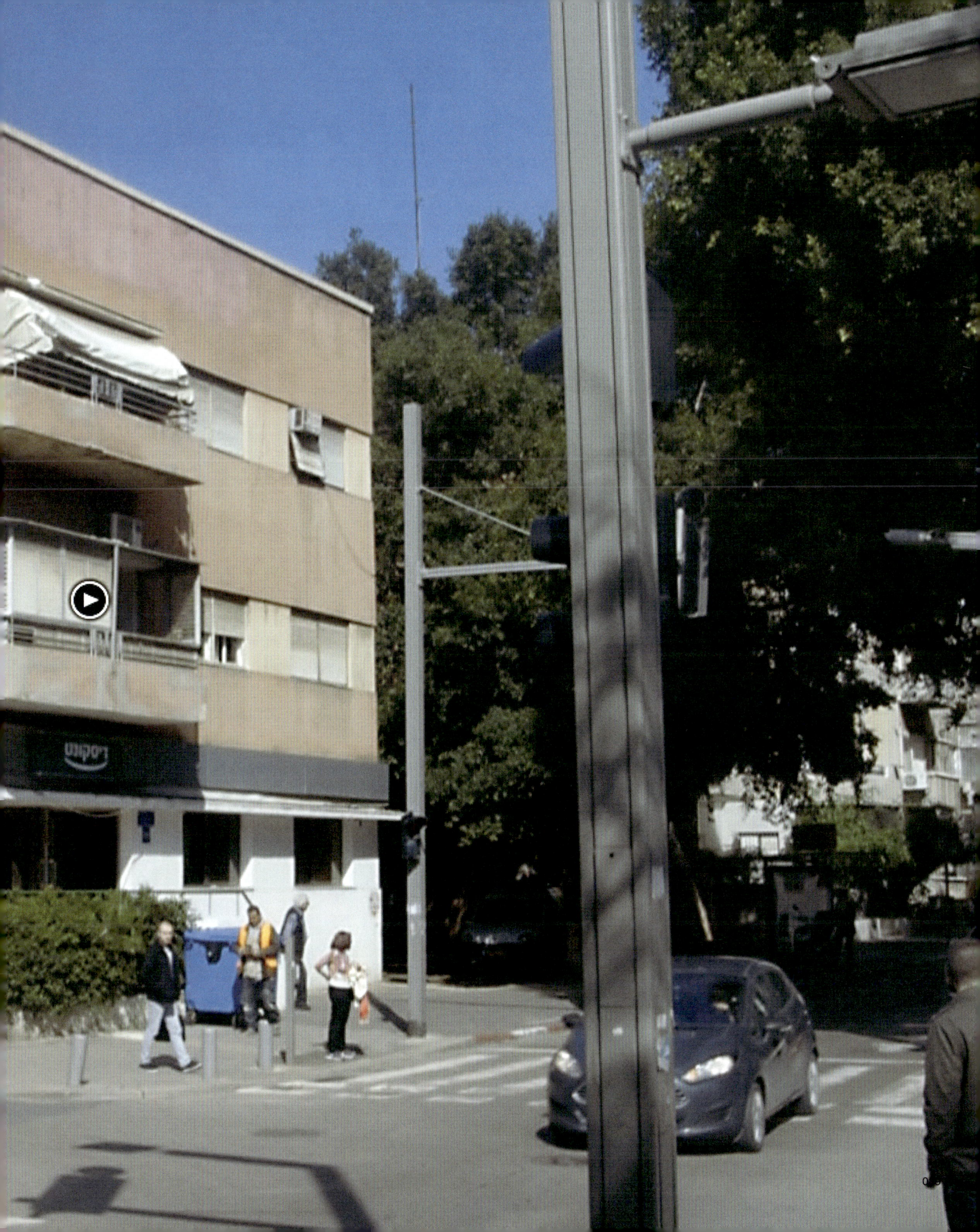
דיסקונט

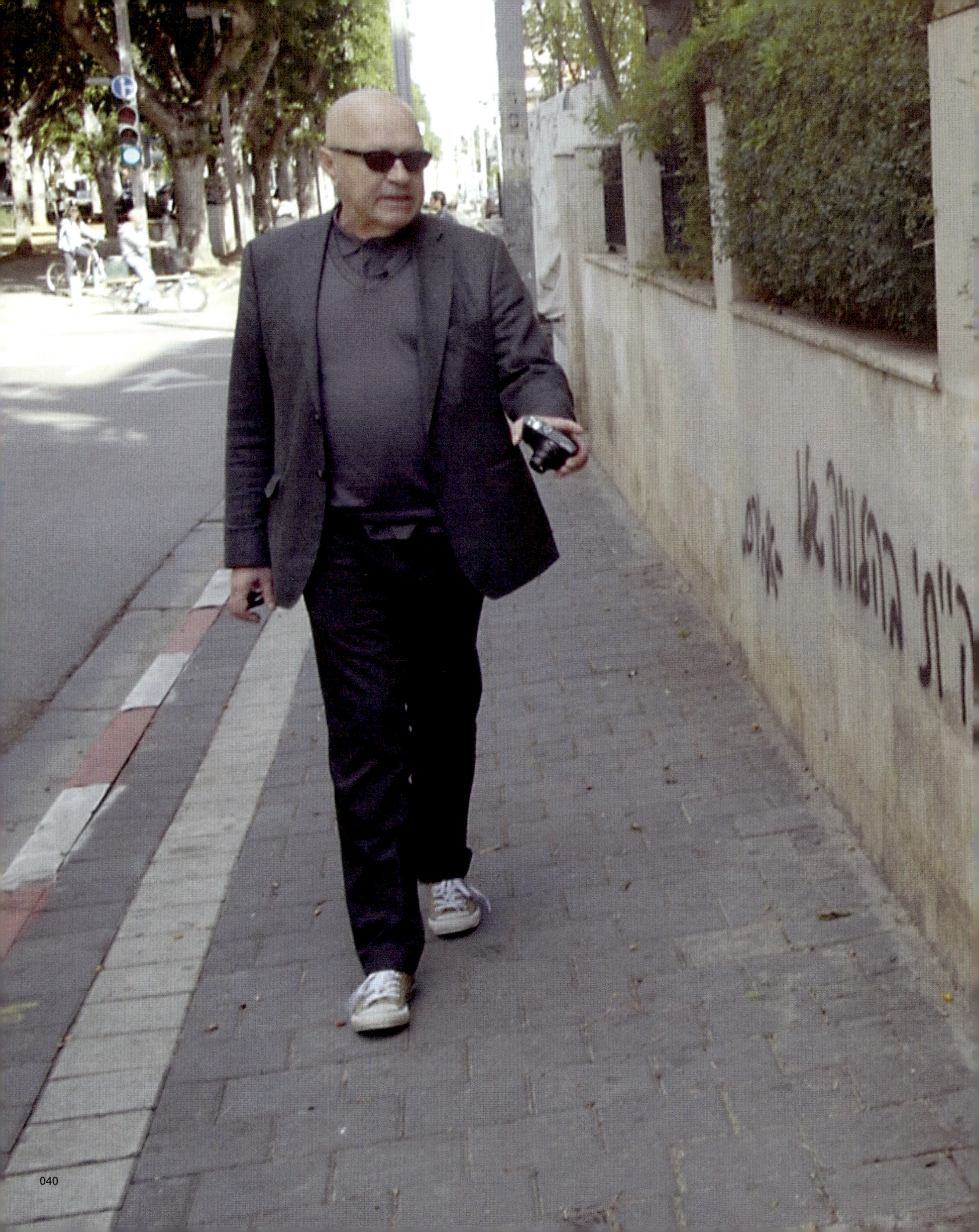

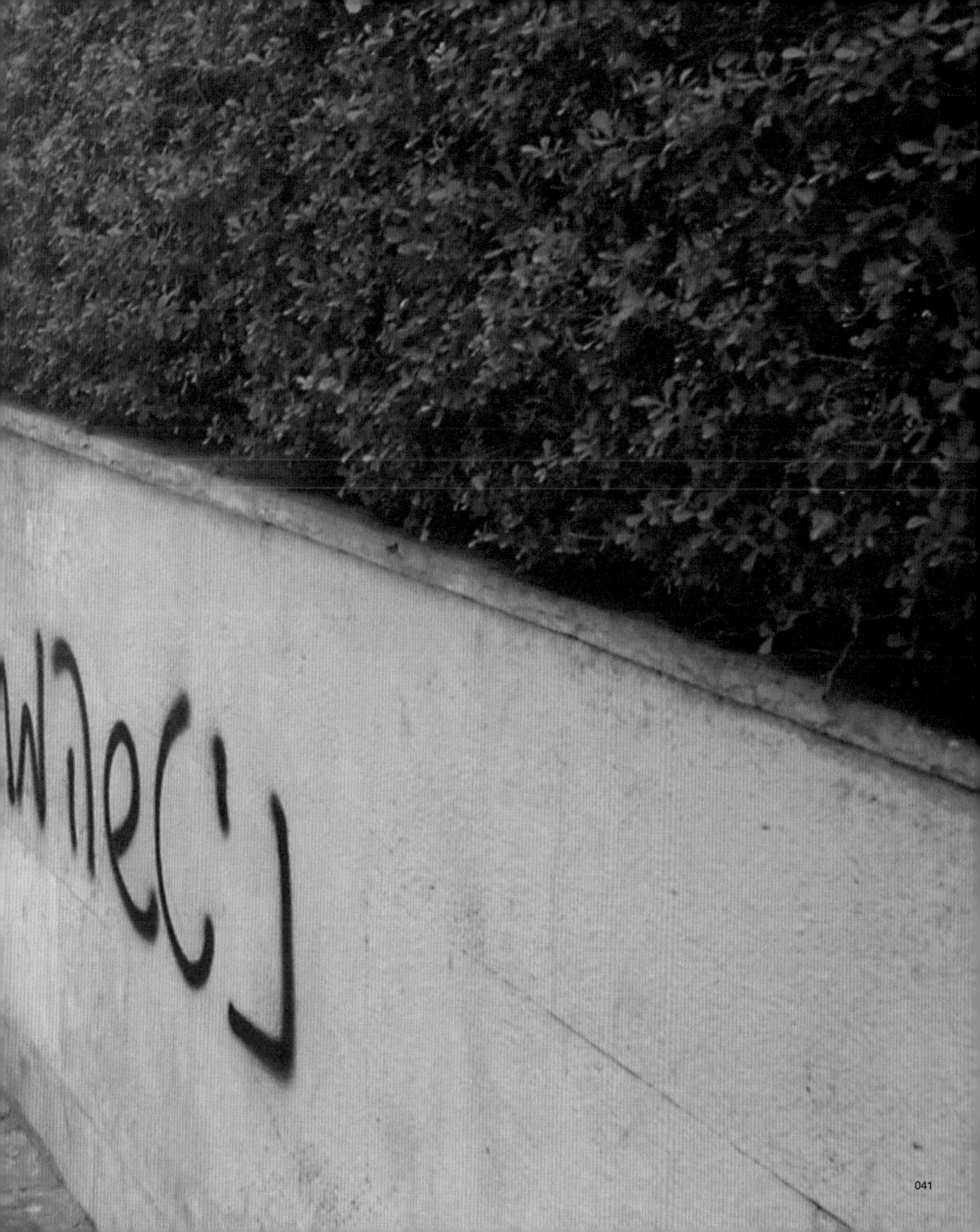

Political Correctness and the Public Sphere
Galia Bar Or

Any More Questions?

"Any More Questions?" Three words followed by a question mark are not a conventional opening for an essay, nor are they a conventional title for a work of art. More than anything, they communicate a strange sense of an ending that precedes the beginning, while resembling a rhetorical question asked by a spokesperson in relation to an event that remains open. Yet especially when related to the public sphere, this question is a catalyzing force in the work of Olaf Metzel, who chose the title *Noch Fragen? (Any More Questions?)* for the new version of his installation, which is being exhibited at the Mishkan Museum of Art, Ein Harod.[1] The discomfort, moreover, does not end with the title. The work, which winds like a wall around four supporting pillars in a central and brightly illuminated gallery, forms a disturbing hybrid between interior and exterior worlds, while underscoring certain questions: What is the meaning of this strange internal wall surrounded by four walls, a protective wall within a museum's protective walls? And, more importantly, can there exist a dialogue between an art grid[2] and what appears as an improvised "grid" born of conflicts and confrontations on the streets? Is such a dialogue between a grid and a "grid" probable? This seems to be the decisive question that Metzel is concerned with throughout his oeuvre; speech that is alive and kicking, which is not detached from the present or ensconced within an aesthetic, self-enclosed world. How possible is it to entertain such a dialogue between different and distinct languages? Another allusion to this dialogue can be found in Metzel's earlier work *Sprachgitter* (*Language Grid*, pp. 059, 062–63), in which a picture frame found by chance served as the point of departure for an installation at the synagogue in Stommeln, Germany. In this installation, an intricate wooden lattice was enlarged into a monumental frame and anchored in the ceiling. Yet what does it frame? A space of absence. More than a boundary, the lattice is itself a threshold space, a language threshold, punctuated by signs in the form of gaping holes that can also be read as symbols. A similar reading may be applied to the frame circumscribing the four pillars in the installation *Any More Questions?* at the Mishkan Museum of Art, Ein Harod.

"Language Grid," which has recently become an Internet-related term, is inextricably related to the work of the poet and intellectual Paul Celan, who chose the title *Language Mesh* for one of his poems, as well as for the book in which it was published in 1959.[3] Like Celan's poetry, Metzel's work appears to be randomly assembled and to lack a structural order—as if a giant hand had cast down a collapsing mountain of debris and readymades. Yet, like Celan's poems, this seemingly random assemblage is in fact based on a carefully planned and deeply embedded structure. Metzel's works capture an inner tension in a language that encapsulates experience with its ruptures and injuries, temporality and effacement.

Moment, Monument

... that there may be speech, of earth,
of ardor, of
things with eyes, even
here, where you read me blind,

even
here,
where you
refute me,
to the letter.[4]

So "that there may be speech," according to Paul Celan, requires "things with eyes," the eyes of time and eyes of the "self" that is disassembled in the poem like a collapsing installation, halting at the end of broken lines.[5]

This poem similarly resonates in a site-specific installation that Metzel created in 1987, whose title is the date of an event that had taken place six years earlier. The title *13.4.1981* marks a point on a temporal continuum—the eruption of riots that led to a significant shift in the public sphere. The violent events that took place on that day were no longer aimed at symbolic representatives of the establishment, but rather constituted a mass attack, which indiscriminately hit homeless people, passersby, and shopping centers. Metzel's collapsing Cyclops, with a single eye made of a shopping cart raised on a pole, stands on legs made of police barricades, and points to a specific time and place: to the eruption of forces coming from below and imposed from above, echoing perspectives of both the past and the future, the present continuous of a monument/moment of warning.

The sculpture described above resonates with a sense of transience rather than eternity, refusing the kind of aesthetic finish that would result in a unified texture and a normative language and thus underscoring the futility of the term "monument." As such, it undermines the process of restoration offered by official memory, which appropriates and embalms history so as to bridge over the abyss. Metzel preserves the vestiges of what was distorted or crushed, creating a fragile equilibrium on the verge of collapse. This precision is achieved by means of the "language mesh," which is infused with temporality as an inseparable part of its living, always fragile contexts.

Olaf Metzel's work touches upon the essential core issues of contemporary art, including "site-specificity." This term has historically addressed questions about dependence and differentiation, about social, cultural, and environmental contexts versus the singularity of the artwork—"a part of" versus "apart from," to use Andrew Benjamin's terms.[6]

In recent decades, this emphasis on contextuality has taken a social, pedagogical, and community-oriented turn. Yet although one cannot argue that Metzel's work is not social/political, it refrains from the reproduction of reality, and avoids the pedagogical pitfall and moralizing; and above all, it is free of ideologism and political correctness. Olaf Metzel's work operates with determination within the language mesh, while overturning the tradition of fine art like a double-edged sword thrust from within the present.

Turkish Delight

The installation *Any More Questions?* touches, as noted, upon "incorrectness" as a catalyzing force; yet the incorrect dimension of this exhibition, which is concealed at its center, has yet to be exposed. It is time to reveal that the "frame" or wall composed of netting and baseball bats, which extends down to the ground, also offers a glimpse of what lies beyond it: to the viewer's great surprise, at the heart of this installation is a statue of a naked woman wearing a traditional Turkish headdress.

The title, *Turkish Delight*, points to a specific Oriental sweet, known in Turkey and elsewhere as *rahatlokum*. Although at this point incorrectness seems to have already, run several red lights, let us first pause to observe the statue: its dimensions are strange, somewhat smaller than those of the human body, and its process of creation seems to have followed the academic method taught for hundreds of years at academies of fine arts, like the one at which Professor Olaf Metzel has been teaching for close to thirty years. The basis for this kind of work is countless hours of drawing from a live, nude model (*Akt* in German). Metzel worked on this sculpture using a classical method: he sculpted it out of a soft material, and the hand's contact with the sculpture can still be felt—unlike the mechanical casts used today. The sculpture was then cast and finished by the book, yet the "classical" quality inherent to the method does not result in a sense of harmony. The woman's pose refutes the conventions of the classical nude; in addition to the absence of *contrapposto*—the body's slight rotation off-axis and upward in order to represent the quintessential Beautiful—this body actually pulls downwards. The Nude has become Naked. The "beautiful" is now nothing but human fragility centered on a single vertebra, the waist that must withhold the body's pressure. The surrounding wall of netting now seems less like a protective wall and more like a laurel wreath presented to the collapsing woman—see *Stammheim* (ill. pp. 057, 094). It echoes the urban public sphere, the traces of destabilization and the disrupted order; at the same time, the trembling born of the physical effort produces another bodily logic, one that expropriates power and authority and allows antagonism to filter into the public sphere. The laurel wreath and the naked figure hint at the breaches in this sphere, while the title illuminates the stigmas existing within the language that discloses debasement and humiliation. Critical thinking has already identified the dark shadow aspects of the term "nude," of the "sublime" whose upward thrust is rooted in power relations and is related, among other things, to voyeurism.[7] It has similarly attended to the term "odalisque," with its embodiment of oppression and its special reference to Oriental women. It is this very space, in the museum sphere that is at once protective and non-protective, that Metzel operates without discounts, interpretations or explanations about Left and Right, East and West. His *Turkish Delight* stands naked and barefoot on the exposed floor tiles with a scarf wound around her head, surrounded by a fence. Her naked body, which bears none of the signs of belonging provided by dress, bespeaks humiliation or female empowerment, while the headdress defines the naked body as "other." Hannah Arendt revealed the dilemma of the refugee's visibility and identity in her foundational essay "We Refugees" (see pp. 014, 015, 098–099). The dilemma is one of visibility, since refugees have no place. The other's body, and especially the body present in the public sphere, enhances the sense of discomfort. It is identified as a disturbance to the order, as a source of pollution, as the contemporary discourse on refugees clearly reveals.[8]

Metzel's second visit to Israel took place at a difficult time—a time in which refugees were being fated to be expelled. During his earlier visit he toured cities and kibbutzim, experienced the Bauhaus architecture created by the movements of refugees and displaced persons, as well as its mutations and the debased vestiges of the myth of progress. He created new works and has come back to exhibit at the Mishkan Museum of Art, Ein Harod, in a building that is all space and light, a beneficial functionalism that creates a threshold sphere. It is in this sphere that Metzel anchors the installation *Any More Questions?* which builds upon the transient foundation that relates body and mind. He touches upon an explosive element that is incompatible with the dictates of political correctness. He avoids labels that aim to create a protective space, alluding instead to those breaches in which afflictions that seemed to belong to other times now reappear.

1 First presented 1998.
2 A grid that Metzel masterfully examines in his drawings and sculptures.
3 Paul Celan, *Die Niemandsrose. Sprachgitter. Gedichte.* Frankfurt a. M., 13th edition. The German term *Sprachgitter* was translated into English by Joachim Groschel as *Speech-Grille* (1971), and later as *Language Mesh* by Michael Hamburger (1988).
4 See Paul Celan, "O Little Root of a Dream," translated by Nikolai Popov and Heather McHugh, https://www.poets.org/poetsorg/poem/o-little-root--dream (accessed April 13, 2018).
5 In Celan's poems, eyes connote time, "the eyes of time," see Shira Wolosky, pluto.huji.ac.il/~wolosky/CELANTR.doc (accessed April 13, 2018).
6 This key notion of dialectical logic appears in Andrew Benjamin's writings in a number of contexts, including architecture. The site-specific discourse has shifted its emphasis from its initial phenomenological conception (with its emphasis on materiality and experience) to the "discursive paradigm" that was formulated in the late twentieth century. See Miwon Kwon, *One Place After Another: Site-Specific Art and Locational Identity* (Cambridge, MA: MIT Press, 2002).
7 Laura Mulvey,"Visual Pleasure and Narrative Cinema," *Screen*, vol. 16, (Autumn 1975), pp. 6–18.
8 Zygmunt Bauman, "Strangers" in *Thinking Sociologically* (Cambridge, Mass. Basil Blackwell, 1990), pp. 54–70; Sara Ahmed, *Strange Encounters: Embodied Others in Postcoloniality* (London and New York: Routledge, 2000).

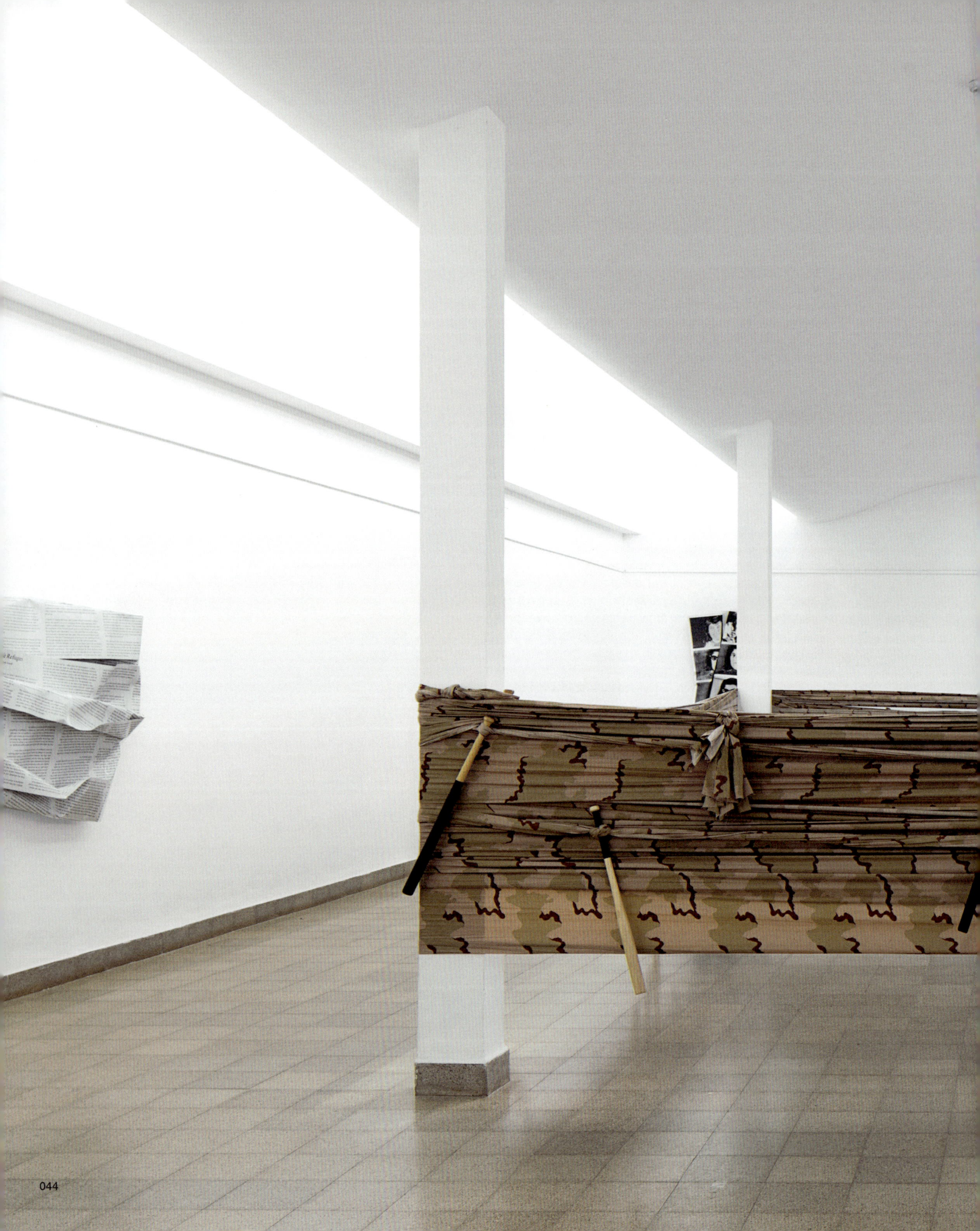

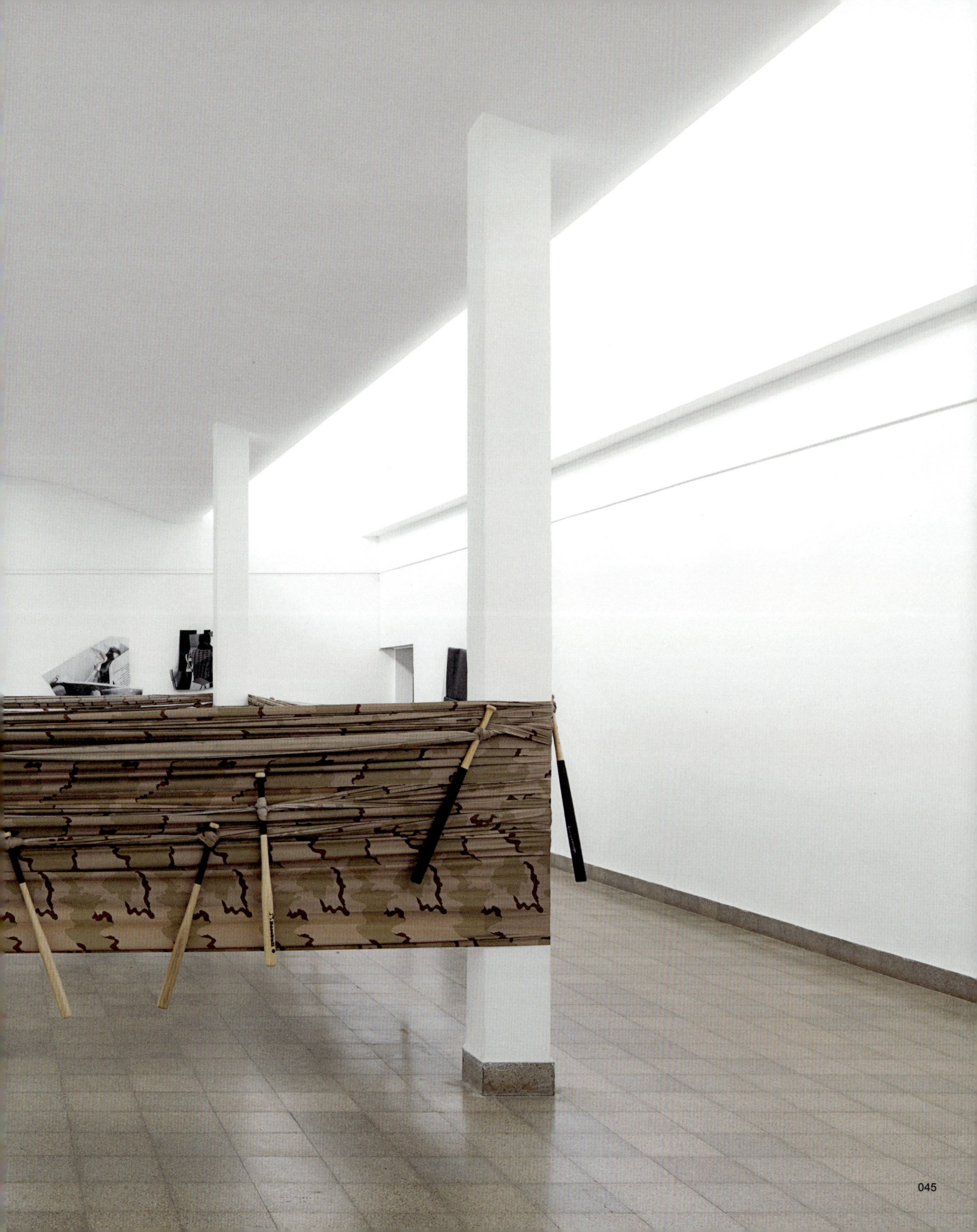

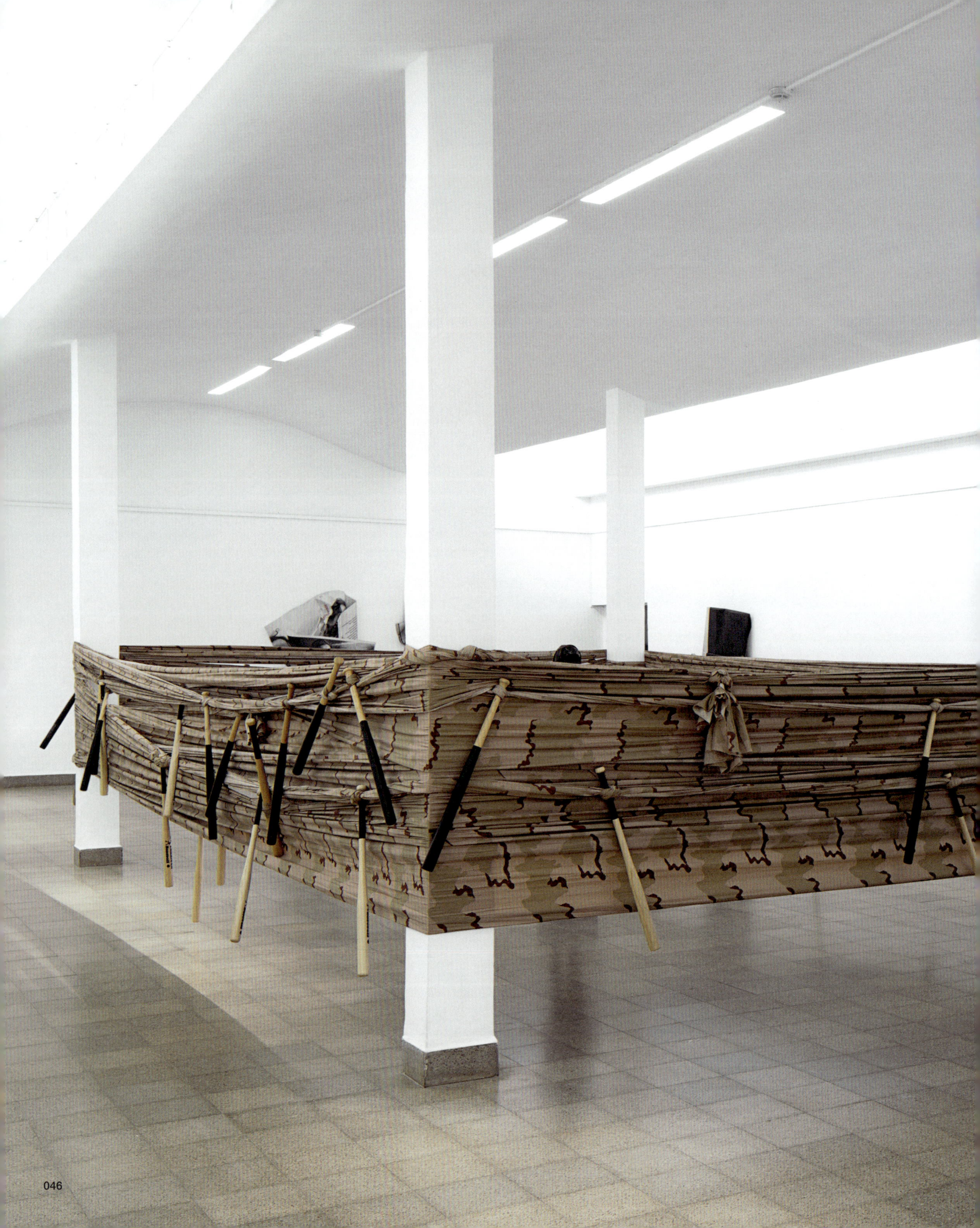

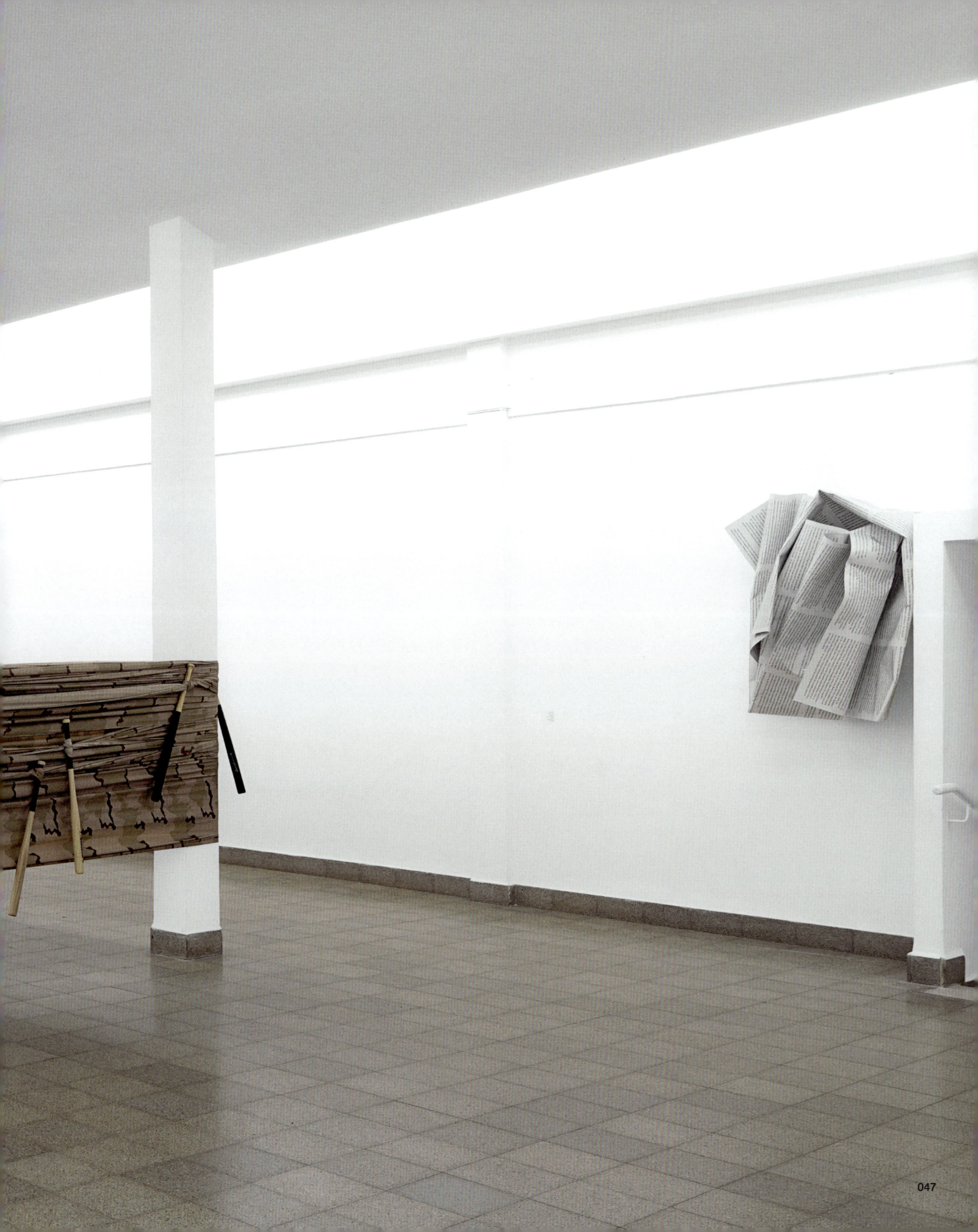

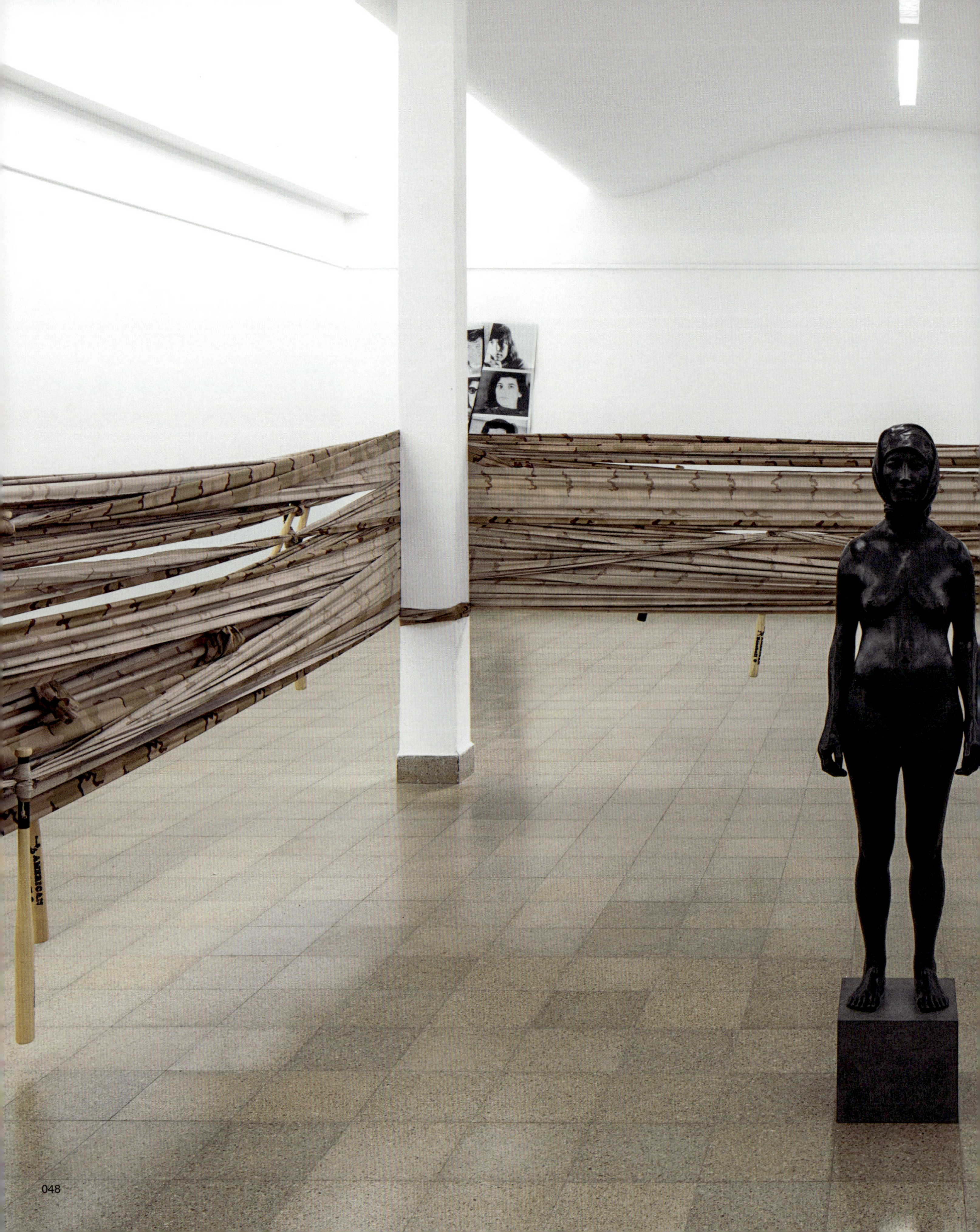

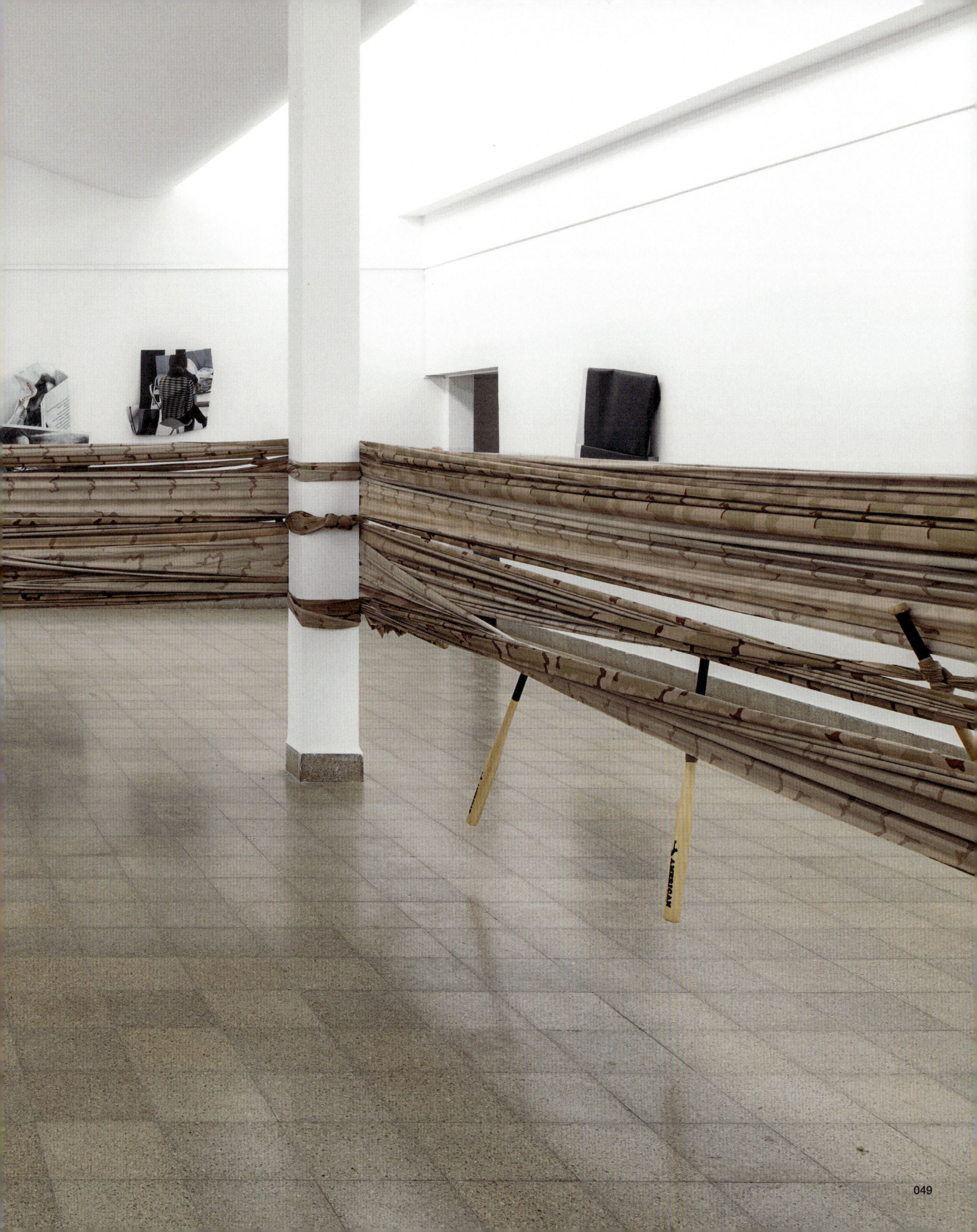
AMERICAN

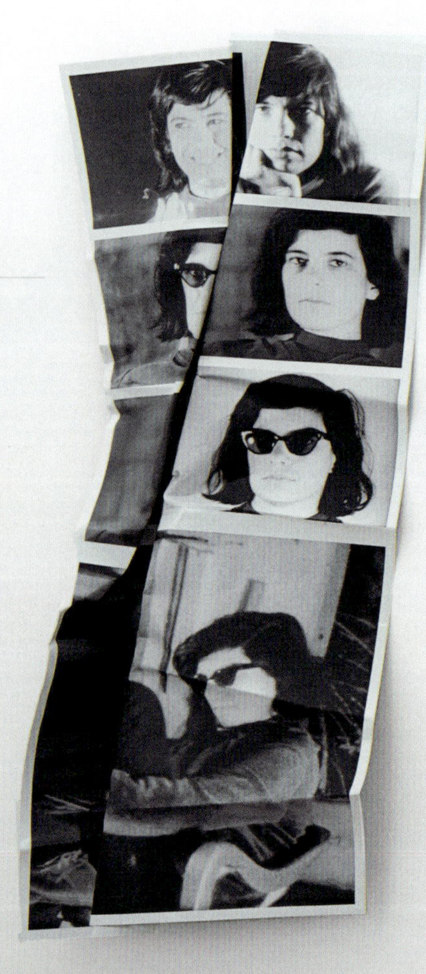

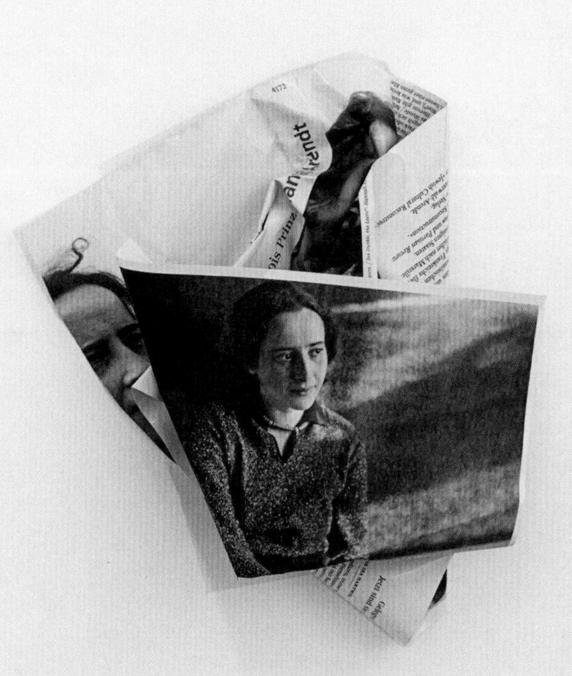

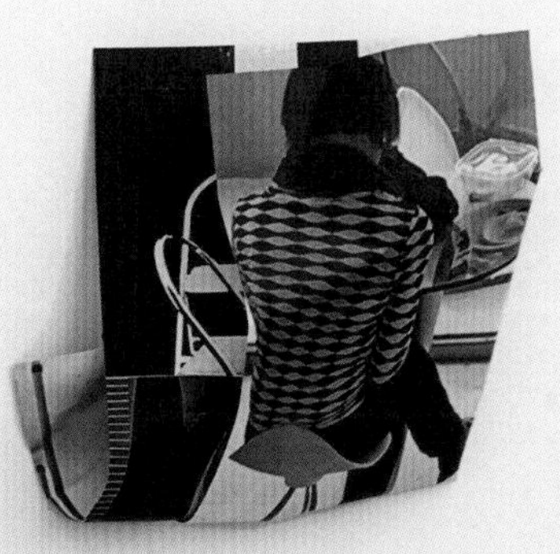

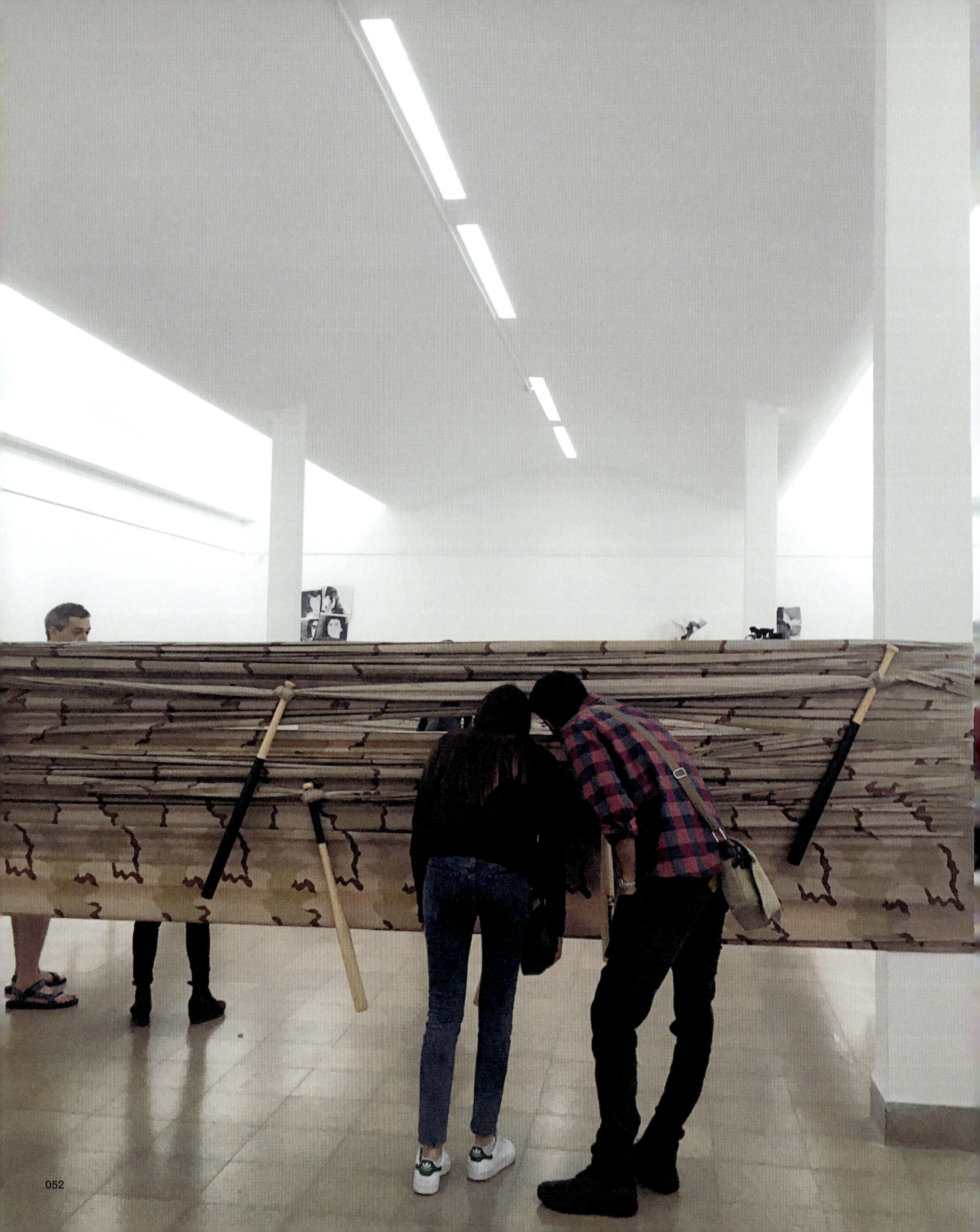

13.4.81
Christoph Heinrich

The Berlin sculptor Olaf Metzel (b. 1952) is not an artist who makes monuments commemorating or warning against war or National Socialism. Instead he devotes himself in autonomous artworks to current sociopolitical topics, such as xenophobia and terrorism, real estate speculation and production conditions in a market economy. Metzler is one of many artists to engage with such topics related to everyday social reality. But above and beyond that he also engages with the formal and contentual aspects of the monument.

His reference to the structures and functions of the monument is most evident in his what is surely most spectacular work *13.4.81*.

13.4.81—A Monument?

The sculpture *13.4.81* was made to mark the occasion of the 750th anniversary celebrations of Berlin's Sculpture Boulevard on Kurfürstendamm. In its very dimensions the work is monumental: on an area measuring ten by nine and a half meters and with a total height of about eleven meters, the artist wedged together a large number of white-and-red traffic barriers and a shopping trolley, piling them up to form a construction that was both artful and—in view of its apparent instability—highly perilous. The barriers and the trolley, like the cobblestones attached to the plinth, were enlarged to more than twice their actual size.

The site at which this work was erected, Joachimstaler Platz, is not only an important traffic hub, but has also been a gathering place and venue for countless clashes between protesters and police since the time of the student unrest. Metzel refers explicitly to one of those protest marches. It was sparked by the rumor of the death of one of the RAF prisoners on hunger strike and resulted in 500 mostly young "sympathizers" destroying 70% of the shop windows on Ku'damm within just a few minutes in the night from the 12 to 13 April 1981. By the time the police arrived, most of the protesters had absconded using public transport or disappeared into the crowds of residents out walking on the Boulevard. Metzel combines this event with a pictorial idea he found—literally—on the street: after a public rally he photographed a heap of barriers, cobblestones and a shopping trolley piled up on the periphery by policemen. This "random sculpture" provided the nucleus for Metzel's monument.

The pointed reference to the place, the title alluding to a concrete historical event, the generally comprehensible signs and their monumental enlargement all prompt us to speak here of a "monument." It may well be that 200 shattered shop windows, the lootings and the swift disappearance of the demonstrators in the underground are not events worthy of a memorial. Yet 13.4.81, and with it the sculpture referring to that date, point beyond the concrete event to a fundamental conflict: politicians and daily newspapers assessed the events of that weekend as symptomatic of the increasing violence of the riots in the early eighties during which the aggression was not, as it had been up till then, directed primarily at symbols and representatives of state authority but unleashed indiscriminately and arbitrarily on passersby and locals. That escalation brought with it another of the numerous attempts to toughen the law on demonstrations and led to a louder call for "a firm hand." The political restraint of the Berlin SPD Senate at the time toward the so-called "squatter scene" was severely criticised and interpreted by the opposition as a weakness. Tolerance and laissez-faire only encouraged destructive forces; that "fateful policy" could only be encountered by restricting and prohibiting demonstrations.

...

The artist refrains from all moralizing. He rejects the "purposeful commemoration" necessary for a monument or memorial. To anyone seeking edifying warning he brusquely points out, "I remember!" After all, on the Kurfürstendamm one could also think of "the Queen's visit, Café Kanzler, shopping, or Kempinski."

Metzel polemicizes against "garbled monument structures" and refuses the didactic impetus of memorials. At first glance, the towering signs with which he marks the place give every passerby legible pointers to two different but related aspects of urban life. The shopping trolley—the vehicle of goods transfer from retailer to so-called end user—refers to prosperity and its values: the freely available consumer goods, trade, possession and mobility. The barrier used by the "guardians of the peace" serves to protect these very values during violent clashes between groups of the population who question them.

During the demonstration on April 13, 1981, however, that so clearly connotated consumer vehicle was misappropriated so as to transport the cobblestones being used as ammunition. Correspondingly, the police instruments of protection were repeatedly transformed into weapons during escalating clashes—as for example in 1985 in a demo in Frankfurt during which a demonstrator was killed by a water cannon. That event occurred at the time Olaf Metzel was creating his sculpture *13.4.81*, and he points to it by means of a newspaper extract on the working wall 1 accompanying this project. The unambiguousness of the signs, imperative for the didactic function of the monument, is shattered here, giving rise to irritation and disorientation.

In *13.4.81*, Olaf Metzel makes quite clear formal references to the monument and in doing so varies the vocabulary of the traditional monument: he makes allusions to the traditional plinth in isolated cobblestones at the foot of the sculpture and generally in the towering wedges. In the history of the monument, the plinth determines, through its height, the distance from what is worthy of commemoration and the person commemorating. A high plinth removed the honored person from the trivial sphere of the commemorator, a low plinth let the hero climb down temporarily from his Olympus to hold out his hand benevolently to the person honoring him. Metzel's plinth however is burst open; the stones are lying about. This plinth is not a hieratic block but rather a climbing frame that is calling out to be appropriated. And the shopping trolley that crowns the

Excerpts from: *Denkmal als Motiv und Funktion (Monument as Motif and Function)* by Christoph Heinrich

13.4.1981
1987
Steel, concrete,
stainless steel, pigment
115 × 900 × 700 cm

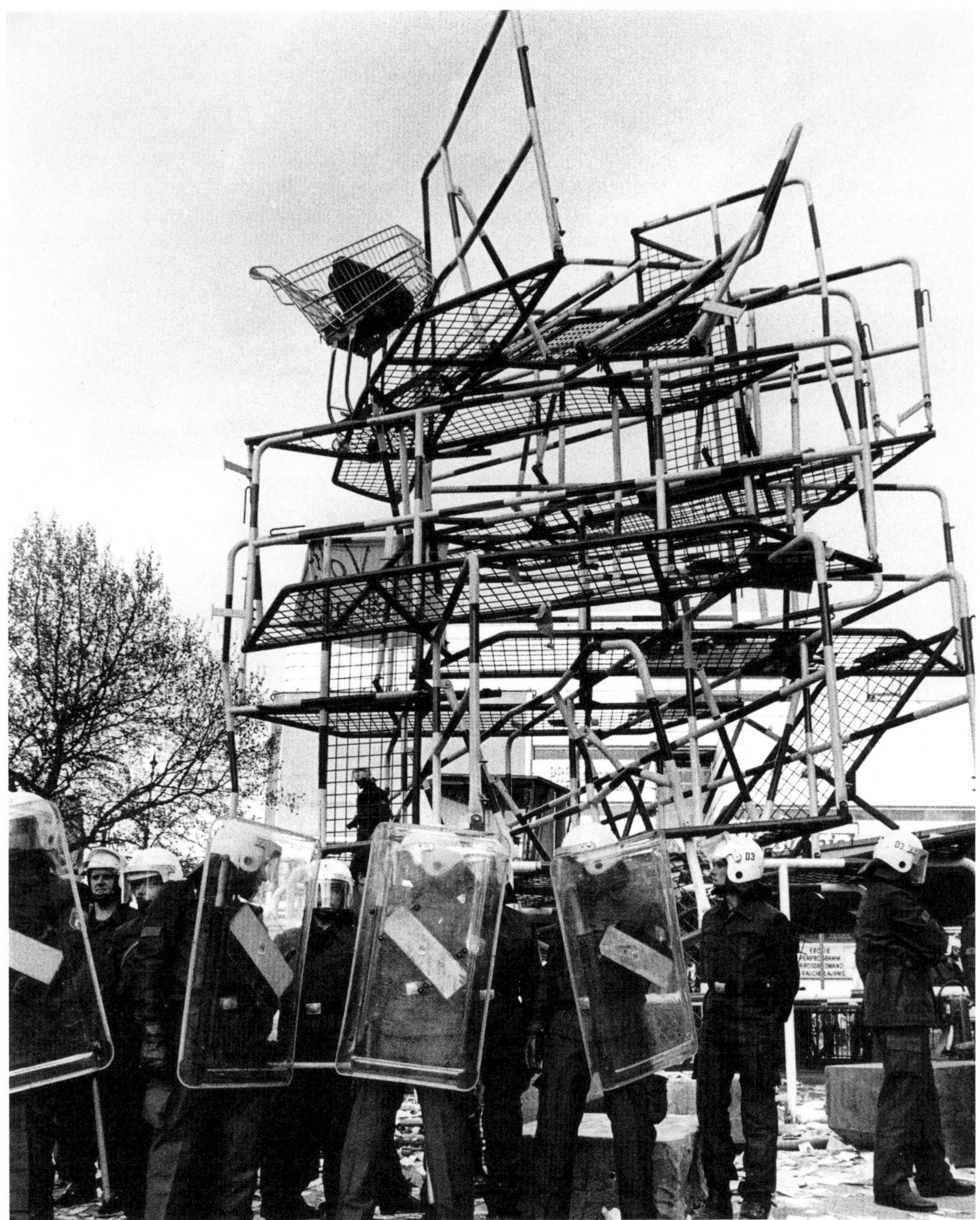

sculpture is anything but festive—instead, it teeters involuntarily through being wedged. Attempts to read this construction hierarchically, for example as an "anti-monument" in the sense of a pithy polemic, are misleading.

With *13.4.81*, Metzel thus confront viewers with a mesh of signs that is only ambivalent at second glance and seems simpler than it is. The artist provokes his viewers, his allusions to monumental forms luring them not least into contradiction, while he himself rejects any confessional manifestation.

Anonymous Writing on the Wall
Christoph Heinrich

Stammheim 1984

A wreath of honor rests against a bleak wall. From afar it looks like a traditional wreath, the type of woven wreath of laurel leaves used at state ceremonies or even cast in bronze and found at traditional monuments. On closer inspection this first impression turns out to be deceptive. The wreath is made of green-colored cement and appears wrought with deep grooves. Brown traces of rust indicate rebars exposed in some places. A name is written on the wall above the wreath to the right, in large capital letters of some one and a half meters: STAMMHEIM.

In Olaf Metzel's work *Stammheim*, made for Stuttgart's Württembergischer Kunstverein in 1984 for inclusion in a West German artistic landscape series, *Kunstlandschaft BRD*, the artist transformed the terrace of the art museum into a work of art. Even today, many Germans still automatically associate the Stuttgart suburb of Stammheim with the discussion about the court case that dragged on for years of the Red Army Faction (RAF) members incarcerated at the correctional facility there. The court wing constructed especially for this purpose was the scene of the spectacular trial against the leading RAF members, during which the question arose time and again of where punishment within a juridical ethos ends and revenge by the authorities on their opponents begins. Stuttgart-Stammheim is also the place where four RAF members were found dead in their cells. The official coroner's verdict that the prisoners had committed suicide was repeatedly doubted.

In his work, Olaf Metzel uses the highly charged place name and thus inevitably refers to the circumstances associated with it. Does this mean his wreath is a provocative hero's tribute to the "martyrs" of Stammheim? Should the courtyard with the sleek concrete wall call to mind the "specially built stronghold" or "Stammheim fortress"—as the courtroom wing and penitentiary were called by the media? Is it a reminder of the prisoners serving a sentence there—as a flyer proclaimed in the year the artwork was made—"walled in in a high-security mausoleum," "buried alive" for the rest of their lives?

With wreath and writing, Metzel clearly delves into the realm of the traditional monument. Originally a symbol of power, war and peace, the laurel wreath's use to distinguish military achievement and honor the dead was already a practice in ancient times. Although wreaths continue to be used in our day to decorate civil graves as well, this wreath in its environment reminds us of military-honor funerals or official wreath-laying ceremonies.

In his work, Olaf Metzel lays a wreath in honor of the Stammheim dead—clearly a provocation, given that distinguishing the Stammheim prisoners and dead with the official signs of honor is neither based on social consensus, nor does it create identity. Therefore it does not meet the requirements for monuments and wreath-laying. Moreover, Metzel's wreath is three to four times larger than a traditional wreath. Such exaltation would normally be a sign of increased significance, of monumentality—if the wreath were of bronze. However, it is made of concrete and so is not a monument but a trompe l'oeil, a fake, a trick.

Through its material, the monumental wreath of honor carries its sweeping gesture ad absurdum and expresses an angry rebellion. However aggression not only emanates from it, but was obviously wrought into it. The wreath made of rigid, deeply grooved material with its protruding rusty rebars threatens to inflict injury and simultaneously expresses its own injury. It was wrought with an electric cutting disk—a process involving vehement aggression and destructive force, which Metzel has processually integrated into other pieces as part of the artworks.

The dedication of this ostensible monument is not expressed in solemn lettering—as would normally be the case for a monument—but is applied on the wall in capital letters without a stencil. And yet the writing is not what one considers to be typical "graffiti." It does not purport to be the result of an illegal cloak-and-dagger operation, as is the case with spray-painted graffiti; instead it is a provocative, yet calm and systematically executed and thus conscious naming of the place. Moreover, the evenly sized capital letters reveal no personal handwriting and account for the anonymous character of the writing.

Writing and wreath suggest a tribute to the prisoners and the dead in Stammheim. However, both the visitor to the exhibition and the pedestrian who discovers the wreath and the writing upon peering through the hedges of the adjacent palace garden wonder who is paying this tribute—who acknowledges responsibility for this act. A wreath normally represents an acknowledgment by the person who lays it, with the writing defining that person's acknowledgement. But who can be presumed to have laid this wreath—state representatives full of sanctimoniousness, or anarchists making a failed appeal to pathos?

The person who did not actually lay the wreath here, but had it hoist over the art museum building by a crane, is easy to identify: the artist. The work is not a publicly commissioned monument but an autonomous work of art—created without lengthy planning and consensus-building in the public arena. Metzel later reported that, on the way to the exhibition venue, he read a commentary in *Der Spiegel* magazine on the judgment against Peter-Jürgen Boock. The discussion about the sentence and the prison conditions of the prisoners serving their time in Stammheim had been heating up for quite some time. The Chief Federal Prosecutor Rebmann was quoted in *Der Spiegel* article as saying that a petition for clemency by Boock could not be discussed before the "first decades of the next century." The artist then decided to create a work of art about Stammheim.

Although the place for this "monument" may initially appear arbitrary, it has been very deliberately chosen. The building wall clad in polished concrete tiles, the copper roof with its patina and the atmosphere in the no-protest zone around the neighboring state parliament building or Landtag, where police units patrol with beeping radio devices, all inspired Metzel. "This immediately triggered in my mind the association with a mausoleum."

Taken from: "Anonymous Writing on the Wall—about two works by Olaf Metzel" by Christoph Heinrich in *Olaf Metzel*, pp. 16–19.

Stammheim
1984
Württembergischer Kunstverein,
Stuttgart

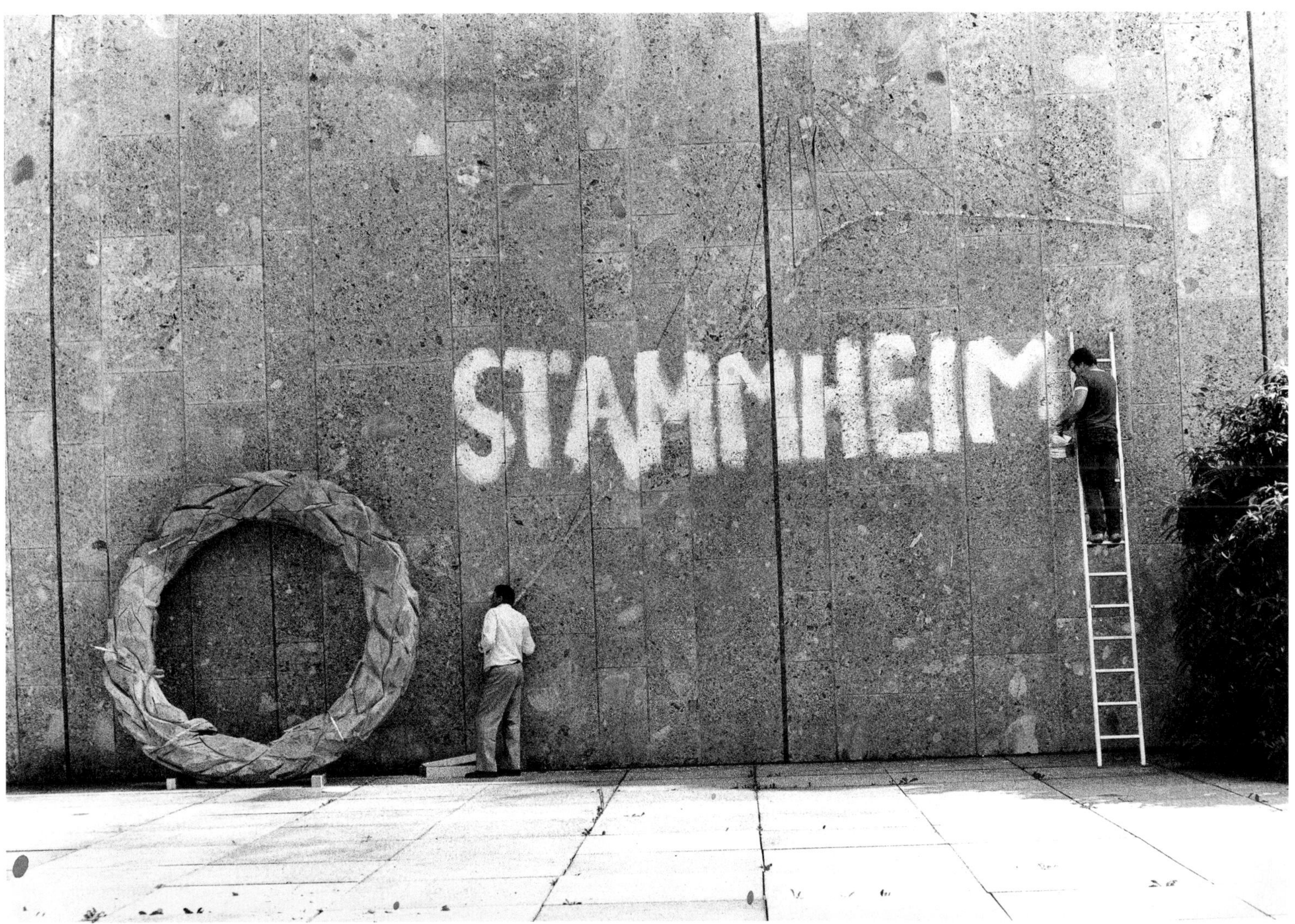

The somewhat functional value of the place, however, is even more essential than this atmospheric character. Naturally integrated into its environment and visible and accessible through the adjacent park's bordering hedges, this exhibition venue ensures that people beyond the exhibition public come in contact with the artwork, though it remains installed on the art museum's grounds. It is at this junction—between the museum's protective space and public space—that Metzel sets up his "explosive device," from his concealed holdout of artistic freedom.

Metzel transforms the concrete terrace of an exhibition building without any character or history to speak of into a monument by means of just two interventions—a concrete wreath and writing. However he refuses to give the observer any handy formula. Although the monument form is provocative in this context, its ambiguity makes it difficult to take a stance. Metzel's work repeatedly lures the observer into snares of significance; it is a kind of teaser with a serious background. Although it sets in motion associations and allusions, one cannot call this multifaceted and caustic work a "monument in remembrance of..." or a "memorial to warn against...." It remains ambiguous, even if it refers to a very specific political context. Sender and recipient cannot be identified—wreath and writing are anonymous—an anonymous annoyance.

Synagoge Stommeln
Hans Belting

The small synagogue near the market square of Stommeln—saved, forgotten, and rediscovered—has long made a name for itself in the art scene. In the nineteen-nineties, Jannis Kounellis became the first in a long line of international artists who once a year create an installation not just on these quiet premises, but for them. The installations are guests that are remembered, each with its own aesthetic idea, and each with its own interpretation of the place.

The first time I visited Stommeln in August 2009, Olaf Metzel had installed a new work the day before. He himself had seen the room empty, whereas I had no choice but to see it through his eyes, as his work had taken charge of the room and was dominating it. It seemed as if it had always been there and become part of the room, and it always kept the upper hand in guiding my vision. It made sense to me only in place, while the place in turn made sense only with this presence added so recently.

In my view, the small Jewish prayer room presented itself as a simple cube, with three windows each on two of the walls. The only partition is the gallery mounted on the wall above the entrance and bisecting it; the only accent is the Torah niche in the main wall opposite; both have been reconstructed in dark wood. The even, whitewashed ceiling was now supplemented by a rectangle made of ash wood and structured like a scaffold or grid that framed an empty center—this being Olaf Metzel's artwork. From the first moment I was unable to rid myself of the impression that I was looking at an empty frame, that is, a frame that remains without an image and yet references the image in its absence. Perhaps the location itself contributed to the impression, because a Jewish prayer house is inconceivable without the Jewish ban on images (defined in the second commandment of the Decalogue) and its sufferance of books only. It banished Yahweh forever from any man-made image (and what else could an image of God be?).

So it was quite fitting that the artist, who could not possibly have been aware of my idea, talked of having bought a small old wooden frame with holding strips, that is, a back-loading frame, some time ago, and that it had inspired him in this work. I realized later that he had been guided by a formal approach. The shape of the frame may also have intrigued him. It breaks down a geometric drawing into several layers and makes it three-dimensional, only to recall the plane with its empty interior from which the four-sided frame separates itself. Along the very same lines, Metzel created a colored sketch of the facade of the Palazzo dei Diamanti in Ferrara. The work captured the multidimensional order of things on a building surface—remaining strictly within the planar grid and yet displaying the shades and semi-shades of the raised crystalline "diamonds"—reproducing it again on a piece of paper. You could interpret this as a metaphor for the ambivalence between personal design (plane) and public effect (space) that pervades the art Metzel uses for the public realm.

But let us remain for a moment with the image that is present in its absence, present by proxy, as it were. My impression was confirmed when I discovered another work in the Hamburg Catalogue of Olaf Metzel's sketches. The work dates back to 1984 and bears the title *Stammheim*, a place name that was familiar to everyone at the time. Among the handwritten notes on this sheet you will find the entry "The veil of Saint Veronica." The association of the crown of thorns suggests itself here, yet the text simultaneously refers to the absence of the face—that is, of the image—in the empty center. Formal interests also had their say, for instance, when next to this woven object the words "diagonal on top" appeared, implying a conversion of the spatial aspect into a three-dimensional work. Thus, the sketch becomes a draft design. At the same time, the association with an absent picture is endorsed by the artist himself.

In *Stommeln*, the impression of an empty picture frame conveys itself only to viewers on the ground floor, that is, when they stand directly below it. Instead of a wooden ceiling, you see here a wooden frame, and you see it on the ceiling where you would otherwise not expect any picture. However, the frame is also a "pars pro toto" of the ceiling as it frames it from inside, as it were, and repeats it on a smaller scale in the center. This would turn the entire ceiling into an image. All of the ceiling? The spot below the integrated gallery commands only a partial view of the ceiling. You see a rectangle that is limited on three sides by walls and by the viewer's location on the fourth. This field of vision is fringed by walls on three sides only. This is exactly the measuring unit which Metzel's frame—as the twice-repeated frame shape—uses as a reference. From the proportions alone, a compelling consonance between location and work is created. The frame bestows a center to the ceiling that is not the center of the room but the center of vision.

The impression you get when ascending to the gallery is radically different. The frame shape disappears, and in its place you see a suspended shape that lowers itself deeper into the room than a frame could possibly do. You behold a staggered structure made of stalactite-like holding strips between which the whitewash of the ceiling remains visible everywhere. It is hard to imagine a more contrary aspect of one and the same work. Up on the gallery, the plastic principle has replaced the framing one. Up close, the pull of the perspective that viewers below the frame are exposed to gives way to the impression of a highly complex organism consisting of a large number of small structures that interlock with each other and appear to form several frames stuck inside of each other. Using computer simulation, they were created in such a way that they turn out to have been the artist's primary consideration. Their multi-dimensional geometry presents the transition from light to shadow and the aspect of various spatial axes, causing the room to be geometrically constructed and at the same time to be encrypted as we lose sight of the greater picture. It is in the nature of geometry to remain impenetrable to the passing gaze and to open only successively as it is analytically decoded.

Geometry as an image alternative, withdrawing from the viewer's gaze and refusing images, took the role of a cosmic signature in the visual culture of the Middle East. Such associations, which are unlikely to have inspired the artist, bring me, the viewer, into play because I may give myself to speculation

Sprachgitter (Language Grid)
2009
Ash wood
95 × 410 × 376 cm
Installation view Synagoge Stommeln

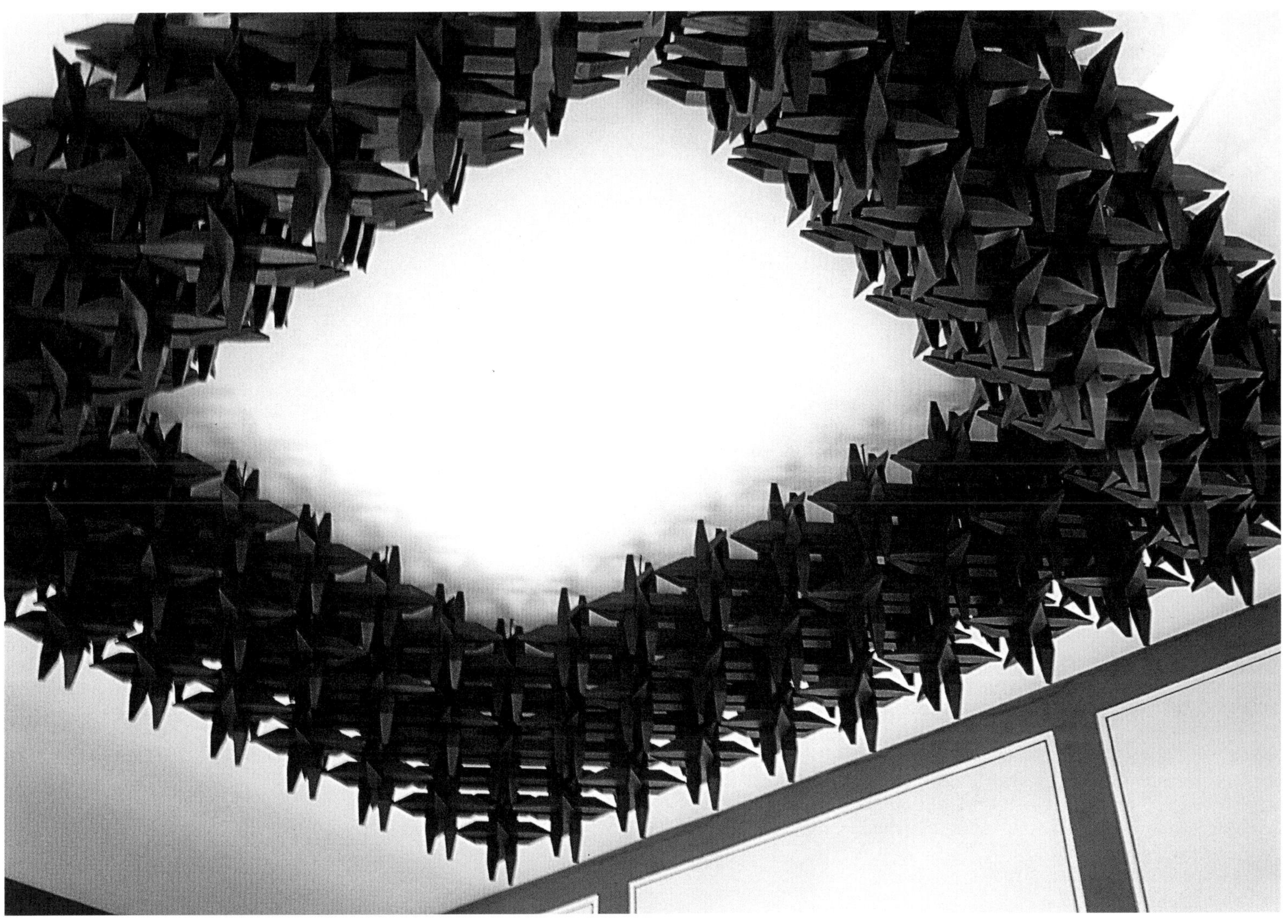

precisely because I did not design this work. Let me elaborate by giving two examples. For one thing, there is Solomon's Temple in Jerusalem as described in the Bible. It preoccupied many artists, none of which were permitted to create an image of it though. The splendour of its fit-out was unparalleled, yet limited to the decoration of the walls and implements because the edifice was consecrated to the Invisible One. And then there is the Arabic-Islamic architecture, culminating in a type of ornamental corbel that was used in recesses and the underside of domes, and that was called Muqarnas. This decorative device was the work of mathematicians, with architects providing the drafts and tradesmen translating the drafts from the plane into the third dimension without abandoning the geometric design. The individual segments of the design, its cells, turned into luminous honeycombs, filter light through from above. The location where Olaf Metzel's installation is on display thus invites viewers to read semantic ambiguity into a formal issue. The more abstract the form, the greater the urge to commit it to memory via interpretation. Among other things, we find here a temptation that the image causes in its very absence.

Language Grid
Olaf Metzel

Brad Pitt speaking Italian in the film *Inglourious Basterds* is certainly amusing. Quentin Tarantino rather subtly uses multiple languages, for structural, as well as artistic purposes. No mess, but language as an interface becomes a pivotal element.

"Create artist, do not talk!" this part of a quote by Goethe is known to many, but few know how it continues in the next line: "Your poem is but a breath."

Two very different examples that are being tackled when the work presented is titled *Sprachgitter (Language Grid)*, and one is speaking out loud.

Why not talk to yourself? After all, rules are made to be broken, which is actually much easier than to stick to them.

And by the way it, the title, might also be about speechlessness or the limitations of language and its respective vocabulary. Provocations, aggressions, ideas, rules, taboos. We are tired of hearing about many things, and there are a lot of misunderstandings.

An article appeared in the newspaper *Welt am Sonntag* on August 23, under the heading *Wörter und tiefe Wunden* (Words and Deep Wounds). It is about the conflict between Jews living here: Are they "Jews in Germany" or "German Jews"? Identity, migration and exile are the key words. There are always more questions than answers.

"Even if you insist on being my enemy—you will not manage to make me yours," Thomas Mann wrote to the composer Arnold Schoenberg during their Californian exile. I will not go into detail here about the conflict between the Jewish composer and the noble Nobel Prize winner. Even if, or rather, because he so finely phrased his sentences, there is something that connects the two: their shared language.

Looking at a grid from a distance, slightly blurred, one perceives it as a composition of points. Is it about boundaries? Maybe I should not speak of a grid, but rather a frame. For discussions. Or do we talk only about conditions, about the shape the argument takes?

In early May, when I read the correspondence between Ingeborg Bachmann and Paul Celan, what stuck to my mind was, besides the "question of the direction of the clock," also the term "Language Grid." Of course, there are no coincidences, especially not when you are invited to visit a synagogue to create a work of art there.

Located in a courtyard on the marketplace in Stommeln, I was impressed by its hidden location, tranquility and seclusion, and even more impressed upon entering the former prayer room. The simple, clearly structured surrounding windows, interspersed with red glass, the gray basalt floor, unadorned, the wooden balcony, and in the center, also made of dark wood, the shrine for the Torah scrolls. The walls are inconspicuously framed in color. If one looks up—at the flat ceiling—nothing. An area where you could insert a new work into the room to create a connection between shrine and balcony. As if it had always been part of the synagogue, perhaps a wooden ceiling? Anyway, something made of similarly dark tinted wood. Not a counterpoint, not a deliberate artistic accent, but something that appears integrated.

"Language Grid," an ambivalent term. Sounds hermetic, like a barrier, although it has almost always to do with permeability, with structures, perhaps a network? Communication after all, as one would call it today? No mesh, rather a grid?

Around 1990, I had made drawings based on designs I had developed in the late seventies. I did not know then how I should translate these and similar contexts into three dimensions.

Is this place—a former synagogue—the right place? Is it possible, in this place, to develop a structure that encompasses a real space, and, at the same time, opens it? Irrespective of history? Are terms such as iconography and semantics relevant? Are there basic elements, perhaps arranged crosswise, that form an autonomous structure?

If you engage extensively with a formal solution, you experience your surroundings in an almost restricted way, or rather, more precisely targeted way. I recently held a small old wooden snap frame in my hands. No picture, only the frame, that's it. Simple and very plain. I bought it immediately. Often you leave an idea, a text, a project for years, and still often think back to it. You don't know what to do. And then there's this one moment where everything comes together, like a mosaic—I had this moment in a former synagogue.

Speech on the occasion of the opening of *Olaf Metzel. Sprachgitter*, Synagoge Stommeln, October 4, 2009.

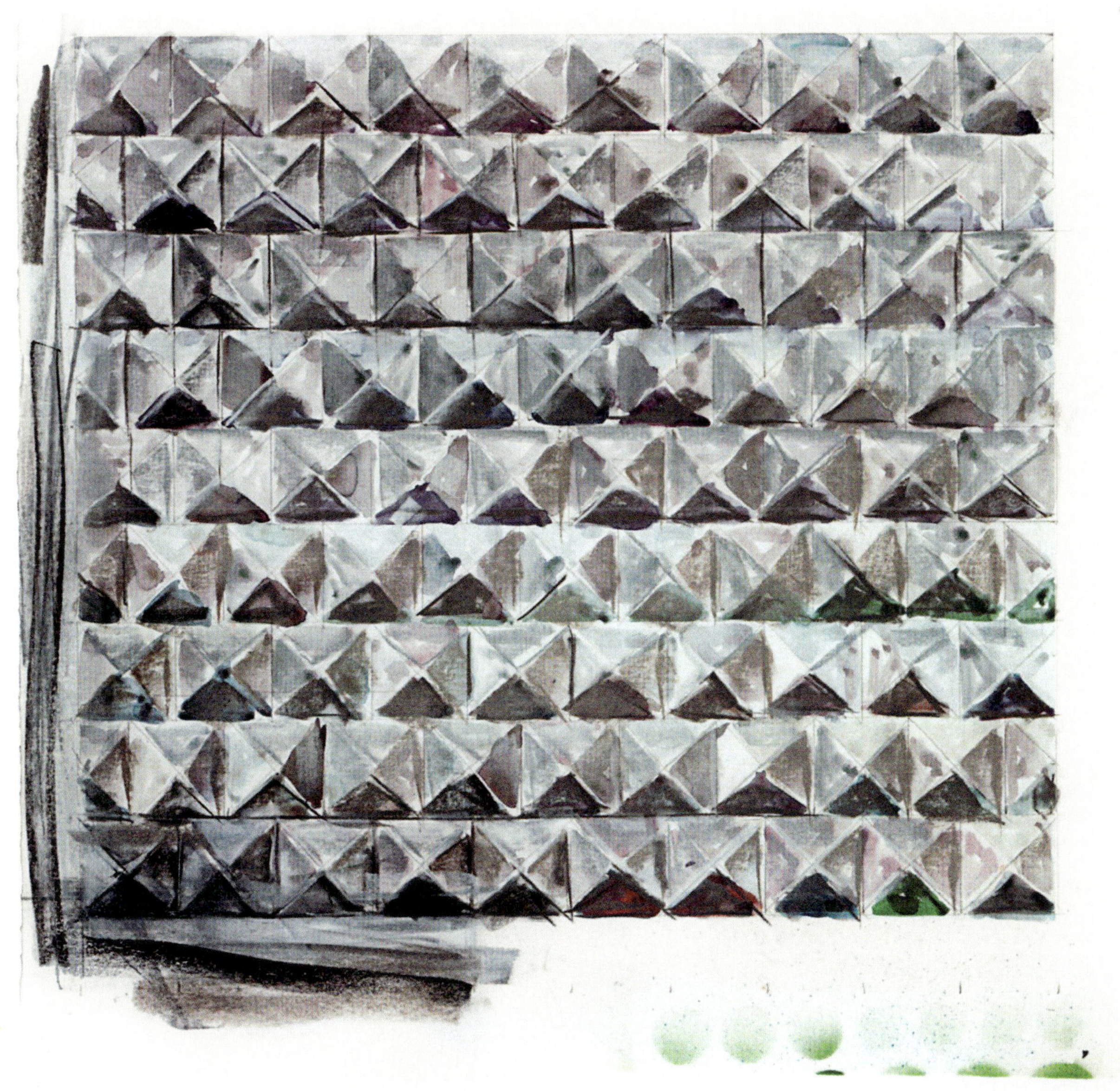

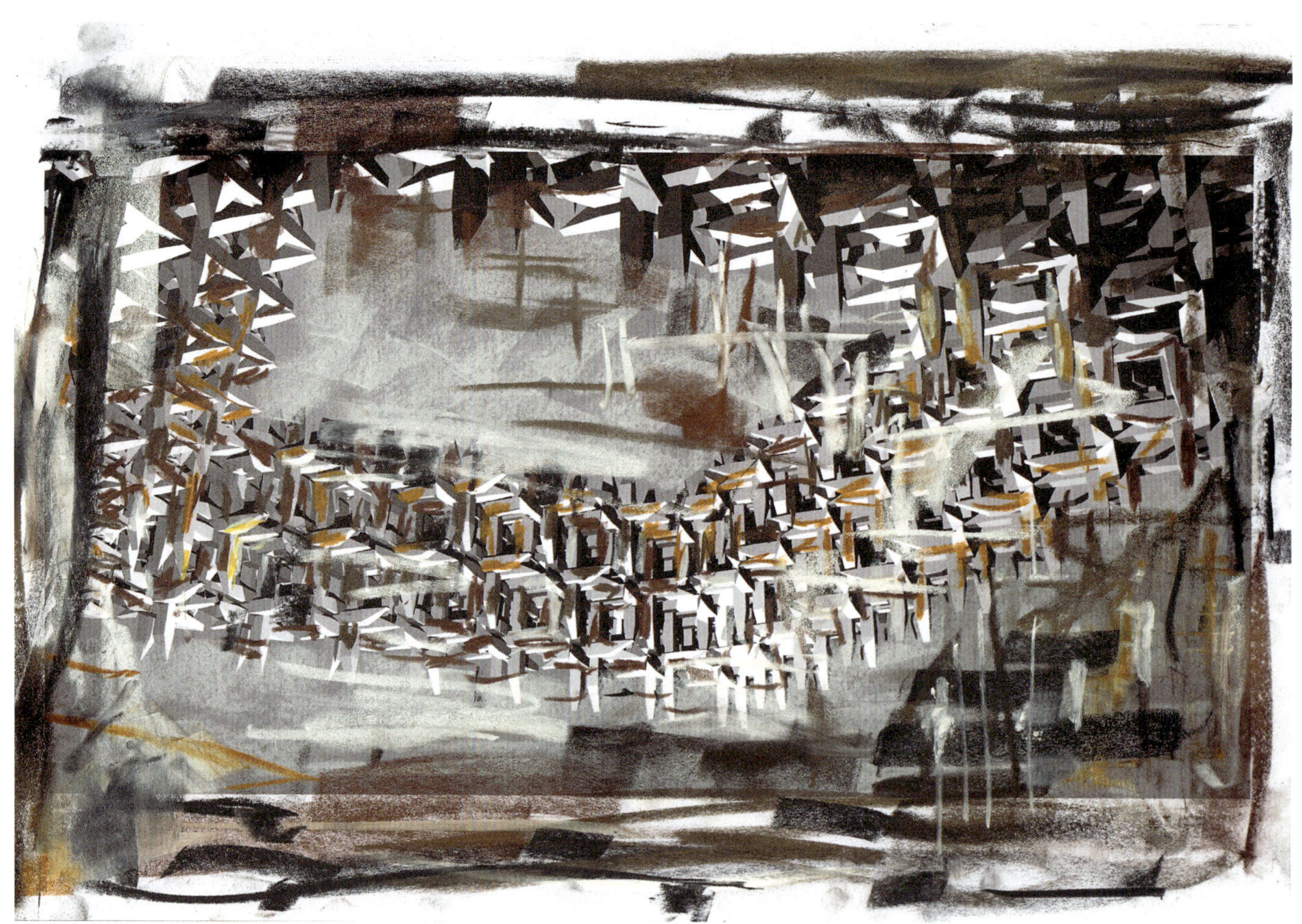

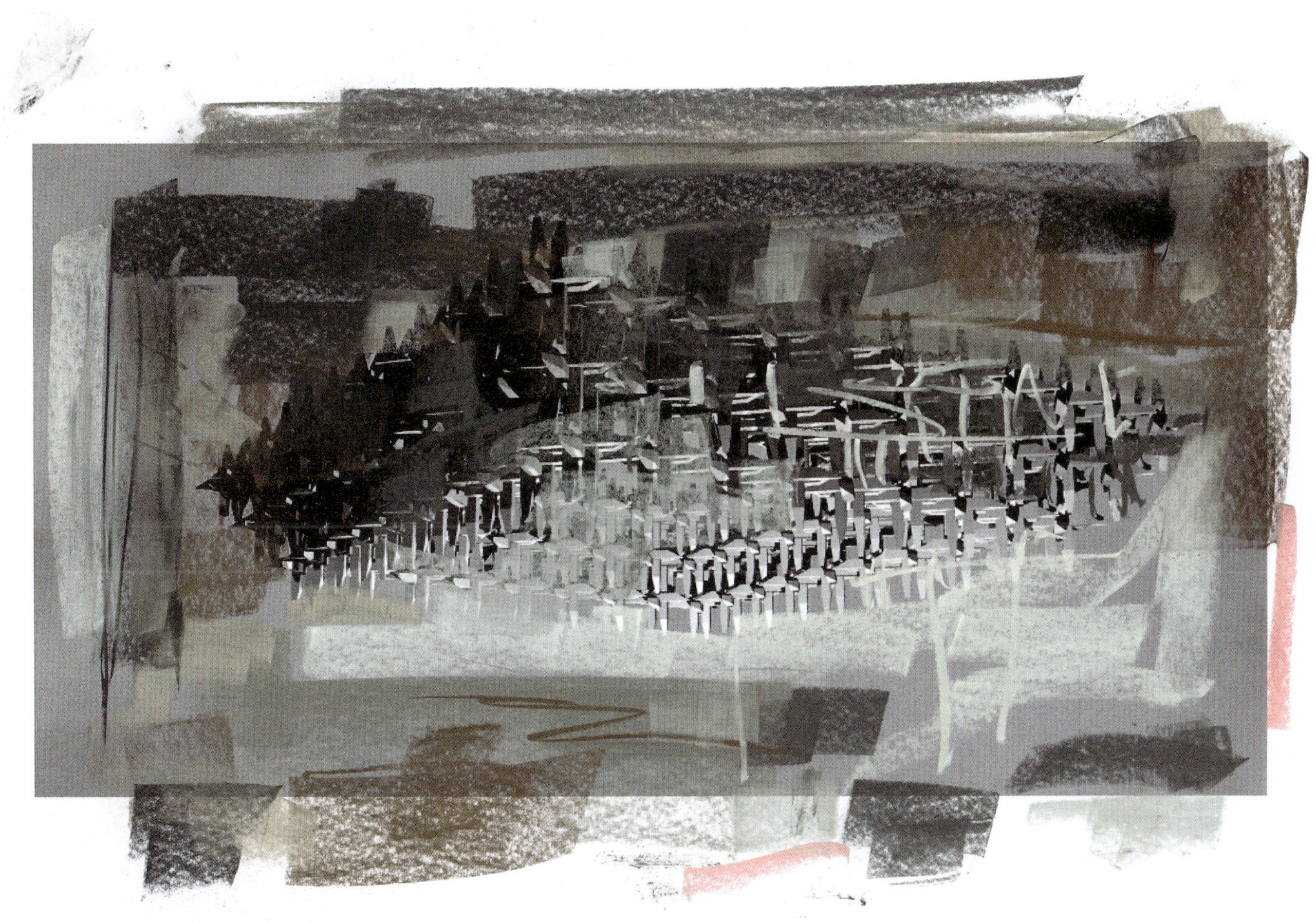

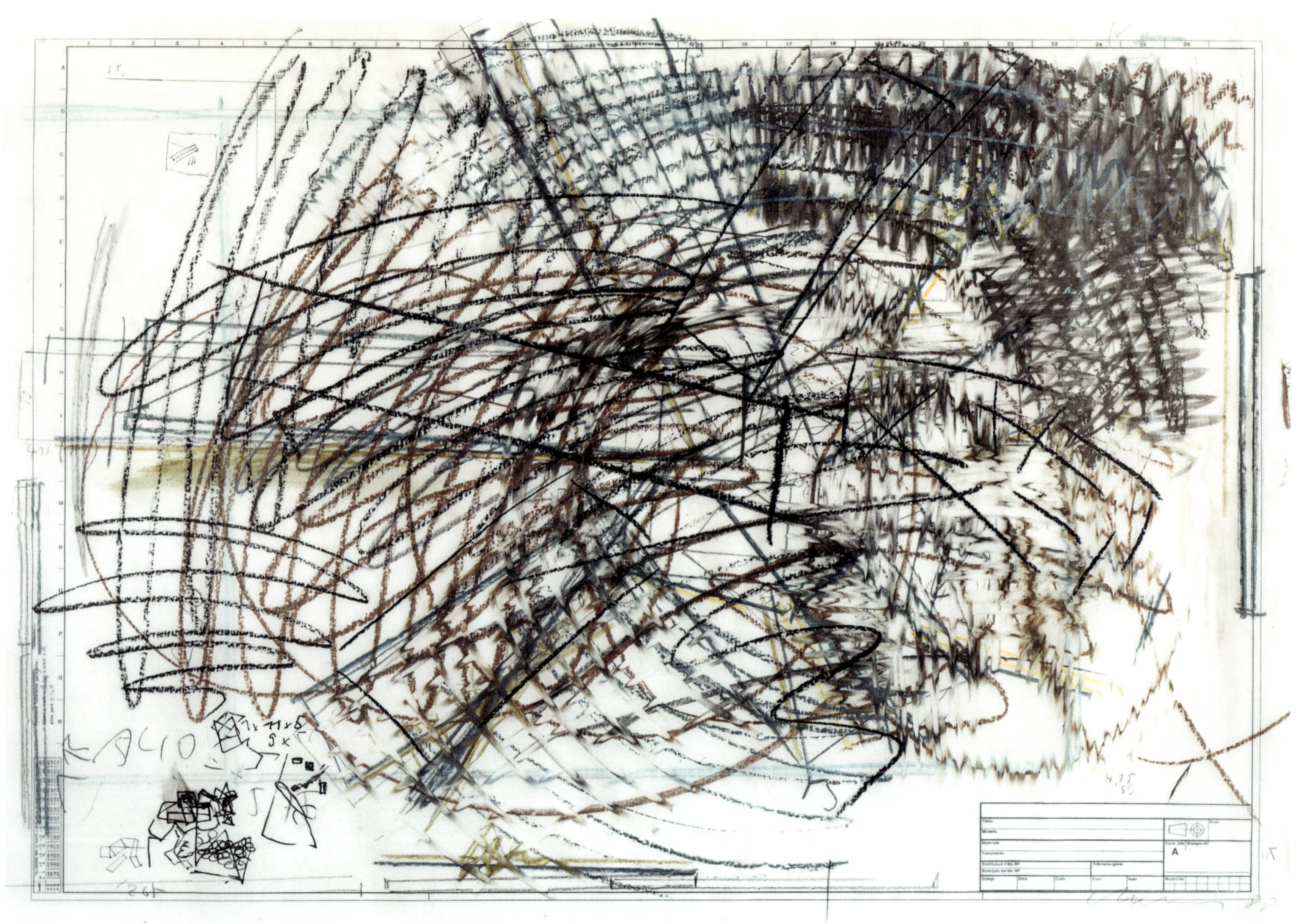

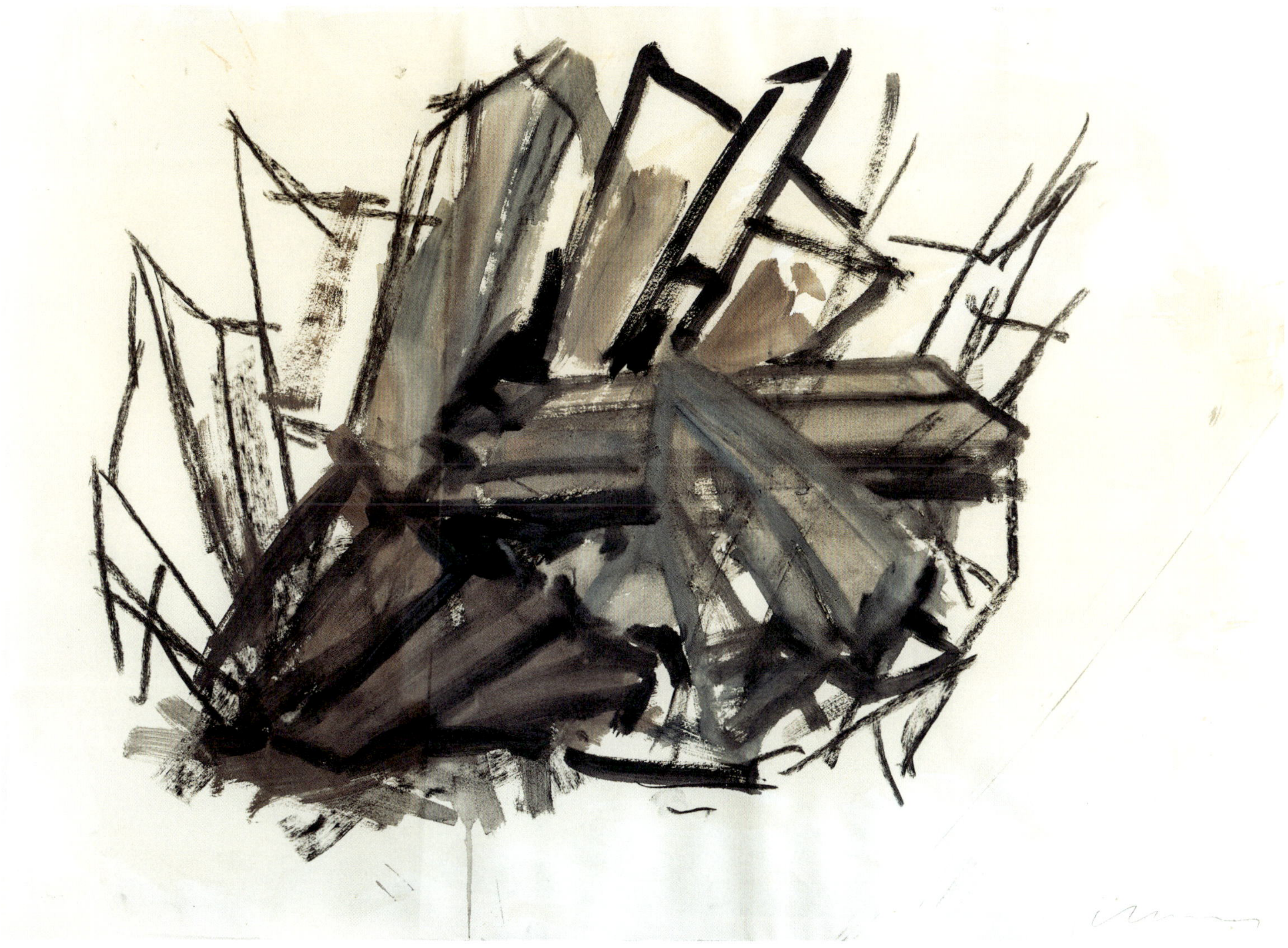

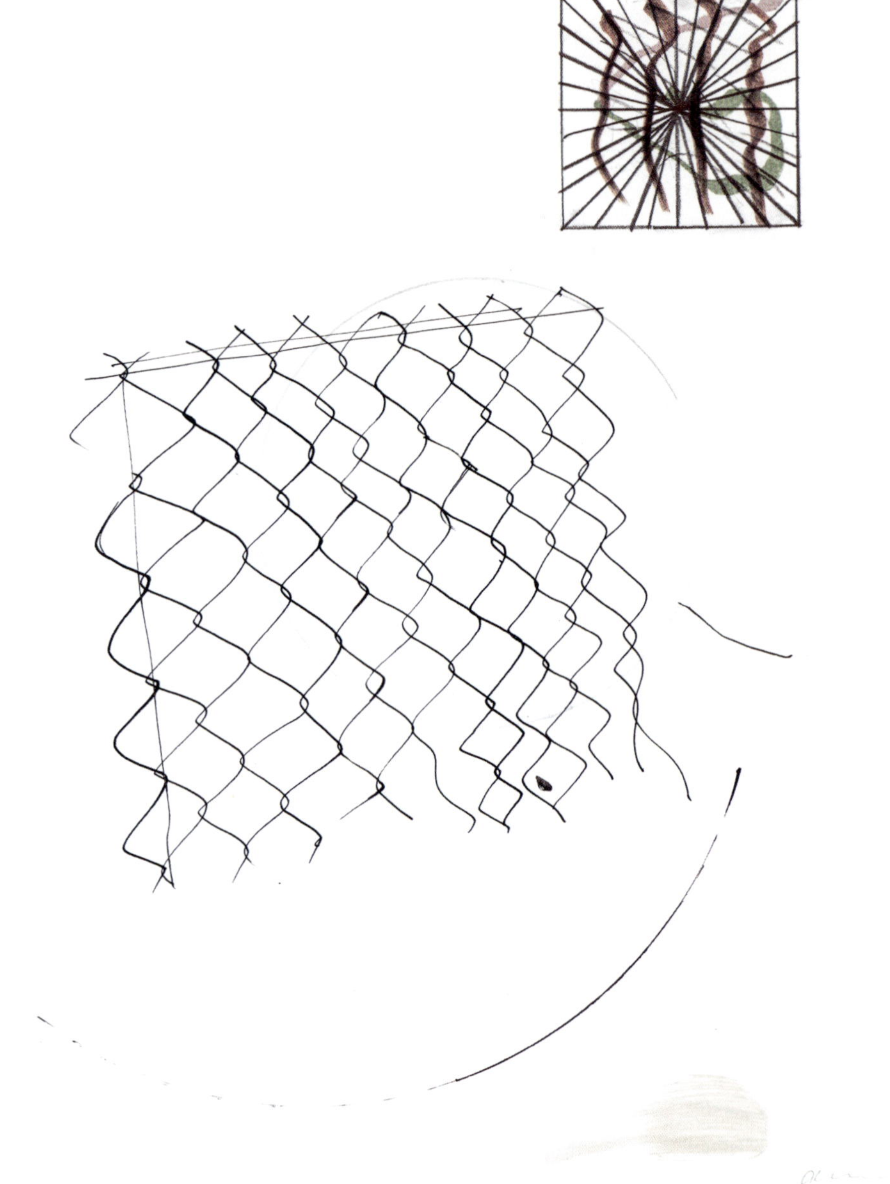

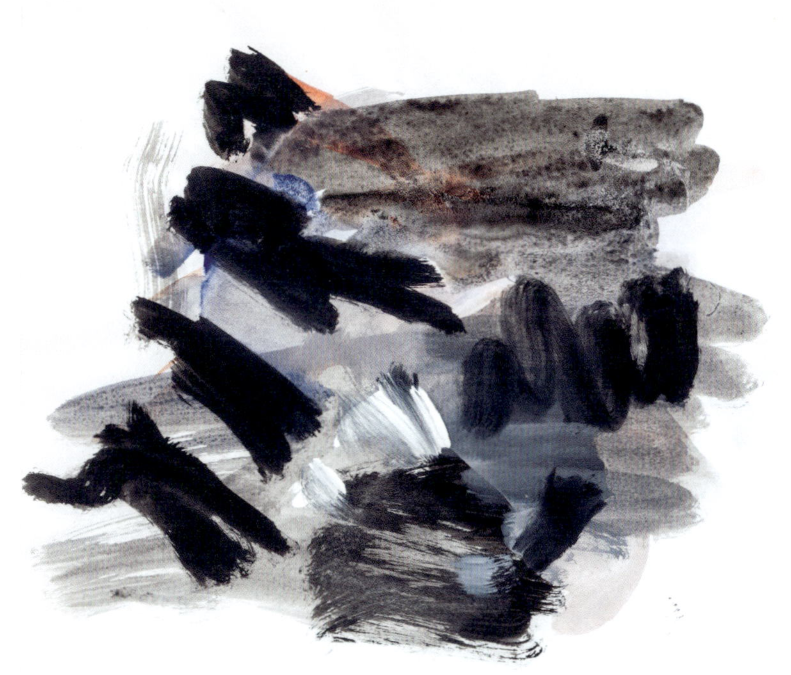

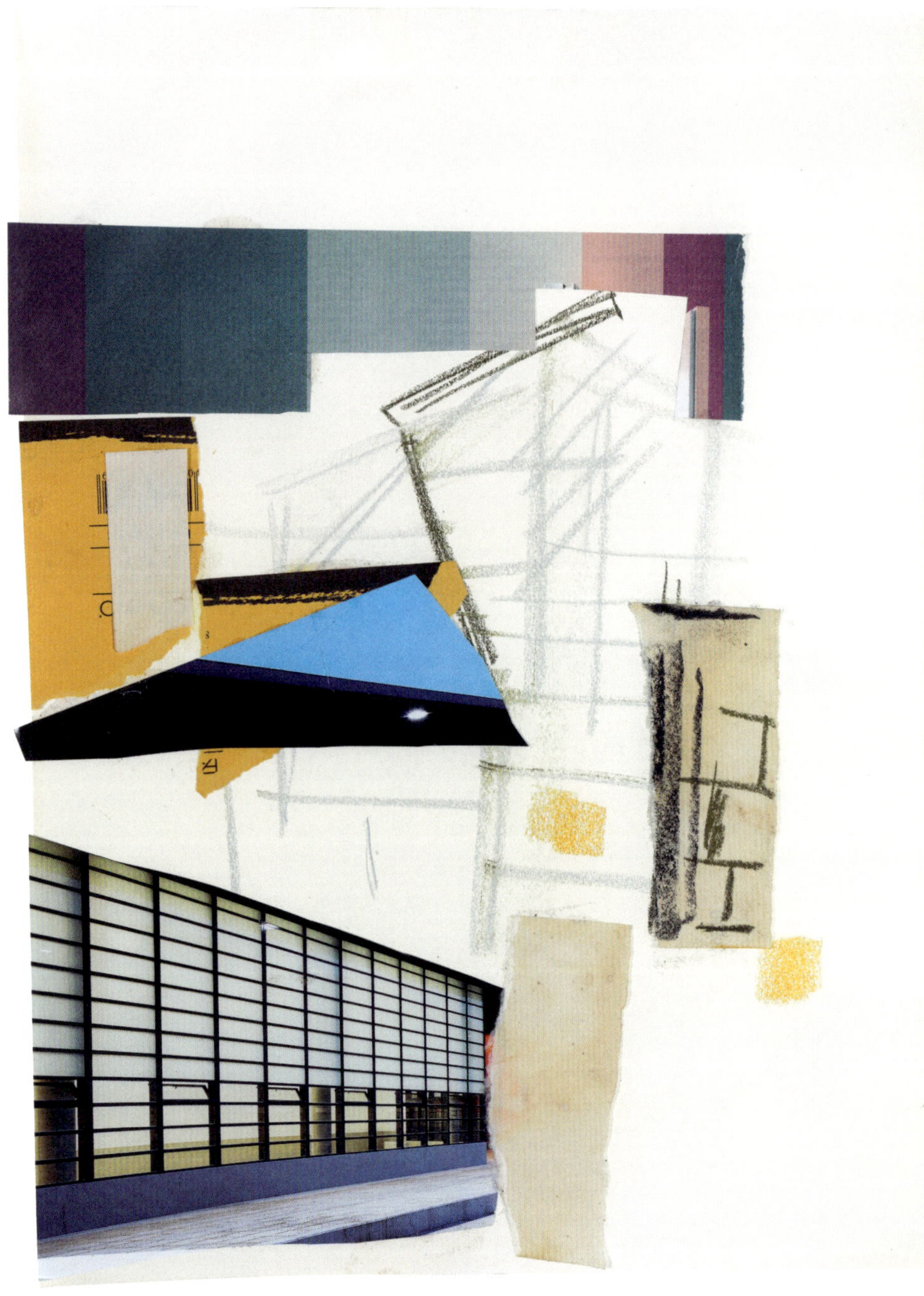

Social Wallpaper (4) 2017

טפט חברתי (4)

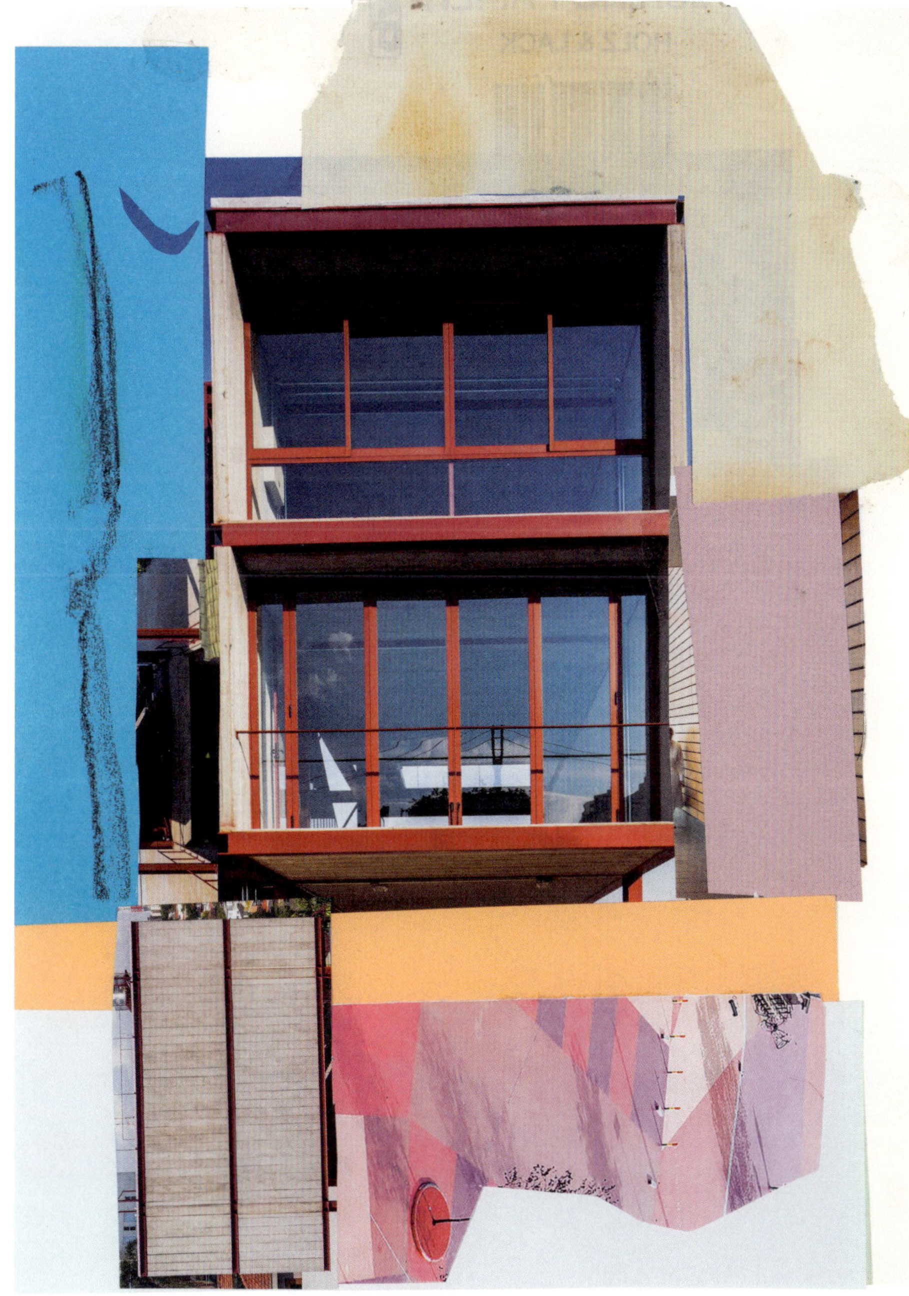

Good Fences Make Good Neighbors
Olaf Metzel

In Kreuzberg, so it was said in the past, you had to be careful that people didn't reach out from the cellar window to steal your shoe laces. It was no different in Neukölln. This described a modest neighborhood in West Berlin, one whose population structure rapidly changed in the nineteen-sixties. More and more foreigners, the majority from Turkey, moved into the area. You could also notice this in the street scenes. New cafes and shops were opened, with the appearance and clothing of the new residents completing the picture. I still remember the Maybachufer market. We used to stroll through it after school, driven by a mix of youthful curiosity and trustfulness. The many Turkish market stalls, the smell of spices, the language—it all had something exotic about it—a taxing but also fascinating atmosphere. Since everything was new and somehow different you didn't exactly know how you should behave. But it was exciting at any rate.

Between the two cultures there was a certain reservedness and shyness on both parts initially, but youth of the same age soon became friends with each other. We went swimming together in the Columbia swimming pool and when playing football there were no problems in understanding each other anyway. The girls—who seldom wore headscarves—were self-confident, which of course increased the allure, and every now and again, especially when they were without any chaperones, the atmosphere was charged with sparks of hope. However, there was always something self-evident about the way we and the Turkish girls and boys got along, due also to the typical secrecies we shared. No one invited you to their homes—people kept to themselves at home and tended to close themselves off. Then, as a means of earning some money, I offered tutoring in German.

For all the liberality there was something hermetic about it, what one refers to today as parallel cultures. It was an exciting time that I like to remember, and one that has given me food for thought over the decades. Different lifestyles, finding one's way around in a foreign environment, and Turkish migration (among other things) have since been themes of my works.

We got along, but that was all. They were new neighbors and—as the saying goes—you cannot choose them. Then at the end of the sixties we moved away to a Berlin suburb.

A contribution to the *A Good Neighbor, Storybook*, Istanbul Biennale 2017.

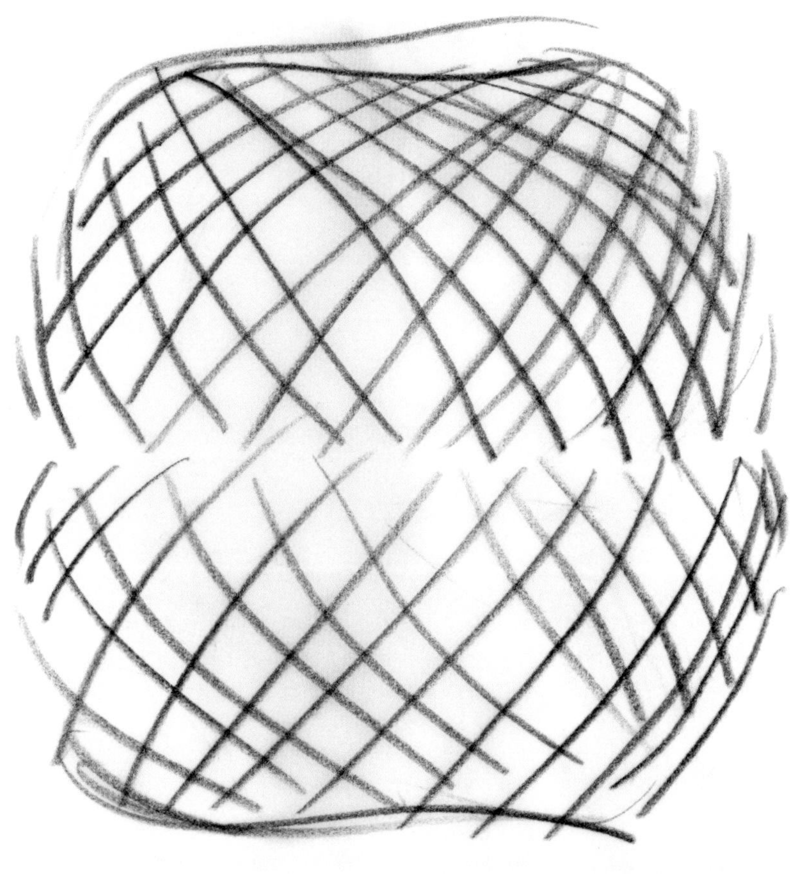

Biography Olaf Metzel

Olaf Metzel lives and works in Munich. He studied at the Free University and University of the Arts in Berlin. Since 1990 he has been professor at the Academy of Fine Arts in Munich, where he served as principal 1995–1999. He has had numerous solo exhibitions in Germany and abroad, including *documenta 8*, Sculpture Projects Munster (1987 and 1997), Sydney Biennial (1984 and 1990), Istanbul Biennial (1995) and São Paulo Biennial (2002). Metzel's prizes include the Villa Massimo Prize (Rome, 1987), the Arnold Bode Prize (Kassel, 1994), the Wilhelm Loth Prize (Darmstadt, 1997), the Art Prize of the City of Munich (2005), the Lichtwark Prize (Hamburg, 2010), and the MFI Graduate Award (Essen, 2014). Public sculptures by Metzel can be seen in Germany, other countries in Europe, and Asia. He has curated multiple exhibitions and published numerous contributions in newspapers and magazines. He is author as well as editor of the art journals *Basisarbeit*, *Rote Zelle*, and *Circus Wols*.

Selected Monographic Catalogues

Olaf Metzel. Skulptur
Cat. Kunstraum München, Munich 1982
Text: Luise Horn

Olaf Metzel
Cat. daad Galerie, Berlin 1984
Texts: René Block, Uwe M. Schneede

Olaf Metzel. Intelligence Service / A.M.T., "Der Fälscher ist der Held der elektronischen Kultur" (Glenn Gould)
Cat. Galerie Rudolf Zwirner, Cologne 1989
Text: Hans Magnus Enzensberger

Olaf Metzel. Drawings 1985–1990
Cat. Westfälisches Landesmuseum für Kunst und Kulturgeschichte, Münster / Kunstraum München, Munich, 1990
Texts: Alexander Dückers, Walter Grasskamp, Luise Horn, Ulrich Wilmes

Olaf Metzel
Cat. Hamburger Kunsthalle, Hamburg 1992
Texts: Hans Dickel, Wolfgang Max Faust, Christoph Heinrich, Luise Horn, Uwe M. Schneede

Olaf Metzel
Kat. Staatliche Kunsthalle Baden-Baden, Munich / Stuttgart 1992
Texts: Wolfgang Hegewald, Jochen Poetter

Olaf Metzel. Zeichnungen und Modelle Zu Projekten im Außenraum
Cat. daadgalerie, Berlin 1995
Texts: Friedrich Meschede, Wieland Schmied, Marius Babias et al.

Olaf Metzel. Freitreppe
Verlag Silke Schreiber, Munich 1996
Texts: Helmut Friedel, Hilmar Hoffmann

Olaf Metzel. Freizeitpark
Cat. Lenbachhaus, Munich 1996
Texts: Diedrich Diederichsen, Bruno Latour, Olaf Metzel / Ulrich Wilmes, Marlene Streeruwitz

Olaf Metzel
Special edition from O. M. Cat, ifa 1996 for the exhibition *Town-Country-River,* Warsaw 1999
Texts (Polish): Tilman Osterwold, Interview Frank Barth with O.M.

Olaf Metzel. Troisième printemps
Cat. Villa Arson, Nice 1999
Texts (French/English): Marius Babias / Olaf Metzel, Florian Matzner

Olaf Metzel, Montag mit Freitag
Ed. Klaus Wolbert, Cat. Institut Mathildenhöhe, Darmstadt
Verlag Silke Schreiber, Munich 2001
Texts: Marius Babias, Maria Eichhorn / Olaf Metzel, Sigrid Hofer, Marlene Streeruwitz, Klaus Wolbert

Olaf Metzel. Reise nach Jerusalem / Musical Chairs
Cat. and Ed. Pinakothek der Moderne, Munich
Verlag Silke Schreiber, Munich 2003
Texts (German/English): Reinhold Baumstark, Bernhart Schwenk

Olaf Metzel. 13.4.1981
Verlag Silke Schreiber, Munich 2005
Texts: Hans Dickel, Alexander Dückers, Wolfgang Max Faust, Walter Grasskamp, Christoph Heinrich, Reinhard Müller, Barbara Straka, Florian Waldvogel, DVD with Rudij Bergmann, *Utopie-Verlust*, First Broadcast ARD 1987

Olaf Metzel. Zeichnungen
Cat. Hamburger Kunsthalle / Staatsgalerie Stuttgart
Verlag Silke Schreiber, Munich 2006
Texts: Leon Krempel, Petra Roettig, Michael Semff, Uwe M. Schneede, Tobias Vogt

Olaf Metzel. noproblem
Von der Heydt-Museum Wuppertal 2007
Texts: Gerhard Finckh, Marlene Streeruwitz, Ayşegül Sönmez, Uwe M. Schneede, Olaf Metzel, Herbert Pogt, Harald Falckenberg

Olaf Metzel. Öffentlichkeitsarbeiten
Hatje Cantz Verlag, Ostfildern 2009
Ed. Fritz Barth
Texts: Rudij Bergmann, Marlene Streeruwitz, Olaf Metzel, Marius Babias, Christiane Hoffmans, Fritz Barth

Olaf Metzel. Noch Fragen?
Cat. MKM Museum Küppersmühle für Moderne Kunst, Duisburg
Weserburg Museum für moderne Kunst, Bremen
Snoeck Verlagsgesellschaft, Cologne 2010
Texts: Walter Smerling, Matthias Winzen, Peter Iden, Daniel Pies, Ayşegül Sönmez

Olaf Metzel. Kaffee Zeitung Zigaretten
Cat. Kunstverein Heilbronn
Snoeck Verlagsgesellschaft, Cologne 2013
Texts: Bodo Fründt, Patrick Lambert, Peter Richter

Gegenwartsgesellschaft
Cat. Hamburger Kunstverein
Distanz Verlag, Berlin 2013
Texts: Raimar Stange, Wolfgang Ullrich, Olaf Metzel / Florian Waldvogel, Friedrich von Borries, Florian Waldvogel, Regina Wamper, Günther Jakob, Felix Ensslin

From the TV to the Fridge
Cat. Kunstraum Innsbruck, for the exhibition *Olaf Metzel. Sozialtapete*
Snoeck Verlagsgesellschaft, Cologne 2015
Texts: Karin Pernegger, Olaf Metzel

Dermaßen regiert zu werden
Cat. Neues Museum – Staatliches Museum für Kunst und Design Nürnberg, for the exhibition *Olaf Metzel. Deutsche Kiste*
Verlag für moderne Kunst, Vienna 2015
Text: Jörg Heiser

Olaf Metzel – Hans von Marées. Eine Annäherung
Cat. Neue Pinakothek
Snoek Verlagsgesellschaft, Cologne 2016
Texts: Michael Diers, Joachim Kaak (Ed.), Konrad Laudenbacher, Bernhard Maaz, Olaf Metzel, Frank Schmidt, Bernhart Schwenk

The Authors

Galia Bar Or
is artistic director of the Pyramida Contemporary Art Center, Haifa, and senior lecturer at Oranim Academic College. As a former director and curator of the Mishkan Museum of Art, Ein Harod she has curated dozens of exhibitions in Israel and abroad, and published numerous books and catalogues in the fields of history and art. In addition to her history of art studies, she obtained her MA for the History and Philosophy of Sciences and Ideas from the Cohn Institute and her PhD from the School of Historical Studies, Tel Aviv University.

Hans Belting
is a German art historian and theorist of medieval and Renaissance art, as well as contemporary art and the visual image. He studied at the universities of Mainz and Rome, and took his doctorate in art history at the University of Mainz. Since 1966, Belting has been teaching as a professor in Hamburg and Heidelberg, and from 1980 to 1992 at the Ludwig-Maximilians-Universität in Munich. From 1992 until his retirement in 2002, Belting was professor at the Institute for Art History and Media Theory at the State College of Design in Karlsruhe. Belting is a member of various scientific academies in Germany and the U.S., including the Heidelberg Academy of Sciences, the Wissenschaftskolleg in Berlin and the order Pour le Mérite of Arts and Sciences. He was elected a Foreign Honorary Member of the American Academy of Arts and Sciences in 1992.

Christoph Heinrich
was appointed Frederick and Jan Mayer Director of the Denver Art Museum in 2010, after serving the museum for two years as Curator of Modern & Contemporary Art. Before joining the DAM, Heinrich was at the Hamburg Kunsthalle, where during his twelve-year tenure, he organized more than fifty exhibitions. Heinrich studied Art History, German Literature and Dramatics in the University of Vienna. He earned his MA and PhD at the Ludwig-Maximilians-Universität in Munich. A knowledgeable art historian, his publications range from contemporary public sculpture to nineteenth- and twentieth-century painters such as Claude Monet, Vincent van Gogh, Francis Bacon, Andy Warhol and Daniel Richter.

Yaniv Shapira
has been serving since 2016 as Director and Chief Curator of the Mishkan, Museum of Art, Ein Harod. Shapira has curated numerous exhibitions in museums in Israel and abroad. From 2004–2009 he was Director and Curator of the Kibbutz Art Gallery in Tel Aviv. During those years, he turned the gallery into the principal art center of thirty local galleries in kibbutzim throughout Israel. He has a BA in Art History and Jewish Philosophy (1995), and an M.A. in Art History (1997) from Tel Aviv University. He is also a graduate cum laude of diploma studies in Museology at the Genia Schreiber University Art Gallery, Tel Aviv University. He is currently completing his PhD dissertation on "Representations of Landscape and Place in Israeli Painting in the 1980s" Tel Aviv University.

Matthias Winzen
has been Professor of Art History at the Saar Academy of Fine Arts since 2005, and Director of the Museum of Nineteenth-Century Art and Technology (LA8) in Baden-Baden since 2009. From 1995–1999 he was Fine Arts Project Manager for the Siemens Cultural Program and from 1999–2005 he was Director of the State Art Gallery in Baden-Baden. He studied at the Dusseldorf Art Academy from 1982–1987 and was a master class student in 1986. From 1988–1995 he studied art history, German philology and pedagogy at the CUNY, New York, and at Ruhr University Bochum, obtaining a doctorate in 1996. In 1994, he was awarded the Carl Einstein Prize for Art Criticism.

אולף מצטל והמחברים

אולף מטצל

אולף מטצל חי ועובד במינכן. הוא למד באוניברסיטה החופשית ובאוניברסיטה לאמנויות בברלין. מאז שנת 1990 הוא מכהן כפרופסור באקדמיה לאמנויות של מינכן, שם כיהן כמנהל בשנים 1995–1999. עבודותיו הוצגו בתערוכות יחיד רבות בגרמניה וברחבי העולם. בין השאר דוקומנטה 8, בפרויקטים לפיסול במינסטר (1987, 1997), בביאנלה של סידני (1984, 1990), בביאנלה של איסטנבול (1995), ובביאנלה של סאו פאולו (2002). הוא זכה בפרסים רבים, וביניהם פרס וילה מאסימו (רומא, 1987), פרס ארנולד בודה (קאסל, 1994), פרס וילהלם לוט (דרמשטט, 1997), פרס האמנות של העיר מינכן (2005), פרס ליכטוורק (המבורג, 2010), ופרס בוגרי MFI (אסן, 2014). פסלי חוצות של מטצל מוצגים ברחבי גרמניה, אירופה, ואסיה. הוא אצר תערוכות רבות וכתביו התפרסמו בספרים, עיתונים ובמגזינים רבים. בנוסף לכתיבתו, הוא משמש גם כעורך של כתבי העת האמנותיים Basisarbeit Circus Wols, Rote Zelle.

ד"ר גליה בר אור

היא מנהלת אמנותית של פירמידה, מרכז לאמנות עכשווית חיפה, ומרצה בכירה במכללת אורנים. כמנהלת ואוצרת משכן לאמנות עין חרוד, אצרה עשרות תערוכות בארץ ובחו"ל ופרסמה ספרים וקטלוגים רבים בתחומי היסטוריה ואמנות. בנוסף ללימודי תולדות האמנות השלימה בר אור לימודי תואר שני במכון כהן להיסטוריה ופילוסופיה של המדעים והרעיונות ודוקטורט בבית-ספר להיסטוריה באוניברסיטת תל-אביב.

ד"ר הנס בלטינג

הוא היסטוריון של האמנות ותיאורטיקן של אמנות ימי הביניים והרנסנס, של אמנות עכשווית ושל הדימוי החזותי. הוא למד באוניברסיטאות של מיינץ ורומא, וסיים את הדוקטורט שלו בתולדות האמנות באוניברסיטת מיינץ. מאז 1966, מכהן בלטינג כפרופסור בהמבורג ובהיידלברג, ובין השנים 1980–1992 באוניברסיטת לודביג-מקסימיליאן במינכן. מאז 1992 ועד לפרישתו ב-2002, כיהן בלטינג כפרופסור במכון לתולדות האמנות ולתיאוריות מדיה במכללה לעיצוב בקרלסרוהה. בלטינג הוא חבר באקדמיות מדעיות שונות בגרמניה ובארה"ב, וביניהן האקדמיה למדעים של היידלברג, המכללה למדעים של ברלין; ומסדר פור לה מריט לאמנויות ומדעים. ב-1992, נבחר בלטינג לחבר זר לשם כבוד באקדמיה האמריקאית לאמנויות ומדעים.

ד"ר כריסטוף היינריך

מכהן מאז 2010 כמנהל המוזיאון לאמנות של דנוור, קולורדו, לאחר שכיהן במשך שנתיים כאוצר לאמנות מודרנית ועכשווית של המוזיאון. קודם לכן, היה אוצר במוזיאון לאמנות של המבורג, שם אצר יותר מחמישים תערוכות במשך תקופה בת 12 שנה. היינריך למד תולדות האמנות, ספרות, ודרמה באוניברסיטת וינה. הוא סיים לימודי תואר שני ודוקטורט באוניברסיטת לודביג-מקסימיליאן במינכן. היינריך הוא הסטוריון בעל ידע עשיר וכתביו עוסקים במגוון נושאים, מפיסול חוצות עכשווי לציירים בני המאות ה-19 וה-20 כגון קלוד מונה, ואן גוך, פרנסיס בייקון, אנדי וורהול, ודניאל ריכטר.

יניב שפירא

משמש מאז 2016 כמנהל ואוצר ראשי במשכן לאמנות, עין חרוד. אצר עשרות תערוכות בארץ ובחו"ל. בשנים 2004–2009 שימש כמנהל ואוצר של גלריית הקיבוץ בתל אביב. במהלך אותן שנים, הוא הפך את הגלריה למרכז אמנות שריכז שלושים גלריות בקיבוצים ברחבי הארץ. הוא בוגר תואר ראשון בתולדות האמנות ובפילוסופיה יהודית (1993–1995) ותואר שני בתולדות האמנות באוניברסיטת תל-אביב (1996–1997). כמו כן סיים בהצטיינות לימודי תעודה במוזיאולוגיה בגלריה האוניברסיטאית ע"ש גניה שרייבר, אוניברסיטת תל-אביב (2002–2003). בימים אלה הוא מסיים את עבודת הדוקטורט שלו על "ייצוגי נוף ומקום בציור הישראלי בשנות השמונים".

פרופ' מתיאס וינצן

מכהן מאז 2005 כפרופסור לתולדות האמנות בבית הספר הגבוה לאמנות יפה של חבל הסאר שבגרמניה. מאז שנת 2009, הוא מכהן גם כמנהל מוזיאון LA8 לאמנות ולטכנולוגיה של המאה ה-19 בבאדן-באדן. בשנים 1995–1999 ניהל את תכנית האמנויות היפות של מרכז התרבות סימנס, ובשנים 1999–2005 כיהן כמנהל גלריית האמנות של באדן-באדן. למד באקדמיה לאמנות של דיסלדורף בשנים 1982–1987 והיה תלמיד בכיתת מסטר בשנת 1986. בשנים 1988–1995 למד היסטוריה של האמנות, פילולוגיה גרמנית, ופדגוגיה ב-CUNY שבניו יורק ובאוניברסיטת רוהר בוכום שבגרמניה. הוא סיים את הדוקטורט שלו בשנת 1996. בשנת 1994 זכה בפרס קרל איינשטיין לביקורת אמנות.

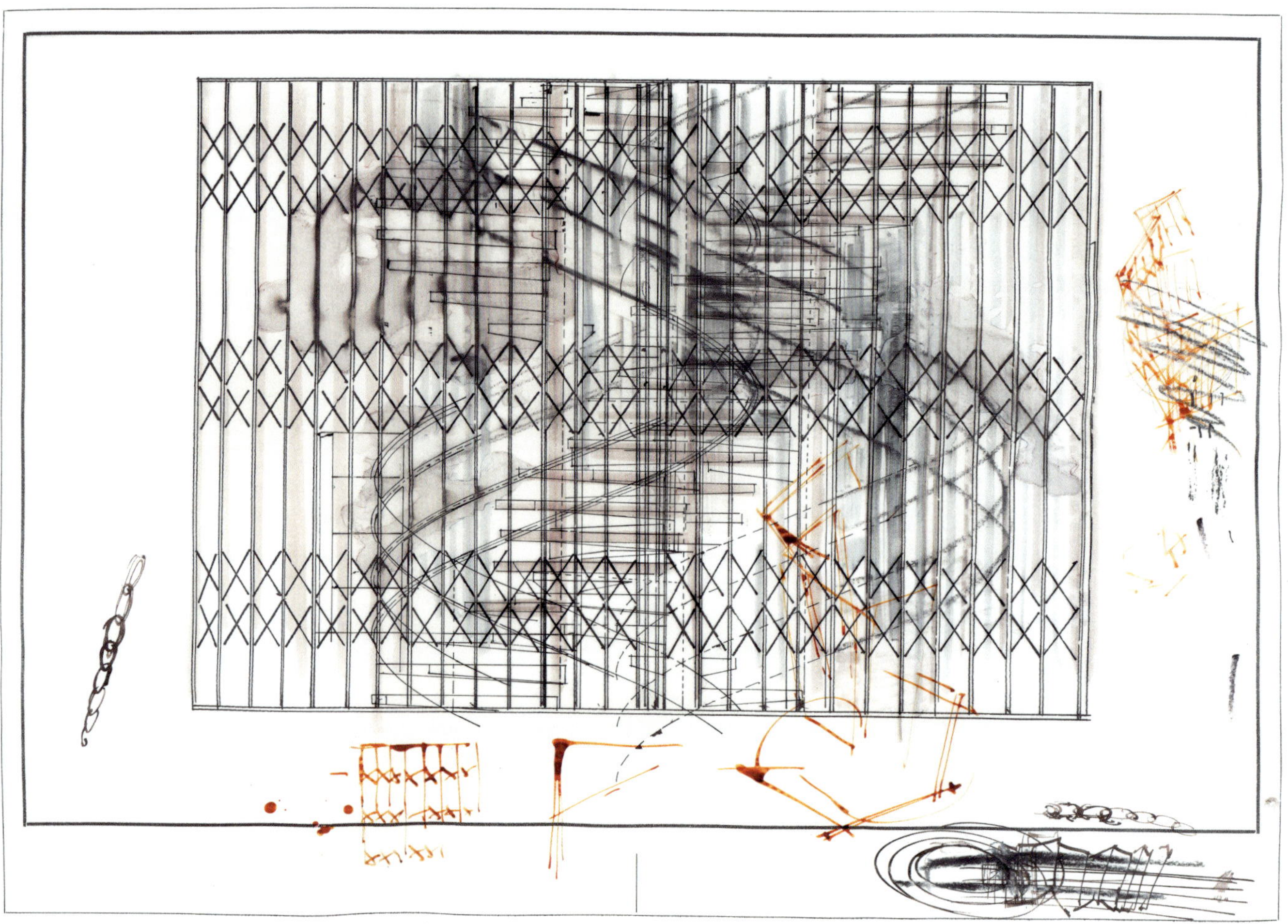

גדרות טובות יוצרות שכנים טובים (פתגם)
אולף מטצל

בשכונת קרויצברג שבברלין, כך היו אומרים בעבר, עליך להיזהר שמא יושיטו דיירי קומת המרתף את ידיהם מהחלון כדי לגנוב לך את שרוכי הנעליים. המצב היה דומה גם בנויקלן, שכונה צנועה במערב ברלין, שאוכלוסייתה השתנתה במהירות בשנות ה-60. מספר הולך וגדל של מהגרים, מרביתם מטורקיה, עברו לגור בשכונה, ופניה השתנו. בתי קפה וחנויות חדשות נפתחו, ומראם הייחודי של התושבים החדשים השלים את התמונה. אני עדיין זוכר את שוק מאיבכאופר (Maybachufer). היינו עוברים דרכו אחרי בית הספר, מובלים על ידי שילוב של סקרנות ילדית ותחושת אמון. הדוכנים הטורקיים, ריח התבלינים, והשפה היו כולם בעלי נופך אקזוטי, והאווירה היתה קשה לעיכול אך יחד עם זאת גם מרתקת: מכיוון שהכל היה חדש ושונה, לא ידעת בדיוק איך להתנהג. אבל בכל מקרה, זה היה מרגש.

בין שתי התרבויות שררו מעין איפוק וביישנות הדדיים, אבל אנחנו הצעירים בני אותו הגיל התקרבנו במהירות. שחינו יחד בבריכת השחייה "קולומביה", ובכל מקרה לא התקשינו להבין זה את זה כששיחקנו כדורגל. הבנות-שכמעט אף פעם לא חבשו רעלות-הקרינו בטחון, שכמובן הגביר את קסמן, ומדי פעם, במיוחד כשלא היו להן מלווים, נטען האוויר בניצוצות של תקווה. היה משהו מובן מאליו באופן שבו הסתדרנו עם בני ובנות המהגרים, שהיה קשור גם לסודות הטיפוסיים שחלקנו. יחד עם זאת, איש לא הזמין אותך לביתו-אנשים נטו להסתגר בדלת אמותיהם. באותה תקופה, כדי להרוויח כסף, הצעתי שיעורים פרטיים בגרמנית. למרות הליברליות שאפיינה את יחסינו, היה בהם משהו הרמטי, שכיום היה זוכה להגדרה "תרבויות מקבילות". היתה זו תקופה מרגשת שאני נהנה להיזכר בה, והיא עוררה בי מחשבות רבות במהלך העשורים שעברו מאז. סגנונות חיים שונים, היכולת למצוא את דרכך בסביבה זרה, וההגירה הטורקית היו מאז לנושאים בעבודותיי.

הסתדרנו, אבל זה בעצם היה הכול. הם היו שכנים חדשים, וכפי שגורס הפתגם-שכנים אי אפשר לבחור. בסוף שנות ה-60, עברנו לפרבר של ברלין.

מתוך הספר שכן טוב / הביאנלה של איסטנבול, 2017

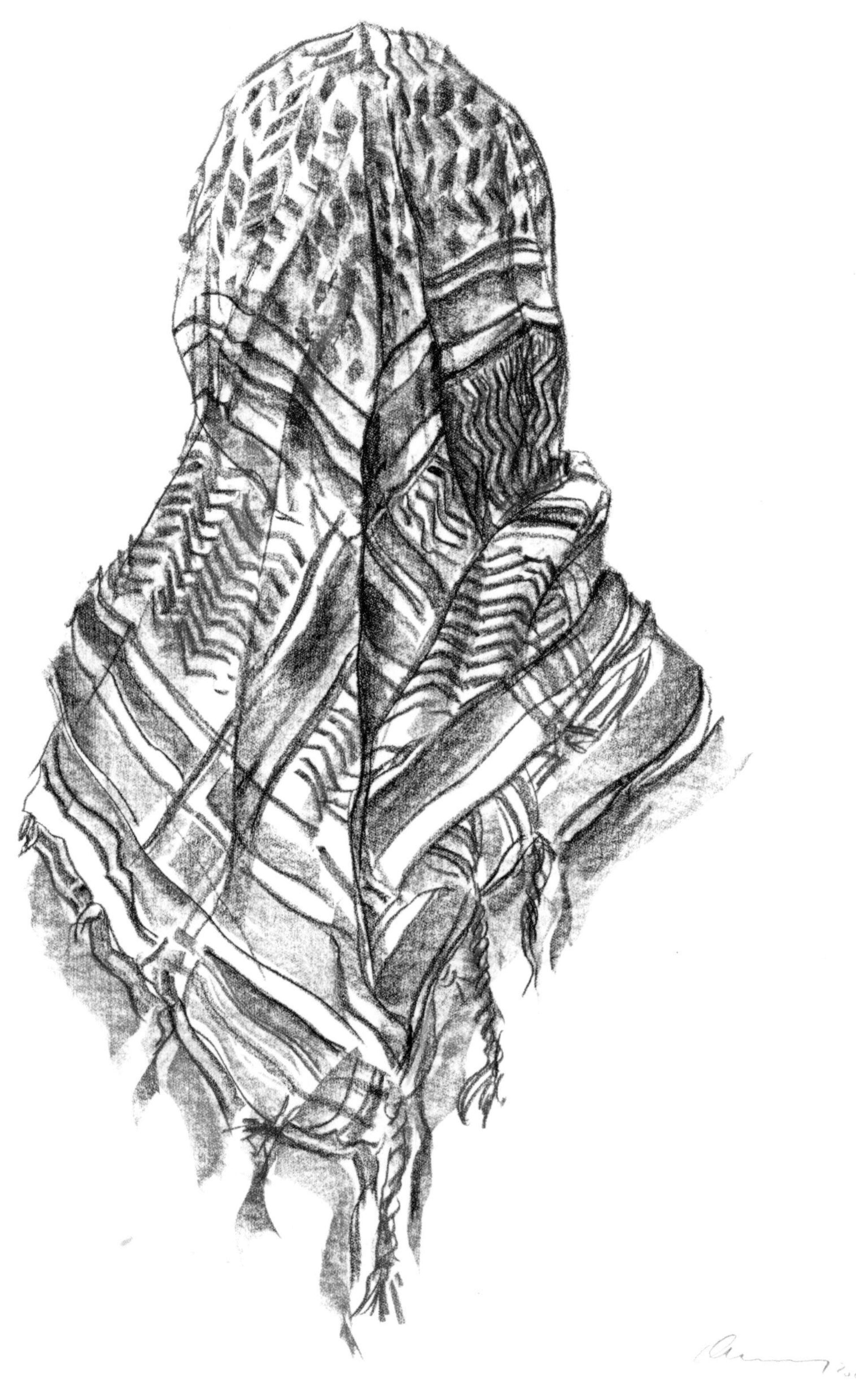

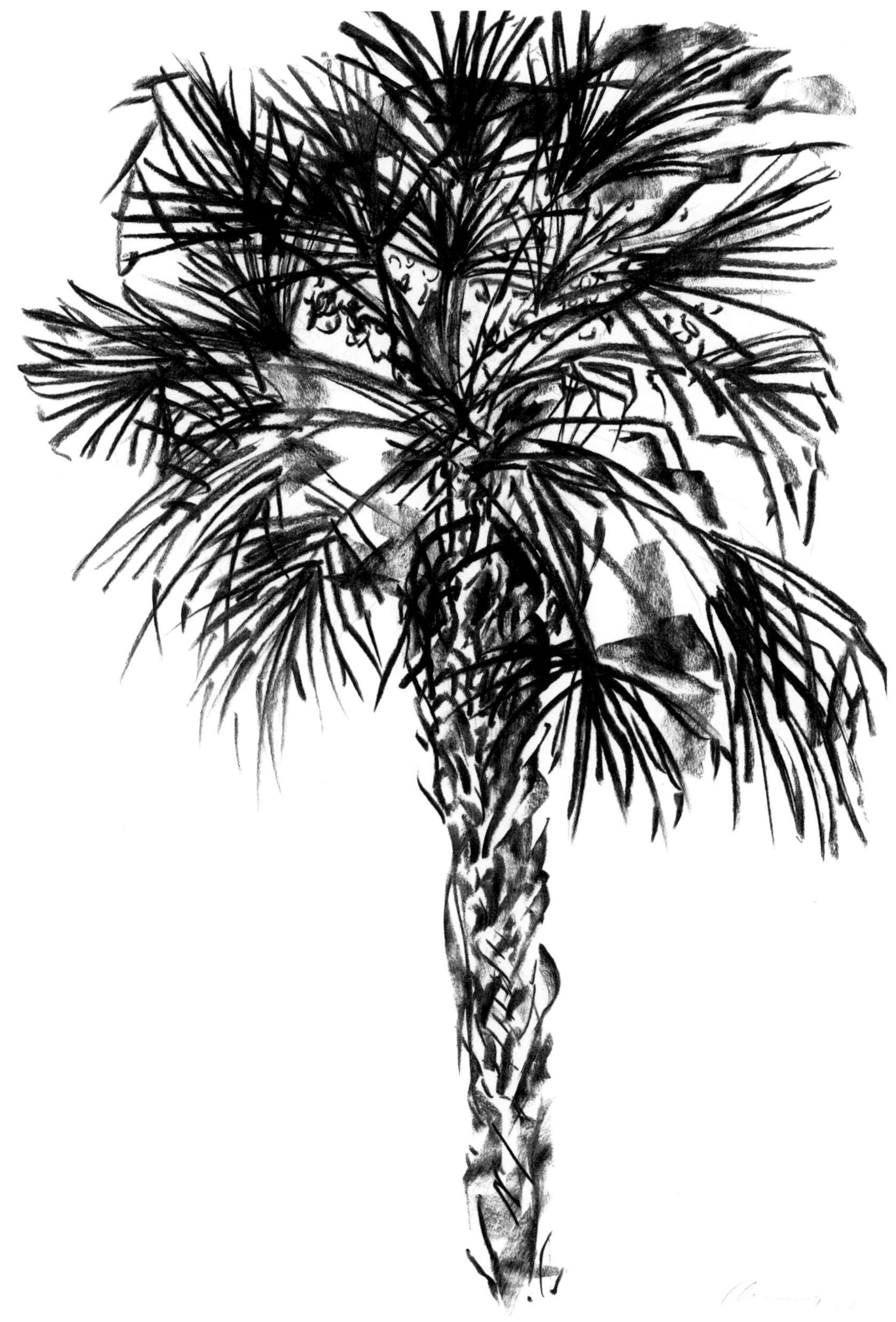

Beretta 1988

ברטה

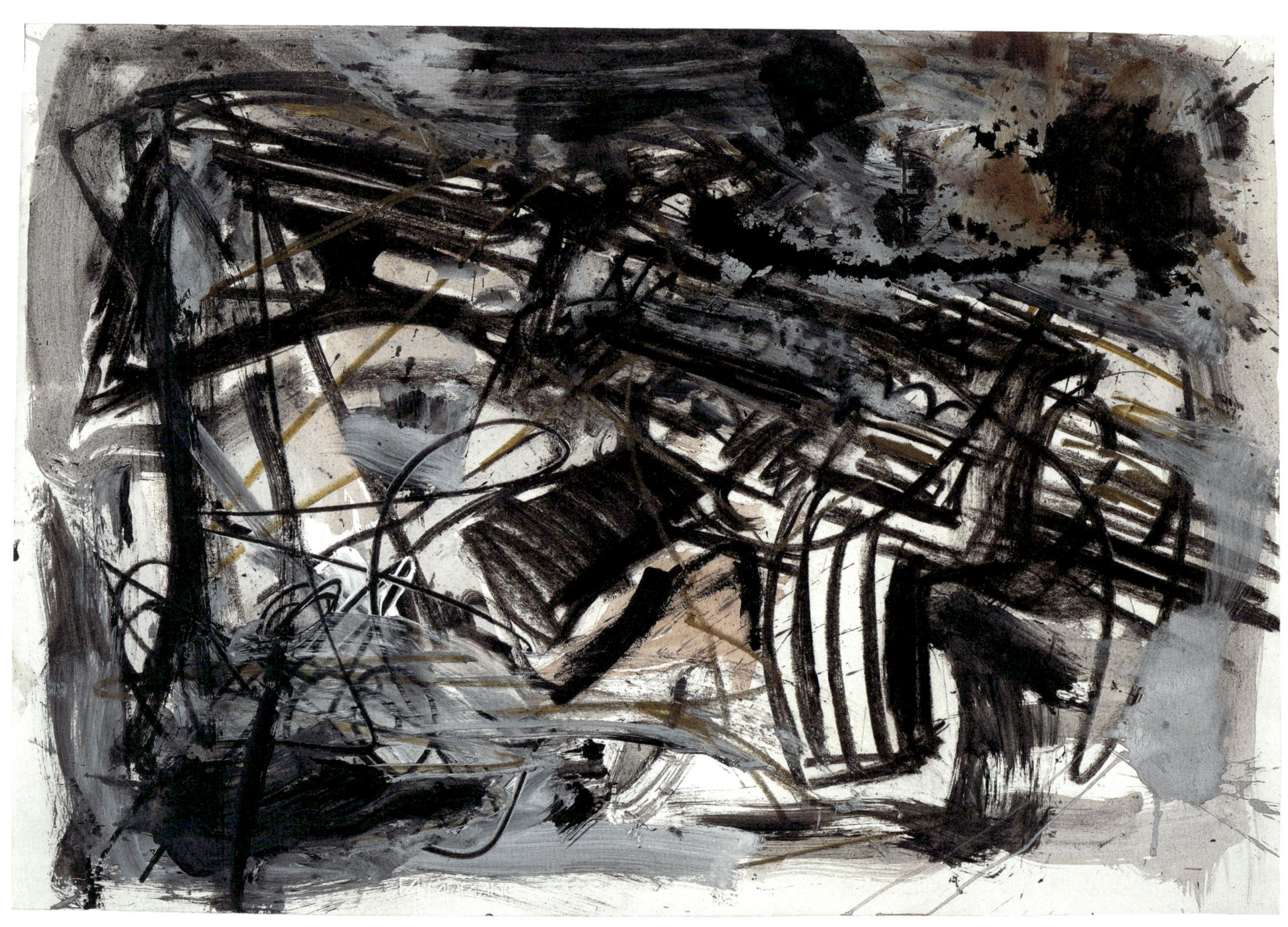

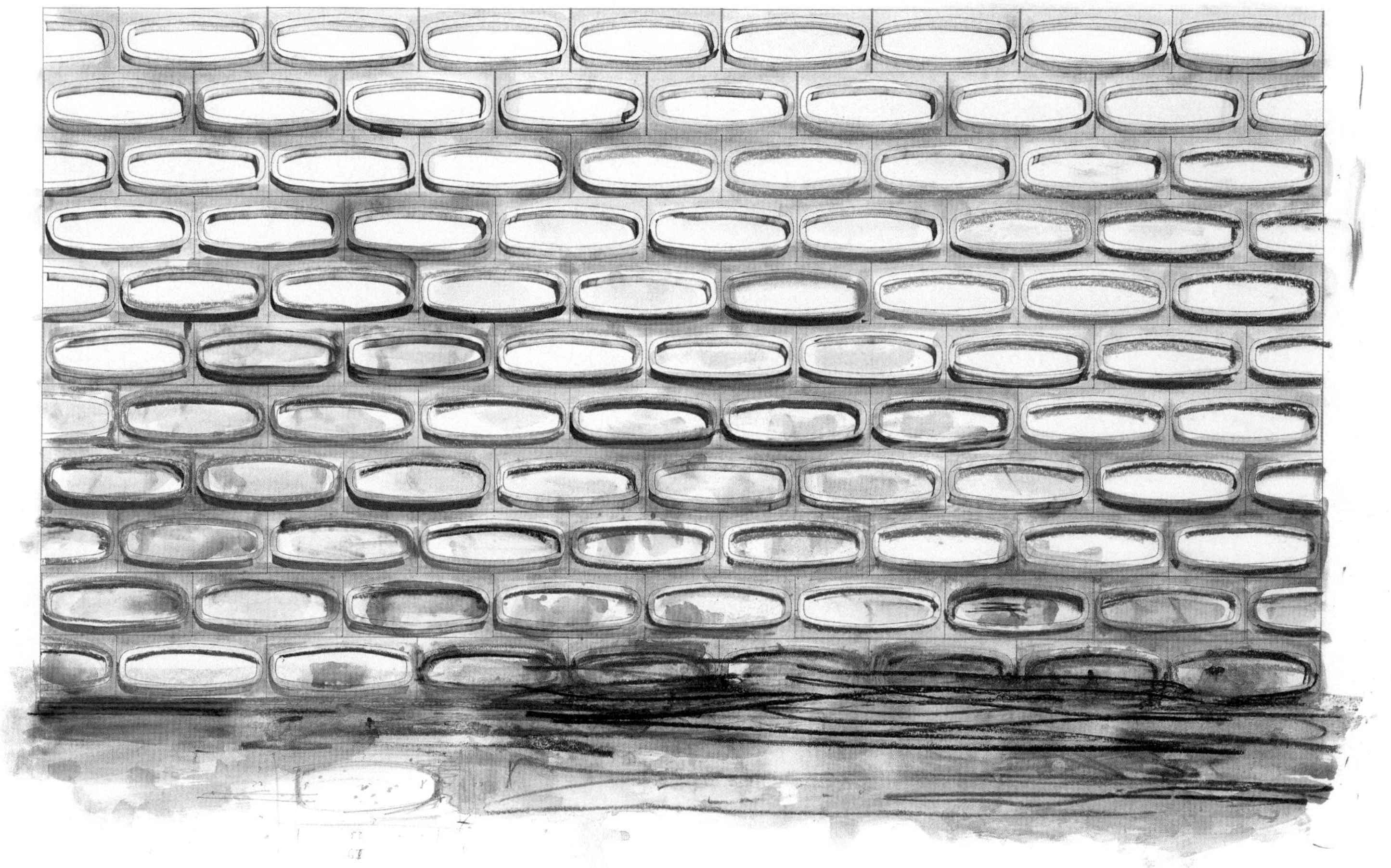

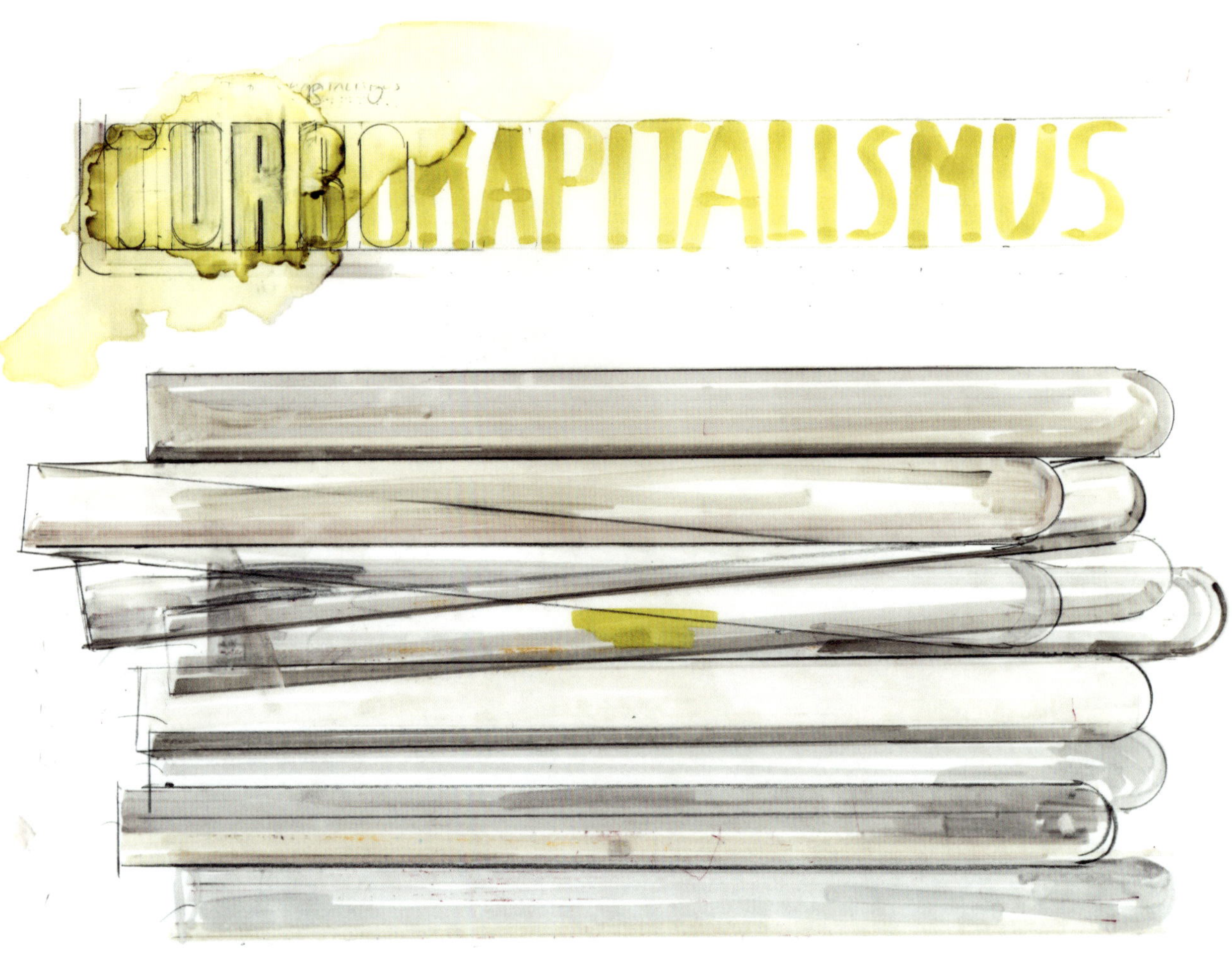
TURBOKAPITALISMUS

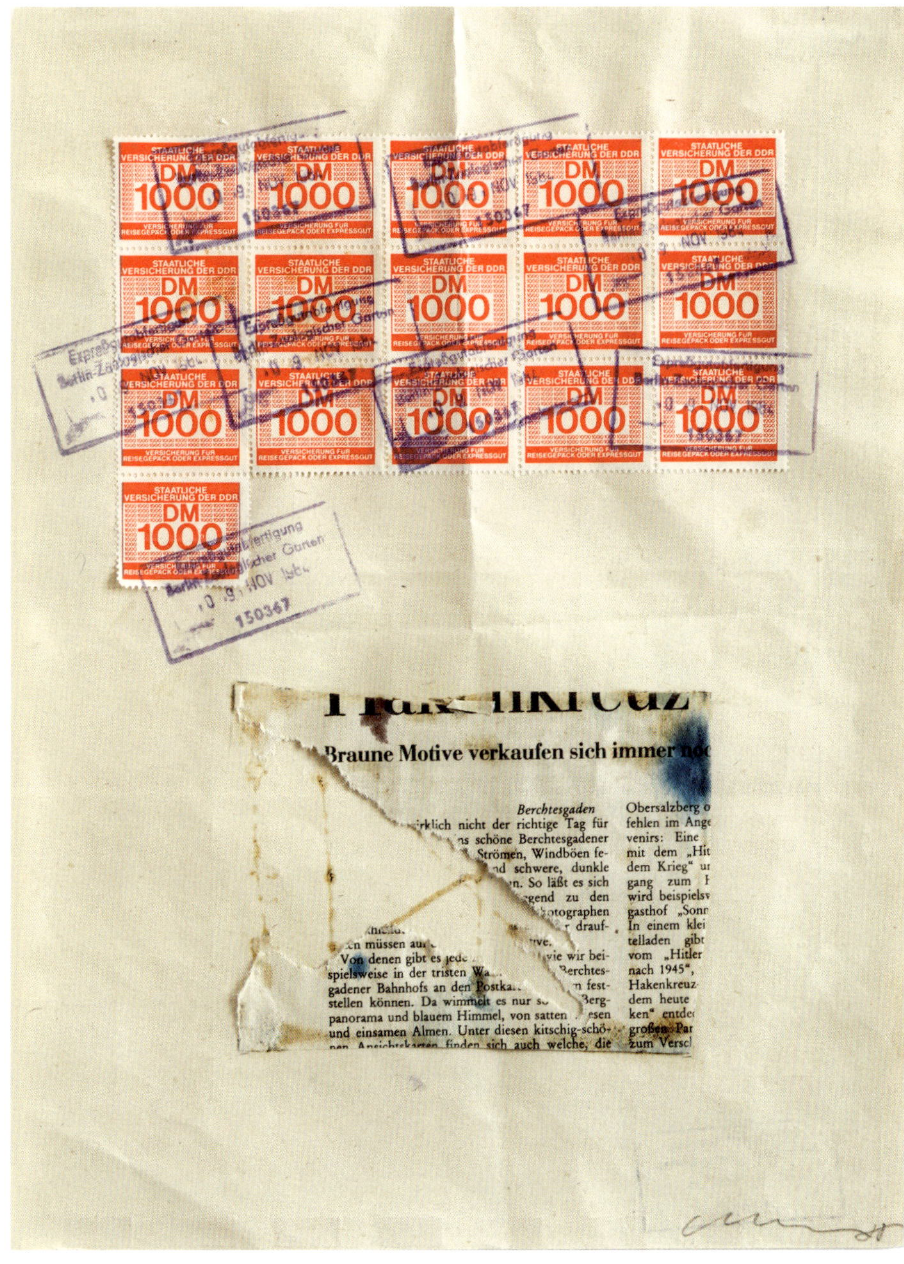
STAATLICHE VERSICHERUNG DER DDR
DM 1000
VERSICHERUNG FÜR REISEGEPÄCK ODER EXPRESSGUT
150367
Braune Motive verkaufen sich immer
Berchtesgaden

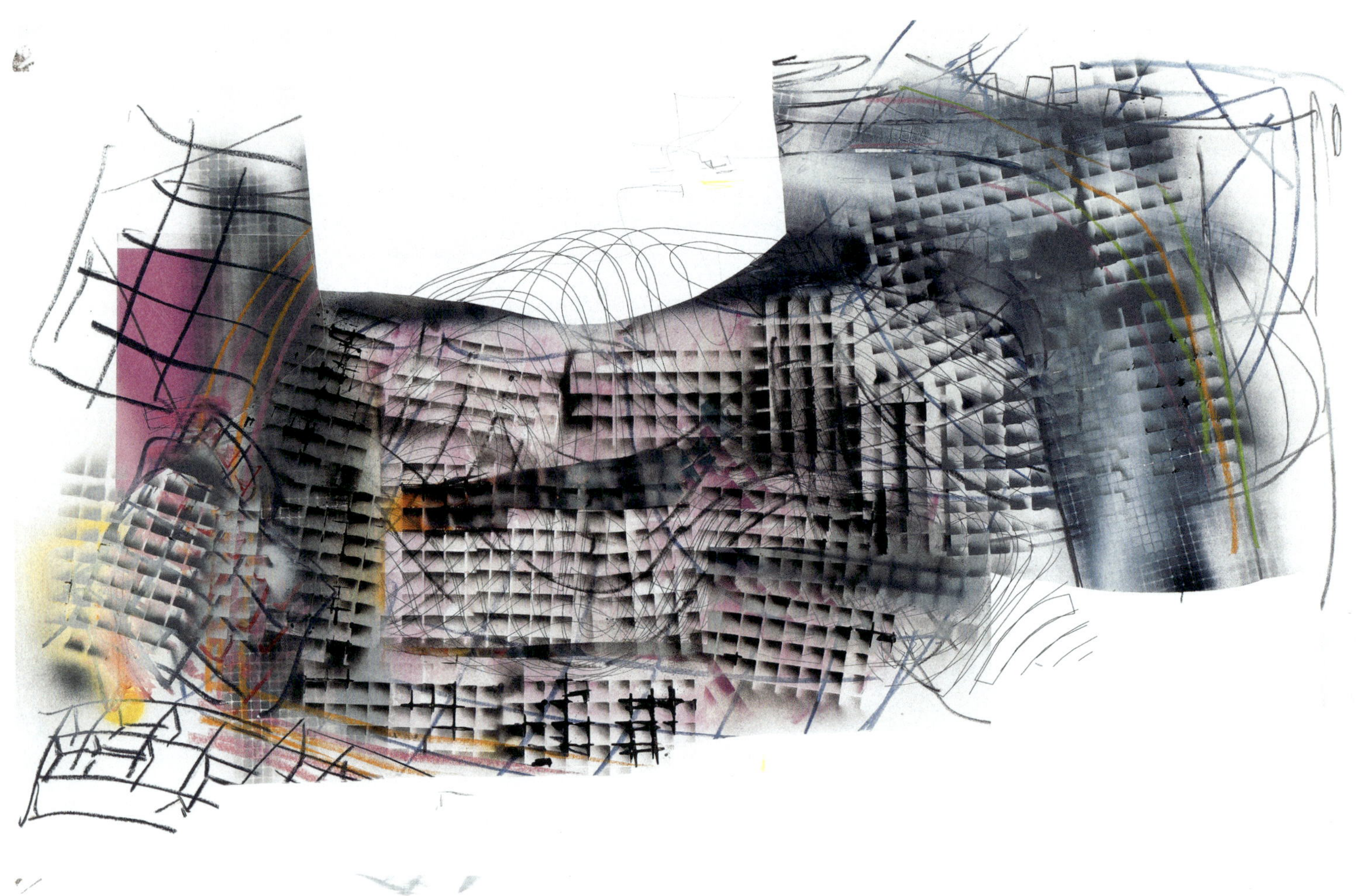

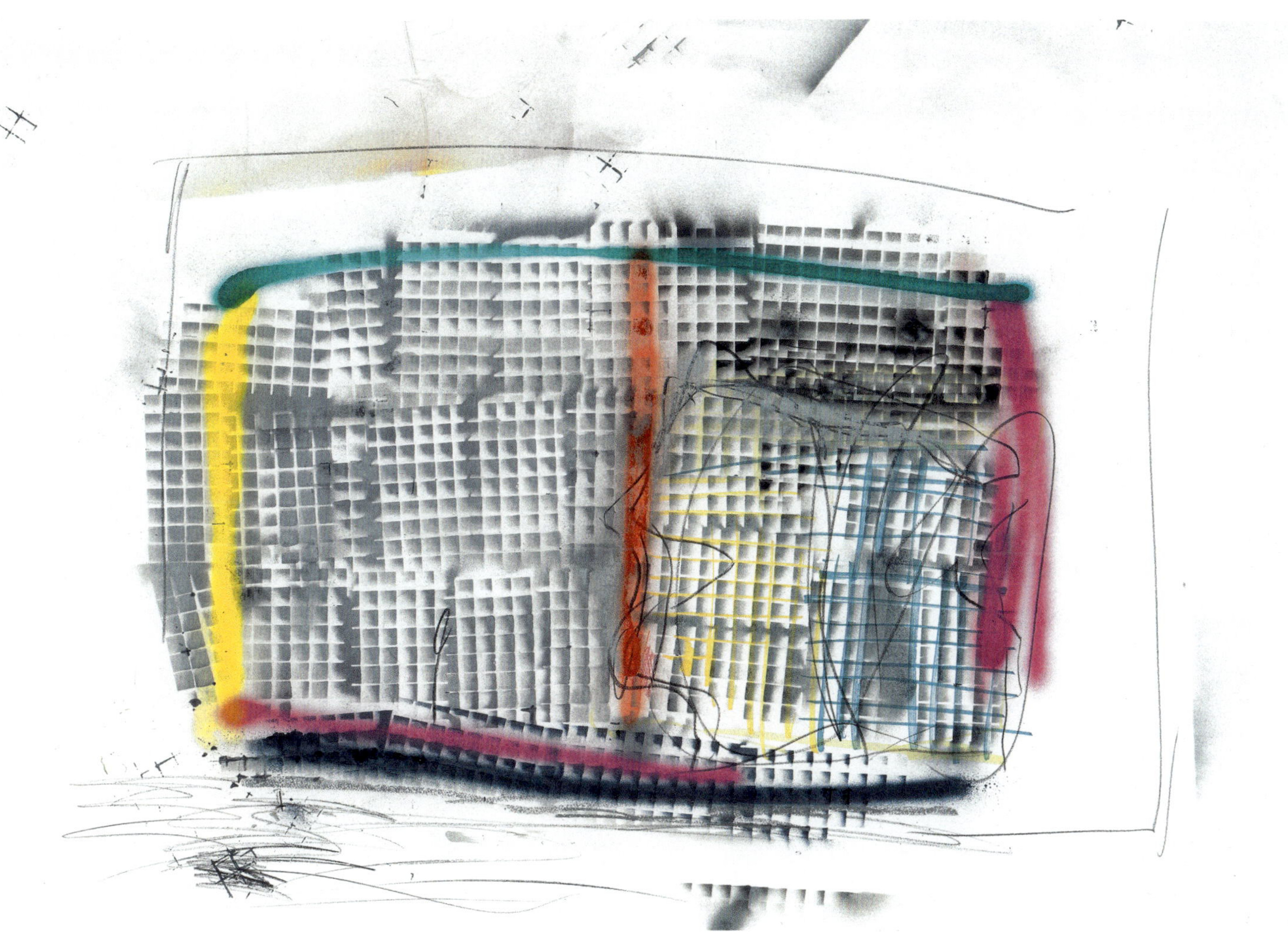

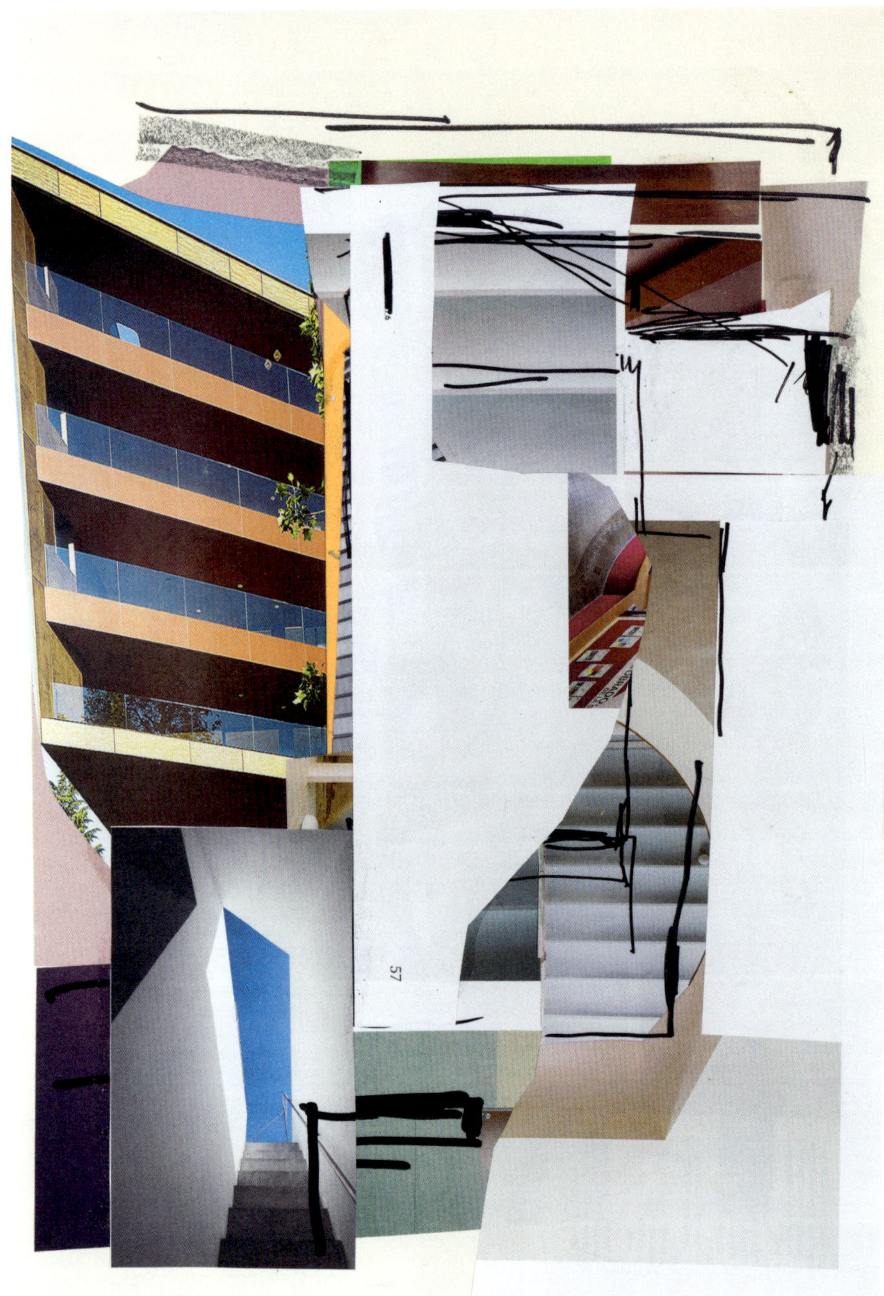

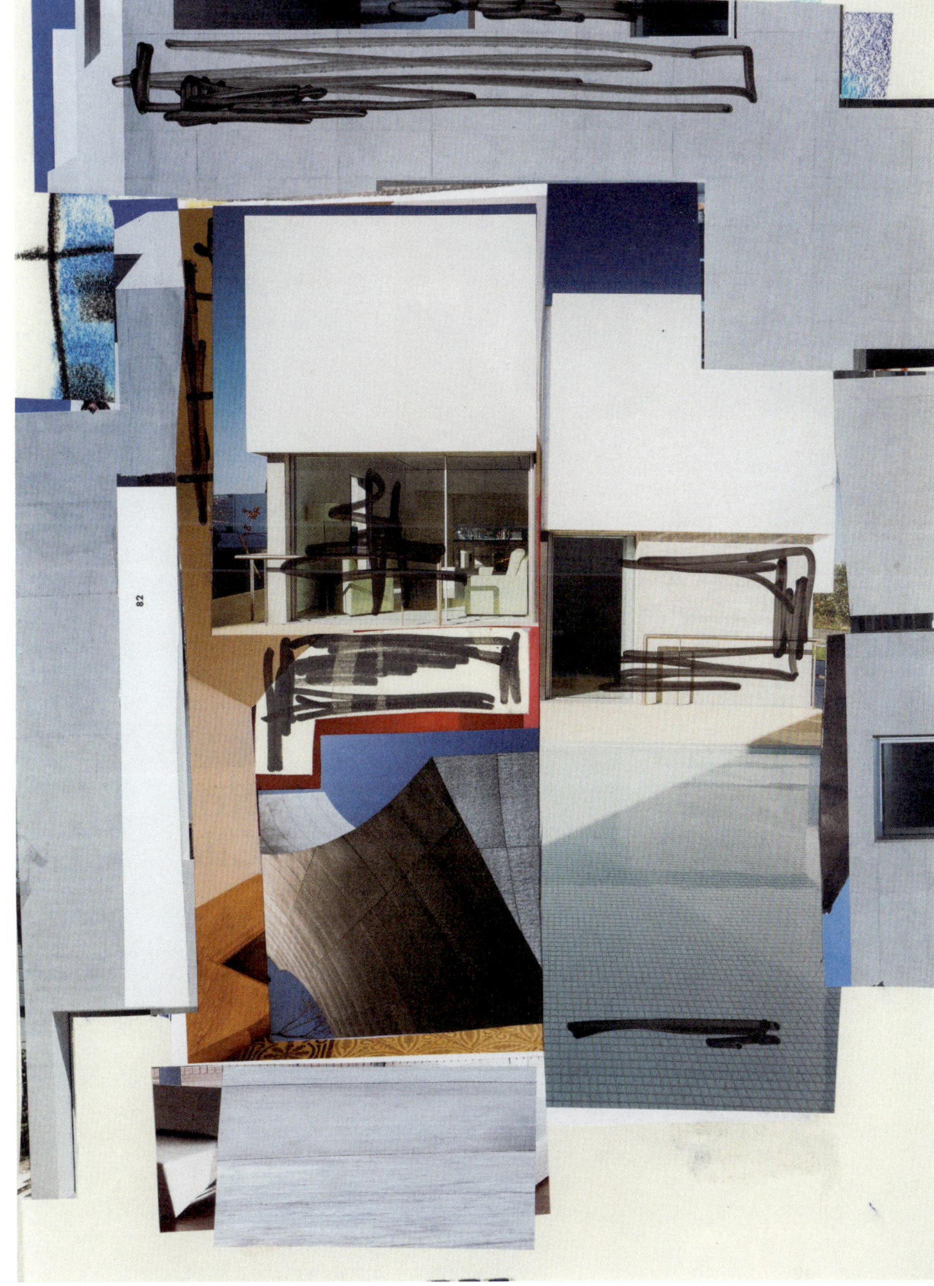

List of Drawings

061
Palazzo dei Diamanti (1)
2009
Pencil, watercolor, pastel on Fabriano cardboard
76 × 57 cm

062
Sprachgitter (Language Grid, draft 1)
2009
Pastel on photocopy
29.7 × 42.2 cm

063
Sprachgitter (Language Grid, draft 2)
2009
Pastel on photocopy
29.7 × 42.2 cm

064
Il balletto della crisi (plot)
1988
Pencil, water pen, Indian ink on transparent paper
63 × 87.5 cm

065
Friedensplan (Peace Plan)
1985
Charcoal, acrylic paint, coffee on cardboard
79 × 106.5 cm

066
Wire Mesh
1998
Pencil, Indian ink, marker, acrylic paint
on Fabriano cardboard
33.1 × 23.9 cm

067
Untitled
1981
Indian ink, opaque white, typewriter
font on computer paper
35.5 × 30.4 cm

068
Social Wallpaper (3)
2017
Newspaper cutouts, charcoal, sandpaper, pastel on paper
42 × 29.7 cm

069
Social Wallpaper (4)
2017
Newspaper cutouts, charcoal, sandpaper, pastel on paper
42 × 29.7 cm

071
No Man's Land
2000
Pencil on transparent paper
41.8 × 29.7 cm

076
Scherengitter (Security Grille)
1993
Pencil, felt pen, ink, Indian ink on tracing paper
42.5 × 60.5 cm

078
Kopftuchstudie (Head Scarf Study)
2006
Charcoal on paper
100 × 70 cm

079
Palm Tree
2002
Charcoal on Fabriano cardboard
100 × 70 cm

080
Beretta
1988
Charcoal, water pen, watercolor, Indian ink on Fabriano cardboard
70 × 100 cm

081
Tegeler Weg
2004
Pencil, colored pen, pastel, wall paint, color spray,
computer print on cardboard
78.5 × 111.5 cm

082
Turbokapitalismus (Turbo Capitalism)
1999
Pencil, marker on tracing paper
41,9 × 59,1 cm

083
Versicherungsmarken (Insurance Stamps)
1985
Postmarked stamps, India ink, newspaper cutout on paper
29.6 × 21 cm

084
Cash Flow (1)
2004–05
Pencil, colored pen, felt pen, India ink,
plastics, color spray on computer print
59.5 × 91 cm

085
Cash Flow (2)
2004–05
Pencil, felt pen, color spray on cardboard
70 × 100 cm

086
Social Wallpaper (1)
2017
Newspaper cutouts, felt pen, pastel on paper
42 × 29.7 cm

087
Social Wallpaper (2)
2017
Newspaper cutouts, felt pen, pastel on paper
42 × 29.7 cm

090
Palazzo dei Diamanti (2)
2009
Pencil, watercolor, pastel and charcoal on Fabriano cardboard
70 × 100 cm

עמ' 061
פאלאצו דיי דיאמנטי (1)
2009
עפרון, צבעי מים, פסטל על נייר פבריאנו
76 × 57 ס"מ

עמ' 062
סורג-שפה (טיוטה)
2009
פסטל על העתק מצולם
29.7 × 42.2 ס"מ

עמ' 063
סורג-שפה (טיוטה)
2009
פסטל על העתק מצולם
29.7 × 42.2 ס"מ

עמ' 064
Il balletto della crisi (מתווה)
1998
עפרון, עט מים, דיו הודי על נייר שקוף
63 × 87.5 ס"מ

עמ' 065
תכנית שלום
1985
פחם, צבע אקרילי, קפה על קרטון
79 × 106.5 ס"מ

עמ' 066
רשת תיל
1998
עפרון, דיו הודי, טוש, צבע אקרילי על נייר פבריאנו
33.1 × 23.9 ס"מ

עמ' 067
ללא כותרת
1981
דיו הודי, עט סימון לבן, גופן מכונת כתיבה על נייר מחשב
אין ממדים במקור
35.5 × 30.4 ס"מ

068
טפט חברתי (3)
2017
גזרי עיתון, פחם, נייר זכוכית, פסטל על נייר
42 × 29.7 ס"מ

069
טפט חברתי (4)
2017
גזרי עיתון, פחם, נייר זכוכית, פסטל על נייר
42 × 29.7 ס"מ

071
שטח הפקר
2000
עפרון על נייר שקוף
41.8 × 29.7 ס"מ

076
סורג מתקפל
1993
עפרון, עט טוש, דיו, דיו הודי על נייר העתקה
42.5 × 60.5 ס"מ

078
איור רעלה
2006
פחם על נייר
100 × 70 ס"מ

079
עץ דקל
2002
פחם על קרטון פבריאנו
70 × 100 ס"מ

080
ברטה
1988
פחם, עט מים, צבעי מים, דיו הודי על נייר פבריאנו
70 × 100 ס"מ

081
Tegeler Weg [רח' ראשי בברלין הקשור לאירועי 1968]
2004
עפרון, עט צבע, פסטל, צבע קיר, ספריי צבע, הדפסת מחשב על קרטון
78.5 × 111.5 ס"מ

082
טורבו קפיטליזם
1999
עפרון, טוש על נייר העתקה
41.9 × 59.1 ס"מ

083
בולי ביטוח לאומי
1985
בולים בחותמות דואר, דיו הודי, גזירי עיתון על נייר
29.6 × 21 ס"מ

084
תזרים מזומנים (1)
2004–05
עפרון, עט צבע, עט טוש, דיו הודי, פלסטיקים, ספריי צבע על הדפסת מחשב
59.5 × 91 ס"מ

085
תזרים מזומנים (2)
2004–05
עפרון, עט טוש, ספריי צבע על קרטון
70 × 100 ס"מ

086
טפט חברתי (1)
2017
גזירי עיתון, עט טוש, פסטל על נייר
42 × 29.7 ס"מ

087
טפט חברתי (2)
2017
גזירי עיתון, עט טוש, פסטל על נייר
42 × 29.7 ס"מ

עמ' 090
פאלאצו דיי דיאמנטי (2)
2009
עפרון, צבעי מים, פסטל על נייר פבריאנו
70 × 100 ס"מ

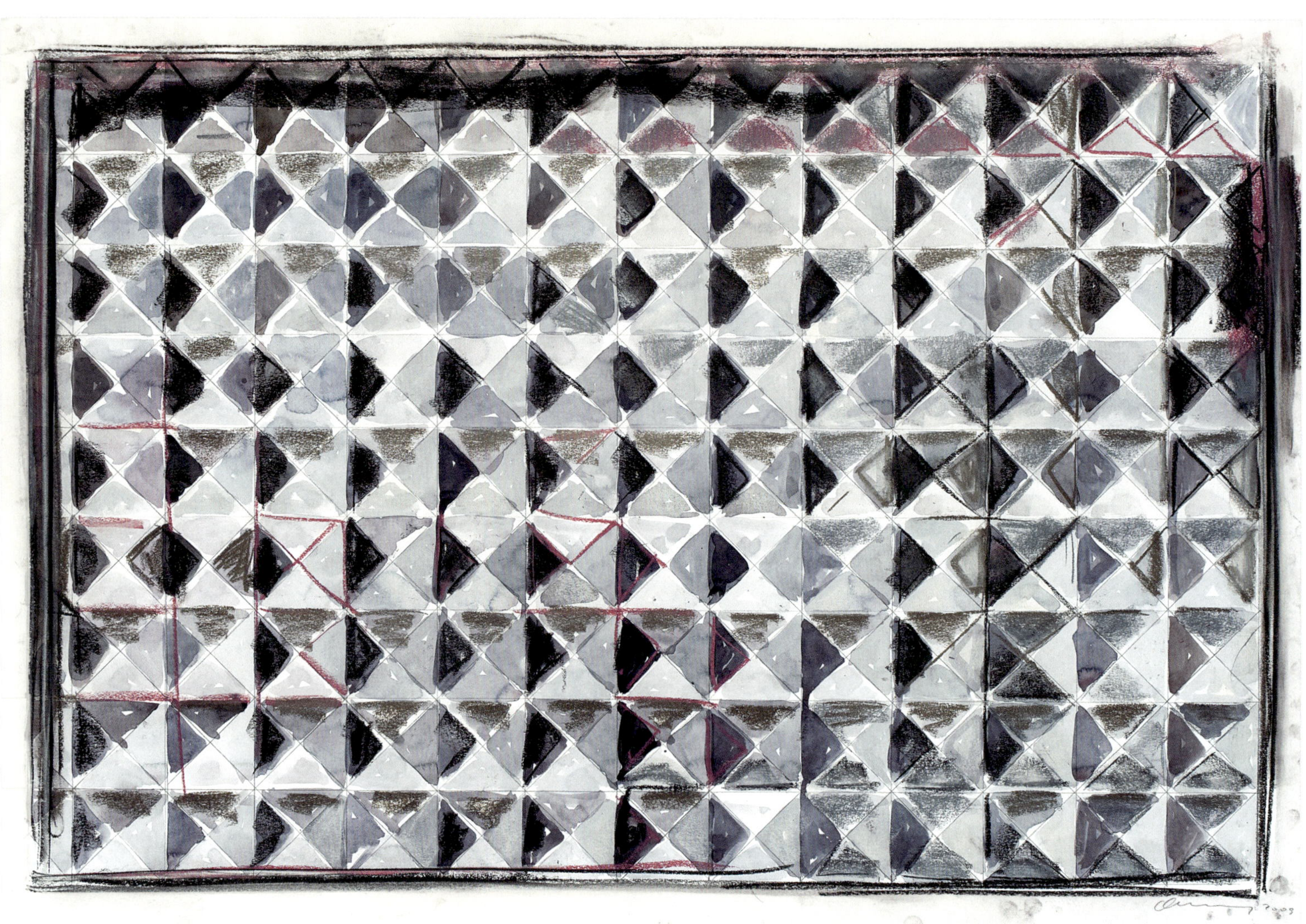

סורג-שפה
אולף מטצל

לשמוע את בראד פיט מדבר איטלקית בסרט "ממזרים חסרי כבוד" (2009) זה בהחלט דבר משעשע. קוונטין טרנטינו משתמש בריבוי שפות בצורה מעודנת למדי, למטרות מבניות ואמנותיות כאחד. הסדר נשמר, אך נוכחותה של השפה כממשק הופכת למרכיב רב-חשיבות.

"צור, אמן, במקום לדבר!" ציטוט זה מדבריו של גתה מוכר לרבים, אך מעטים מכירים את השורה הבאה: "שירך אינו אלא הבל פה."

שני אזכורים אלה, השונים בתכלית, מתקשרים לכותרת העבודה "סורג-שפה". האחד עוסק בדיבור בקול רם-ובעצם, למה לא לדבר לעצמך? אחרי הכל, חוקים נועדו כדי שיופרו, מה שלרוב קל יותר מאשר לקיימם. אגב, הכותרת עוסקת באותה מידה בהעדר דיבור או בגבולות השפה ואוצר המילים שלה. פרובוקציות, אגרסיות, רעיונות, חוקים, נושאים שהם טאבו. עייפנו מלשמוע על דברים רבים, ואי-הבנות צצות בכל פינה.

בשבועון "וולט אם זונטאג" הופיע ב-23.8 מאמר שכותרתו "מילים ופצעים עמוקים". המאמר עסק בקונפליקט של היהודים החיים בגרמניה: האם הם "יהודים בגרמניה" או "גרמנים יהודים"? זהות, הגירה, גלות. השאלות תמיד רבות מן התשובות. "אפילו אם תתעקש להיות אויבי, לא תצליח להפוך אותי לאויבך", כתב תומאס מאן למלחין ארנולד שנברג במהלך תקופת הגלות שלהם בקליפורניה. לא אפרט כאן לגבי הקונפליקט ששרר בין המלחין היהודי לסופר חתן הנובל. למרות, או אולי דווקא בגלל, שמאן ניסח את משפטיו בצורה כה מושלמת, היה משהו שקישר בין השניים: שפתם.

כשאנו מתבוננים בסורג מרחוק, כשהוא מעט מטושטש, הוא נתפס כקומפוזיציה המורכבת מנקודות. האם הוא עוסק בגבולות? אולי במקום לדבר על סורג, עליי לדבר על מסגרת. לשיחות. או שמא אנחנו מדברים רק על תנאים, על הצורה שלובש הדיון?

בתחילת מאי השנה, כאשר קראתי את מכתביהם של אינגבורג באכמן ופאול צלאן, מה שתפס אותי, מלבד "השאלה בנוגע לכיוונו של השעון", היה המינוח "סורג-שפה". מיותר לומר שאין צירופי מקרים, במיוחד לא כאשר אתה מוזמן לבקר בבית כנסת כדי ליצור בו עבודת אמנות.

בית הכנסת ממוקם בחצר המשיקה לכיכר השוק של שטומלן. מיקומו החבוי והשלווה השוררת בו יוצרים רושם עז, הגובר כשנכנסים למה שהיה פעם אולם התפילה: החלונות הבנויים בפשטות, זגוגיות הזכוכית האדומה, רצפת הבזלת האפורה נטולת הקישוטים, הגלריה העשויה עץ, ובמרכז ארון התורה, העשוי גם הוא עץ כהה. הקירות ממוסגרים בצבע בצורה שאינה בולטת לעין. כשמתבוננים מעלה-אל התקרה השטוחה-אין שם דבר. זה מרחב שבו ניתן להכניס עבודה חדשה כדי ליצור קשר בין הארון לגלריה. משהו שייראה כאילו היה תמיד חלק מבית הכנסת, אולי תקרת עץ? בכל אופן, משהו שיהיה עשוי גם הוא מעץ צבוע בצבע כהה. לא ניגוד משלים, גם לא דגש אמנותי מכוון, אלא משהו שייראה כחלק אינטגראלי מהמקום.

"סורג-שפה", מינוח אמביוולנטי. הוא נשמע הרמטי, כמו מחסום, למרות שכמעט תמיד הוא נוגע דווקא לחדירות, למבנים, אולי לרשת? תקשורת אחרי הכל, כפי שהיו קוראים לזה היום? לא רשת, אלא סורג?

בשנת 1990 לערך, ציירתי ציורים שהתבססו על דוגמאות שפיתחתי בשנות השבעים המאוחרות. לא ידעתי אז כיצד לתרגם ציורים אלה והקשרים דומים לתלת-ממד.

האם אתר זה-בית כנסת לשעבר-הוא המקום הנכון? האם ייתכן, במקום הזה, לבנות מבנה שחובק חלל אמיתי, ובו בזמן גם פותח אותו? במנותק מההיסטוריה? האם מונחים כגון "איקונוגרפיה" ו"סמנטיקה" רלוונטיים כאן? האם ניתן לחשוב על מרכיבים בסיסיים, אולי מסודרים לרוחב, שיהוו מבנה אוטונומי?

כשאתה מתעסק לאורך זמן בפתרון צורני, אתה חווה את סביבתך בצורה כמעט מוגבלת, או יותר נכון מכוונת מטרה. לאחרונה החזקתי בידי מסגרת עץ קטנה וישנה, ללא תמונה. מסגרת ותו לא. פשוט מאד. קניתי אותה מייד. לפעמים אתה זונח רעיון, טקסט, או פרויקט במשך שנים, ועדיין חוזר לחשוב עליו לעיתים קרובות, אינך יודע מה לעשות. ואז מגיע הרגע שבו הכל מתחבר כמו פסיפס-אני חוויתי את הרגע הזה במקום שהיה פעם בית כנסת.

נאום בפתיחת התערוכה "Olaf Metzel, Sprachgitter" (אולף מטצל, סורג-שפה). בית הכנסת של שטומלן, 4.10.2009.

סורג שפה
2009
עץ מילה
376 × 410 × 96 ס"מ
מבט על המיצב בבית הכנסת שטומלן

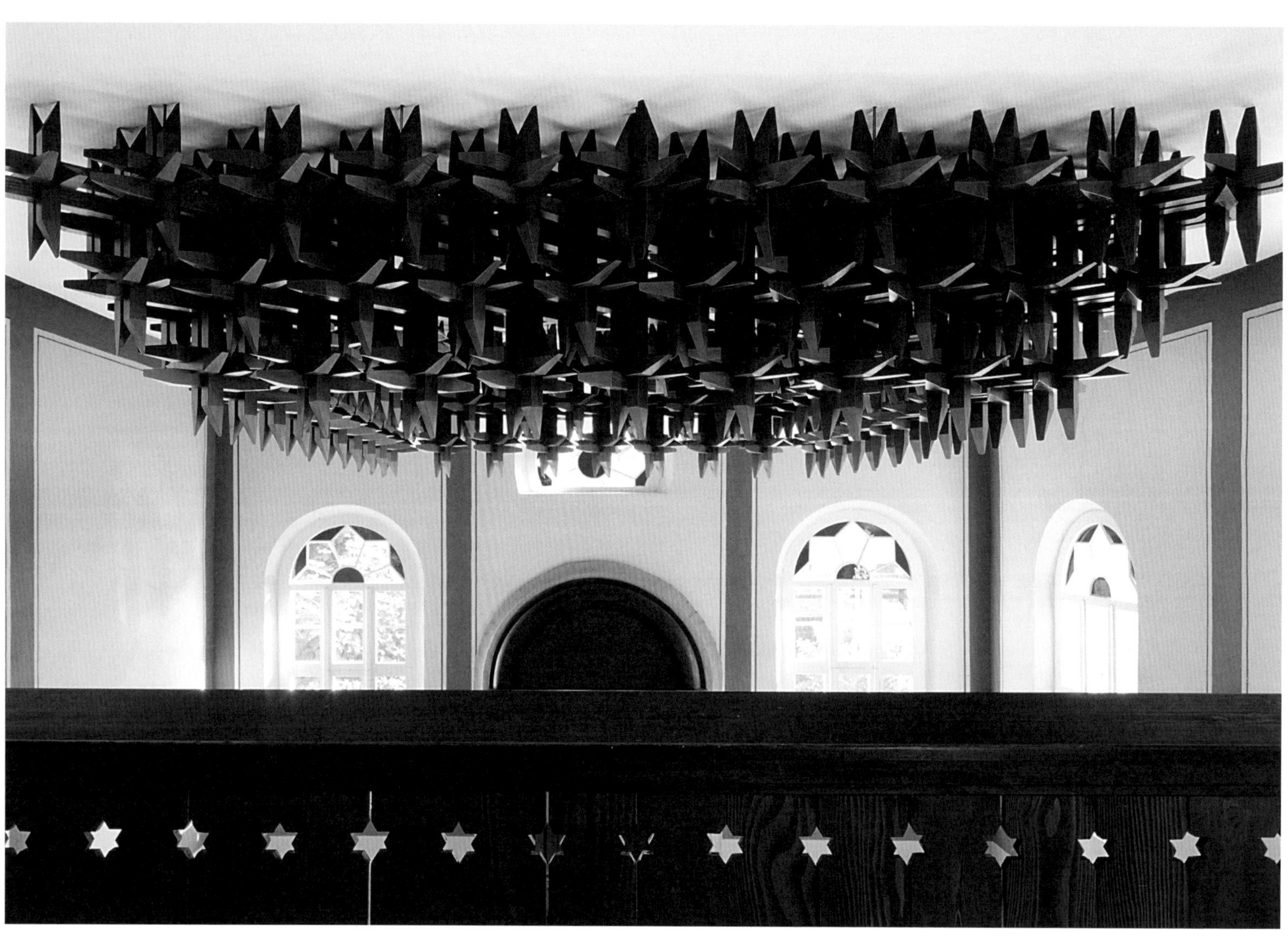

בית הכנסת של שטומלן
הנס בלטינג

בית הכנסת הקטן שבסמוך לככר השוק בעיירה שטומלן – שניצל, נשכח והתגלה מחדש – היה זה מכבר לשם דבר בסצנת האמנות. בשנות ה–90, היה יאניס קונליס לראשון בשורה ארוכה של אמנים בינלאומיים שיוצרים פעם בשנה מיצב – שלא רק שהוא מוצב במקום השקט הזה, אלא מוצב בעבורו. המתקנים הם אורחים שכל אחד מהם זכור בזכות הרעיון האסתטי שלו, ושלכל אחד פרשנות משלו למקום.

בפעם הראשונה שביקרתי בשטומלן, באוגוסט 2009, היה זה יום לאחר שאולף מטצל הציב שם עבודה חדשה. בעוד שהוא ראה את החדר ריק בטרם ההצבה, לי לא היתה ברירה אלא לראותו מבעד לעיניו, כאילו עבודתו השתלטה על החדר ומשלה בו. נדמה היה כאילו היתה שם מאז ומתמיד, חלק בלתי נפרד מהחדר, ותמיד היתה ידה על העליונה כהשראה לחזוני האמנותי. היא היתה נהירה לי רק באותו המקום, ובה במידה היה המקום נהיר לי רק במשולב עם הנוכחות הזו שנוספה זה מכבר.

בעיניי, חדר התפילה היהודי הקטן נראה היה כקוביה פשוטה, עם שלושה חלונות על כל אחד משניים מהקירות. החציצה היחידה היא הגלריה שעל הקיר מעל לכניסייה, החוצה אותו לשניים; הגומחה היחידה היא זו של ארון התורה בקיר הראשי שממול; שתיהן שוחזרו בעץ חום כהה. לתקרה החלקה המטויחת בלבן נוסף עתה מלבן מעץ מילה הבנוי כמו פיגום או גריד הממסגר מרכז ריק – יצירת האמנות של אולף מטצל. מאותו הרגע ואילך, לא הצלחתי להשתחרר מהרושם שאני מתבונן במסגרת ריקה, כלומר מגרת שנותרת חפה מדימוי ובה בעת מציינת את הדימוי בהעדרו, מפנה אליו. אפשר שהמיקום עצמו תרם לרושם הזה, בגלל שאין להעלות אל הדעת בית תפילה יהודי ללא האיסור הדתי על עשיית פסל ותמונה (המופיע כבר בדיבר השני) וללא הסתפקותו בספרים בלבד. האיסור גירש את ה' לנצח מכל דמות מעשה ידי אדם (ואיזו דמות אחרת תיתכן לאלהים?).

על כל הן היה זה אך יאה שהאמן, שכלל לא יכול היה להעלות את הרעיון שלי על דעתו, סיפר לי כיצד קנה פעם מסגרת קטנה וישנה מקורות עץ עם רצועות תליה, כלומר מסגרת למטענים הנישאים על גב, וכיצד נתנה לו את ההשראה ליצירתו זו. מאוחר יותר הבנתי שהנחתה אותו גישה צורנית. צורת המסגרת אולי סקרנה אותו גם היא, בגלל שהיא משכפלת תרשים גיאומטרי למספר שכבות והופכת אותו תלת–ממדי, רק כדי לשוב ולאזכר את המישור עם לבו הריק, שממנו מפרידה עצמה המסגרת בת ארבעת הצדדים. באותו האופן ממש, יצר מטצל איור צבעוני של חזית הפלאצו דיי דיאמנטי בפררה, שלכדה את סדר הדברים הרב–ממדי על משטח של בניין – כולו בתוך הגריד המישורי, אם כי בלוויית הצללים והצללים למחצה של גבישי "יהלומים" מוגבהים – שגם הם הושטחו אל פיסת נייר. ניתן לפרש זאת כמטפורה לאמביוולנטיות שבין העיצוב האישי (מישור) והאפקט הציבורי (מרחב) שעוברת כחוט השני באמנות החוצות של מטצל.

אבל הבנה נשתהה לרגע על הדימוי הנוכח בהעדרו, המתקיים דרך ייצוגו, במובן מסוים. הרושם שלי אושש כשגיליתי יצירה מסוימת בקטלוג המבורג של איורי אולף מטצל – למעשה היתה זו היצירה שהופיעה על כריכת הקטלוג. היצירה מתוארכת ל–1984 וכותרתה "שטאמהיים", מקום שהיה מוכר לכל באותה עת. בין הפתקים שבכתב יד שעל דף זה, תמצאו את המלים "המטפחת של ורוניקה הקדושה". האסוציאציה של כתר הקוצים מתבקשת כאן, אך הטקסט מתייחס בה בעת להעדר הפנים – כלומר הדמות – במרכז הריק. לסוגיות צורניות ניתן מקום משלהן, למשל, כשבסמוך לחפץ ארוג זה הופיעו המלים "אלכסון למעלה", בהתייחס להמרת ההיבט המרחבי לכדי יצירה תלת–ממדית. כך הפך האיור לשרטוט מקדים. בה בעת, האסוציאציה לתמונה ריקה קיבלה את אישורו של האמן עצמו.

בשטומלן, הרושם של מסגרת ריקה ללא תמונה מועבר רק לצופים בקומת הקרקע, כלומר, כשהם עומדים הישר מתחת. במקום תקרת העץ, רואים כאן מסגרת עץ, ורואים אותה על התקרה היכן שבדרך כלל לא היינו מצפים לראות תמונה כלשהי. אולם המסגרת היא גם חלק המעיד על השלם, הלא הוא התקרה, כיוון שהיא ספק ממסגרת אותה מבפנים, וחוזרת על כך בקנה מידה קטן ביותר במרכזה. לאור זאת, התקרה כולה הופכת לדמות. כל התקרה? מהמקום שמתחת לתקרה המשולבת ניתן לראות רק חלק מהתקרה. רואים מלבן עליו סוגרים משלושת צדיו הקירות ומצדו הרביעי מיקומו של הצופה. שדה ראייה זה תחום על ידי קירות משלושה צדדים בלבד. זוהי בדיוק יחידת המדידה שאליה מתייחסת המסגרת של מטצל כמסגרת כפולה. בזכות יחסי הגודל לבדם, נוצר הדהוד משכנע בין המיקום ליצירה. המסגרת מקנה מרכזיות לתקרה שאינה מרכז החדר אלא מרכז שדה הראייה.

הרושם המתקבל בעלייה לגלריה שונה בתכלית. צורת המסגרת נעלמת, ובמקומה רואים צורה תלויה שמנמיכה עצמה עמוק יותר לתוך החדר מכפי שניתן לצפות ממסגרת. לעיני הצופה מתגלה מערך מדורג העשוי מרצועות תלייה דמויות נטיפים שביניהם ניתן לראות את טיח התקרה בבירור בכל מקום. קשה לדמיין היבט ניגודי יותר לאותה היצירה עצמה. למעלה בגלריה, עקרון הפלסטיק מחליף את עקרון המסגור. מקרוב, כוח המשיכה של הפרספקטיבה שאליו נחשפים הצופים מתחת למסגרת מפנה את מקומו לרושם של אורגניזם מסועף מאד, המרוכב ממספר רב של מבנים קטנים המשתלבים זה עם זה ודומה שהם יוצרים מספר מסגרות הנעוצות אחת בתוך השנייה. בעזרת הדמיית מחשב, הם נוצרו באופן שכזה שמתברר כי הם היו השיקול העיקרי של האמן. הגיאומטריה הרב–ממדית מציגה את המעבר מאור לצל ואת ההיבט של צירים מרחביים שונים, באופן שגורם לחדר להיות מובנה גיאומטרית ובה בעת מוצפן בצופן שגורם לנו לאבד את התמוהה הגדולה. מטבעה של הגיאומטריה הוא שאינה חדירה למבט החולף, ושהיא מתגלה רק בהדרגה ככל שהיא מנותחת ומפוענחת.

הגיאומטריה כתחליף לדימוי, המתרחקת ממבטו של הצופה ודוחה מעליה את הפסל והתמונה, קיבלה תפקיד של חתימה קוסמית בתרבות החזותית של המזרח התיכון. אסוציאציות כאלה, שלא סביר שנתנו השראה לאמן, מכניסות אותי, את הצופה, לתמונה כיוון שאני יכול להעמיק בהשערות דווקא מכיוון שלא אני יצרתי את העבודה הזו. אבהיר זאת בעזרת שתי דוגמאות. ראשית, מקדש שלמה בירושלים כמתואר במקרא. הוא שבה את דמיונם של אמנים רבים, אם כי לאף אחד מהם לא הותר לקרום לו עור וגידים. לעיטוריו לא היו מתחרים, אך הם היו מוגבלים לקישוטי קירות ועיצובי ריהוט כיוון שהמבנה מוקדש היה למי שצלמו אינו ידוע. וכאן נכנסת לתמונה האדריכלות הערבית–אסלאמית, שהגיעה לשיאה בזיזי הקיר האורנמנטליים ששימשו בגומחות ובפנים הכיפות, המכונים "עיטורי נטיפות" (מוקרנס בערבית). צורת הקישוט הזו היתה יציר מחשבתם של מתמטיקאים, ואדריכלים סיפקו את השרטוטים אותם תרגמו האומנים מהמישור לממד השלישי בלי לזנוח את העיצוב הגיאומטרי. מקטעי העיצוב השונים, תאיו, הפכו לכוורות מהן נגה האור שהסתנן מלמעלה.

מיקום הצבתו של אולף מטצל מזמין אפוא את הצופים לקרוא עמימות סמנטית לתוך סוגיה צורנית. ככל שהצורה מופשטת יותר, כך מתחזק הדחף לשנגה דרך פרשנות. בין יתר הדברים מתגלה כאן פיתוי שמעוררת הדמות מעצם העדרה.

שטאמהיים
1984
Württembergischer Kunstverein,
Stuttgart
שטוטגרט

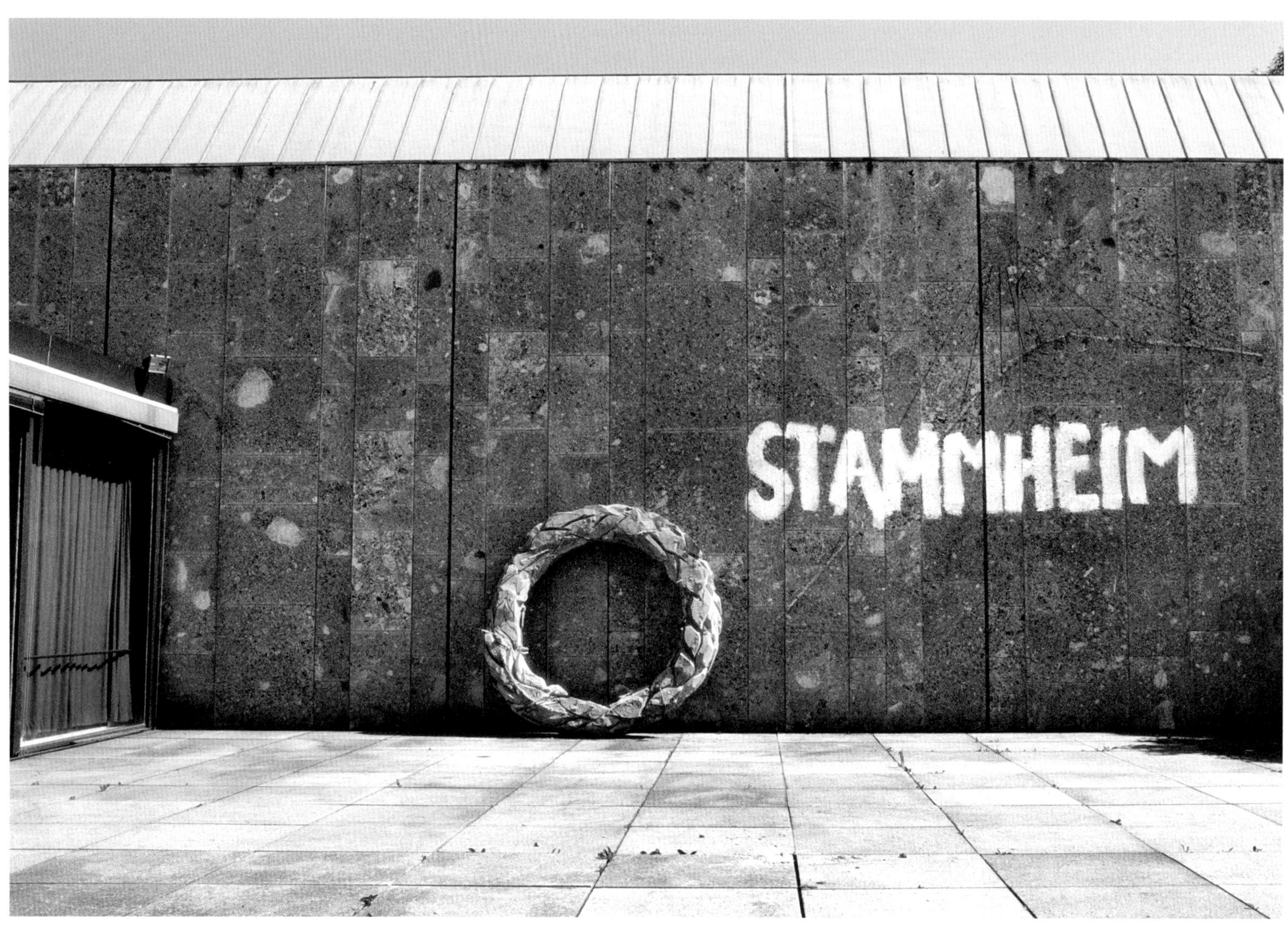

כתובת אנונימית על הקיר
כריסטוף היינריך

זר זיכרון שעון כנגד קיר ריק. מרחוק הוא נראה כמו זר מסורתי השזור מעלי דפנה, מן הסוג המשמש בטקסים ממלכתיים, או אפילו כמו זר יצוק מברונזה המתנוסס על אנדרטות רשמיות. אך מבט בוחן מגלה שרושם ראשוני זה מוטעה. הזר עשוי מבטון ירוק, ונראה מרחוק כחרוץ בחריצים עמוקים. שאריות חלודה חומות מצביעות על מוטות פלדה שנחשפו בנקודות מסוימות. על הקיר מעל הזר מתנוסס מימין, באותיות שגודלן כ-1.5 מטרים כל אחת, הכיתוב הבא: STAMMHEIM.

עבודתו של אולף מטצל "שטאמהיים" נוצרה בשנת 1984 כחלק מסדרת התערוכות "הנוף האמנותי של הרפובליקה הפדראלית של גרמניה", שהוצגה במוזיאון לאמנות של שטוטגרט. אפילו כיום, שמו של הפרבר שטאמהיים שבפאתי שטוטגרט מעלה בזכרון את משפטם של חברי סיעת הצבא האדום ("באדר-מיינהוף"), שהיו אסורים בכלא שזה היה שמו. אגף בית המשפט שנבנה במיוחד למטרה זו הוא המקום בו התקיים משפט הראווה כנגד החברים המובילים בארגון. במהלך המשפט עלתה שוב ושוב השאלה היכן עובר הגבול בין עונש בעל צידוק משפטי למעשה נקמה של השלטונות במתנגדיהם. כלא שטאמהיים הוא גם המקום שבו נמצאו ארבעה מחברי הארגון מתים בתאיהם. הדו"ח הרשמי שלפיו התאבדו האסירים הוטל שוב ושוב בספק, ועדיין לא הוכח באופן ודאי.

בעבודה זו משתמש אולף מטצל בשם טעון, שלא ניתן להתעלם מהנסיבות שבו נודע ברבים. האם משמעות הדבר הוא שהזר שלו מהווה מחווה פרובוקטיבית להרוגי שטאמהיים? האם החצר בעלת קיר הבטון החלק אמורה להזכיר את "המעוז שנבנה במיוחד", כפי שקראה התקשורת לאגף בית המשפט? את "מבצר שטאמהיים", כפי שכונה הכלא בו ריצו האסירים את עונשם? את אותו מבנה שתואר בעלון שהופץ באותה שנה בה נוצרה עבודת האמנות כ"מאוזוליאום שמור ברמת אבטחה גבוהה", שבו הנאשמים "נקברו בעודם חיים למשך כל חייהם"?

הזר והכיתוב מתייחסים בבירור למאפיינים של אנדרטות מסורתיות. זר עלי הדפנה שימש כבר בימי קדם לסמל ניצחונות צבאיים ולכבד את זכר הנופלים. למרות שגם היום משמשים זרים כדי לקשט קברים אזרחיים, זר זה והמיקום בו הוא מופיע מרמזים למפגני כבוד בהלוויות צבאיות או בטקסים ממלכתיים של הנחת זרים.

בעבודה זו מניח מטצל זר לכבוד חללי שטאמהיים-פרובוקציה ברורה בהתחשב בעובדה שהכבוד שהוא חולק לאלו שנאסרו ומתו בכלא אינו משקף קונצנזוס חברתי או שואף לייצר זהות קולקטיבית, כך שאינו עונה על הקריטריונים המקובלים לבניית אנדרטות והנחת זרים. זאת ועוד, הזר של מטצל גדול פי שלושה או ארבעה מזרים מקובלים. אם זר זה היה יצוק מברונזה, ממדיו המונומנטאליים היו משמשים להאדרת האנדרטה ומשמעותה. אך במקרה זה, הזר היצוק מבטון נתפס כאחיזת עיניים, כזיוף או כתכסיס. איכות חומרית זו מאפשרת לזר הזיכרון הענק להעצים את המחווה הגורפת לממדים אבסורדיים, המביעים מרי וכעס. האגרסיה שמשדר הזר טבועה בתוכו: הוא עשוי מחומר נוקשה ומחוספס, שמוטות הפלדה החלודים המזדקרים מתוכו מאיימים לפגוע בעוברים ושבים, בו בזמן שהם פוגעים בזר עצמו. הזר נוצר באמצעות דיסק חיתוך חשמלי-תהליך שמעורבת בו אגרסיה בוטה וכוח הרסני, ושמטצל עשה בו שימוש בעבודות נוספות כחלק מיצירת האמנות עצמה.

ההקדשה המתנוססת כחלק ממה שנראה לכאורה כאנדרטה אינה מופיעה באותיות בעלות מראה רשמי, כפי שנהוג בדרך כלל במקרים כאלה, אלא כתובה על הקיר באותיות דפוס ללא שבלונה. יחד עם זאת, אין מדובר בכיתוב מהסוג המתקרא "גרפיטי". הוא אינו נתפס כתוצר של מבצע סודי ובלתי-חוקי. למרות מראהו הפרובוקטיבי, זהו כיתוב שנעשה באופן רגוע ומתודי, והמתייחס באופן ברור למקום. זאת ועוד, אותיות הדפוס שגודלן זהה אינן מצביעות על חותם יד אישי, ומעניקות לכיתוב אופי אנונימי.

הכיתוב והזר נקראים שניהם כמחווה לאסירים ולמתים בכלא שטאמהיים. יחד עם זאת, הן המבקר בתערוכה והן הולך הרגל המגלה את הזר והכיתוב כשהוא מציץ באקראי דרך הגדר החיה של גינת הארמון הסמוך, יתהו ללא ספק לגבי זהותו של בעל המחווה, הלוקח אחריות על המעשה. זר מייצג בדרך כלל הכרה מצד האדם המניח אותו, בעוד שהכיתוב מגדיר את מהות ההכרה. אך מהי הזהות הנרמזת של מניחי הזר הזה-האם מדובר בנציגים מתחסדים של המדינה, או באנרכיסטים העוסקים במאמץ שווא לעורר תחושת פאתוס אצל המתבונן? האדם שלא הניח את הזר במו ידיו, אך דאג לכך שמנוף ירים אותו מעל בניין המוזיאון, ניתן בקלות לזיהוי: זהו האמן עצמו. העבודה לא נוצרה בעקבות הזמנה רשמית, אלא מהווה עבודת אמנות אוטונומית שלא כללה תכנון ארוך-טווח או יצירת קונצנזוס במרחב הציבורי. מטצל דיווח מאוחר יותר שבדרכו למוזיאון קרא מאמר דעה במגזין "דר שפיגל" שעסק בגזר הדין של פטר-יורגן בּוֹק. לאחר תקופה שבה הדיון בגזר הדין ובתנאי המאסר של הכלואים בשטאמהיים הלך והתלהט, צוטט התובע הפדראלי הראשי רבמאן כאומר שבקשה לחנינתו של בוק לא תידון לפני "העשורים הראשונים של המאה הבאה". זה היה הרגע שבו החליט האמן ליצור את שטאמהיים.

למרות שמיקומה של "אנדרטה" זו נדמה במבט ראשון כשרירותי, הוא נבחר בקפידה רבה. מטצל שאב את השראתו מקיר הבניין המצופה במרצפות בטון מלוטשות, מגג הנחושת המכוסה בפטינה, מהאווירה באזור הסובב את הפרלמנט השכן, שבו חל איסור על הפגנות, ומהשוטרים הנושאים מכשירי קשר רועשים: "זה מיד גרם לי לחשוב על האסוציאציה למאוזוליאום".

אך אופיו הפונקציונאלי למחצה של המקום חשוב אף יותר מהאווירה הסובבת אותו. אתר התערוכה, המהווה חלק טבעי מהסביבה ושניתן לראותו ולגשת אליו דרך הגדר החיה של הגן הסמוך, מבטיח שגם אנשים שאינם חלק מקהל המבקרים הרגיל של המוזיאון יבואו במגע עם עבודת האמנות, למרות שהיא ממוקמת בשטח המוזיאון. סף זה-המפריד בין החלל המגונן של המוזיאון למרחב הציבורי-הוא הנקודה שבה מציב מטצל את "חומר הנפץ" שלו, בעודו חוסה במעוז של חופש הביטוי האמנותי.

מטצל הופך את מרפסת הבטון של בניין התצוגה חסר האופי או ההיסטוריה לאנדרטה באמצעות שתי התערבויות בלבד-זר מבטון וכיתוב. יחד עם זאת, הוא מסרב להעניק לצופה נוסחה קלה לשימוש. למרות שההתייחסות לצורתה המסורתית של האנדרטה נתפסת בהקשר זה כפרובוקציה, המסר הרב-משמעי מקשה על הניסיון לנקוט עמדה. עבודתו של מטצל מפתה שוב ושוב את הצופה להילכד במלכודת המשמעות: היא מהווה מעין "טיזר" נעדר בסיס רציני. למרות שהיא מכילה מגוון אסוציאציות ורמיזות, לא ניתן לקרוא לעבודה רבת-פנים וחותכת זו "אנדרטה לזכר..." או "יד זיכרון המזהירה כנגד...". המסר נותר מעורפל, גם אם הוא מתייחס להקשר פוליטי מסוים מאד. לא ניתן לזהות את מעביר המסר או את נמענו. הזר והכתובת נותרים אנונימיים-טרדה אנונימית.

כריסטוף היינריך, "כתובת אנונימית על הקיר - אודות שתי יצירות של אולף מצטל", אולף מצטל, עמ' 19–16

13.4.1981
1987/2001
פלדה, בטון, פלדת אל-חלד, פיגמנט
700 × 900 × 1150 ס"מ

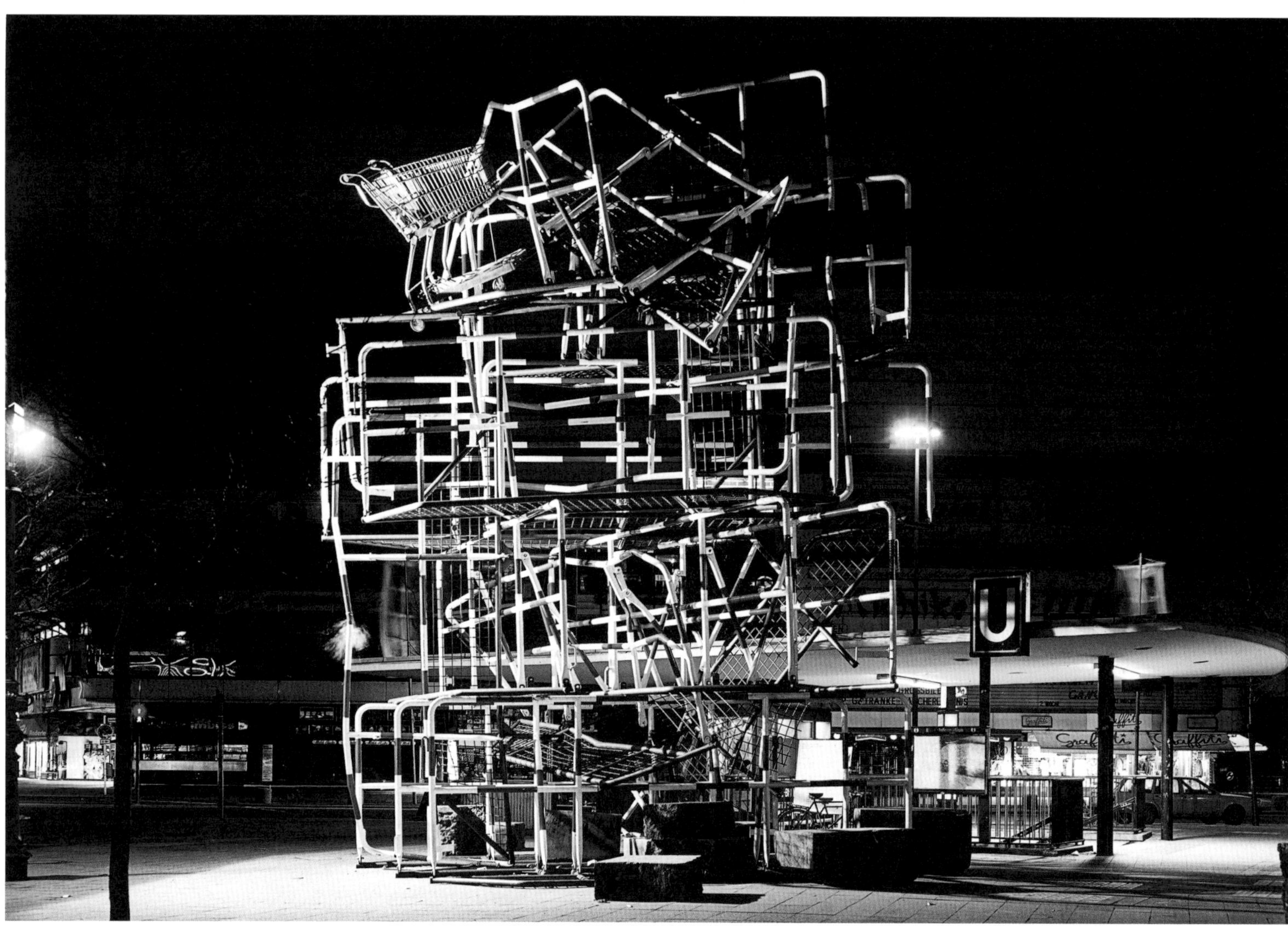

13.4.81
כריסטוף היינריך

הפסל יליד ברלין אולף מטצל (נ. 1952) אינו יוצר אנדרטות זיכרון המוקיעות מלחמות או את השלטון הנאצי. תחת זאת, הוא מתמסר לעבודות אמנות אוטונומיות העוסקות בנושאים סוציו-פוליטיים עכשוויים, כגון שנאת זרים וטרור, ספקולציות נדל"ן, ותנאי הייצור בכלכלת שוק. מטצל הוא אחד מבין אמנים רבים העוסקים במציאות החברתית היומיומית. מעבר לכך, הוא עוסק גם בממדיה הצורניים והתמטיים של האנדרטה. התייחסותו למבנה ולפונקציה של אנדרטות ניכרת במיוחד בעבודתו המרשימה."13.4.81" ר' עמ'

העבודה "13.4.81" נוצרה לרגל יום השנה ה-750 לשדרת הפסלים ברחוב קורפורסטנדאם ("קו-דאם") בברלין. ממדיה של העבודה עצומים: היא משתרעת על שטח של 10x9.5 מטרים, ומתנשאת לגובה של 11 מטרים. היא מורכבת ממספר רב של מחסומי משטרה אדומים ולבנים אותם ערם מטצל יחד עם עגלת קניות ליצירת מבנה אסתטי דחוס ובלתי יציב באופן מסוכן. המחסומים והעגלה, כמו אבני המרצפות המהוות את הבסיס, הוגדלו לפי שניים מגודלם המקורי.

האתר שבו הוצבה עבודה זו, כיכר יואכים שטלר, אינו רק עורק תנועה מרכזי, אלא גם מקום שבו התרחשו אינספור היתקלויות בין מפגינים למשטרה מאז פרוץ מהומות הסטודנטים במהלך שנות ה-70. מטצל מתייחס במפורש לאחת מאותן הפגנות, שהתארגנה בתגובה לשמועה על מותו בשביתת רעב של אחד מאסירי סיעת הצבא האדום ("באדר-מיינהוף"). בתגובה לידיעה זו, בליל ה-12–13 באפריל 1981, ניתצו תומכי האסירים, רובם צעירים, כ-70% מחלונות הראווה בשדרה תוך דקות ספורות. כשהמשטרה הגיעה למקום, רוב המפגינים כבר עזבו או נעלמו בתוך המון התושבים שטיילו בשדרה. מטצל קושר אירוע זה לרעיון ציורי שמצא-תרתי משמע-ברחוב: בתום עצרת ציבורית הוא צילם תלולית של מחסומים, אבני מרצפת, ועגלת קניות שנערמה בשולי האזור על ידי השוטרים. פסל "אקראי" זה היווה את נקודת המוצא לאנדרטה.

ההתייחסות למקום מסוים, שם העבודה המתייחס לאירוע היסטורי ספציפי, הסימנים המוכרים, והגדלתם למידות ענק מכוונים אותנו למחשבה על "אנדרטה". ייתכן שמאחורי חלונות הראווה המנותצים, הביזה, וההיעלמות המהירה של המפגינים שנמלטו אל הרכבת התחתית אינם אירועים ראויים לציון באמצעות אנדרטה. אך התאריך כמו גם הפסל המתייחס לו מצביעים על קונפליקט בסיסי המתקיים מעבר לאירוע הספציפי: הפוליטיקאים והתקשורת ראו באירועי אותו סוף שבוע סימפטום של אלימות גוברת וקשרו אותם למהומות של אותה תקופה, שבמהלכן התוקפנות שהופנתה עד אז בעיקר נגד סמלים ולנציגים של המדינה התפרצה ללא אבחנה והכתה גם בעוברים ובשבים. הסלמה זו גררה בעקבותיה אחד מניסיונות רבים להקשיח את החוקים הנוגעים להפגנות, והובילה לקריאה לשימוש ב"יד חזקה". האיפוק הפוליטי שבו נהג הסנאט בהנהגת המפלגה הסוציאל-דמוקרטית באותה תקופה ביחס לסצנת ה"פולשים" לדירות זכה לביקורת חריפה, והתפרש על ידי האופוזיציה כאות חולשה. סובלנות והימנעות מהתערבות עודדו לדבריה את הכוחות ההרסניים, אותם ניתן לבלום רק באמצעות הגבלות ואיסורים על הפגנות.

[...]

האמן נמנע מהטפת מוסר, כמו גם מסוג "ההנצחה המכוונת" המתבקשת במקרה של אנדרטה או יד זיכרון. בתגובה לכל ניסיון לאתר אזהרה חינוכית, הוא עונה בבוטות, "אני זוכר!" אחרי הכול, בשדרות קו-דאם ניתן לחשוב גם על "ביקור המלכה, קפה קנצלר, קניות, או קמפינסקי".

מטצל מעורר פולמוס כנגד "מבני האנדרטות המעוותים" ומסרב לדחף הדידקטי העומד מאחוריהן. כבר במבט ראשון, החפצים שבאמצעותם הוא מסמן את המקום מכוונים כל הולך רגל אל שני מאפיינים שונים אך קשורים של החיים האורבאניים: עגלת הקניות-האמצעי להעברת סחורות ממוכר לקונה-מתייחסת לחברת השפע ולצרכיה. המחסום שבו משתמשים "האחראים על הסדר" מגן על אותם ערכים במהלך היתקלויות אלימות עם אותם חלקים באוכלוסייה שמתנגדים להם.

אך במהלך ההפגנה שנערכה בתאריך "13.4.81", אותו כלי קיבול צרכני שימש כדי להעביר ממקום למקום את אבני המרצפת ששימשו כנשק. עם העלייה ברמת האלימות שאפיינה את ההיתקלויות, הפכו גם "כלי המגן" של השוטרים לכלי נשק. כך קרה לדוגמא בשנת 1985, כאשר מפגין נהרג מפגיעתו של תותח מים בזמן הפגנה בפרנקפורט. אירוע זה קרה בתקופה שבה יצר מטצל את הפסל, והוא מתייחס אליו באמצעות גזיר עיתון על קיר העבודה "1" המלווה את הפרויקט. המסר הברור של השלטים, שהוא הכרחי למימוש הפונקציה הדידקטית של כל אנדרטה, מאבד כאן את משמעותו, ומוחלף בתחושה של אי-נוחות ובלבול.

העבודה "13.4.81" מתייחסת בבירור למבנה הצורני של האנדרטה המסורתית, תוך שהיא סוטה ממנה. היא מרמזת לבסיס הקלאסי באמצעות אבני המרצפת הבודדות למרגלות הפסל, כמו גם באמצעות הטריזים המתנשאים. לאורך ההיסטוריה של האנדרטה, גובהו של הבסיס קבע תמיד את המרחק בין מושא ההנצחה לבין האדם המנציח אותו, כמו גם את אופי התקשורת ביניהם. בסיס גבוה מרחיק את האדם המונצח מהמרחב הטריטוריאלי של המנציח, בעוד שבסיס נמוך מאפשר לגיבור לרדת באופן זמני מפסגת האולימפוס ולהושיט את ידו בנדיבות אל האדם המכבד את זכרו. הבסיס של מטצל, לעומת זאת, פרוץ לגמרי, והאבנים פזורות לכל עבר. בסיס זה אינו קובייה היראטית, אלא מסגרת לטיפוס שקוראת לעוברים ושבים לנכסה לעצמם. העגלה המכתירה את הפסל אינה טעונה בחגיגיות ממלכתית-ההיפך הוא הנכון, שכן היא מתנודדת בחוסר שליטה. הניסיון לקרוא מבנה זה באופן היררכי, לדוגמא כ"אנטי-מונומנט" המעורר פולמוס, מטעה.

העבודה "13.4.81" מציבה בפני הצופים רשת של סימנים שנדמית במבט ראשון ברורה למדי, ומורכבותה מתגלה רק במבט שני. האמן מתגרה בצופים; הרמזים שהוא מציע לצורות מונומנטאליות מאלצים אותם להתעמת עם הסתירה, בעוד שהוא עצמו דוחה כל אינדיקציה לווידוי.

קטעים מתוך "האנדרטה כמוטיב וכפונקציה". (Denkmal als Motiv und Funktion) לכריסטוף היינריך

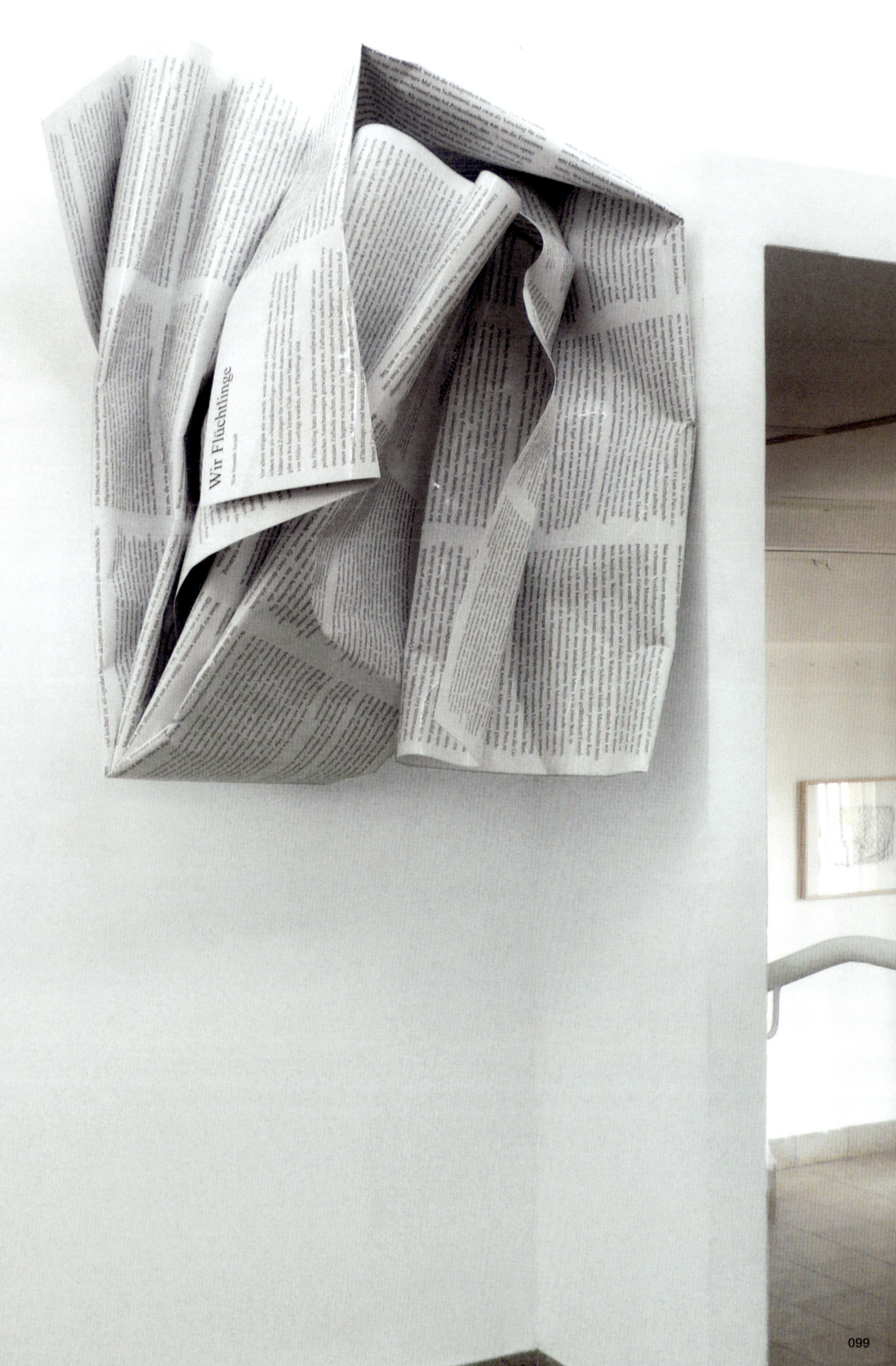
Wir Flüchtlinge

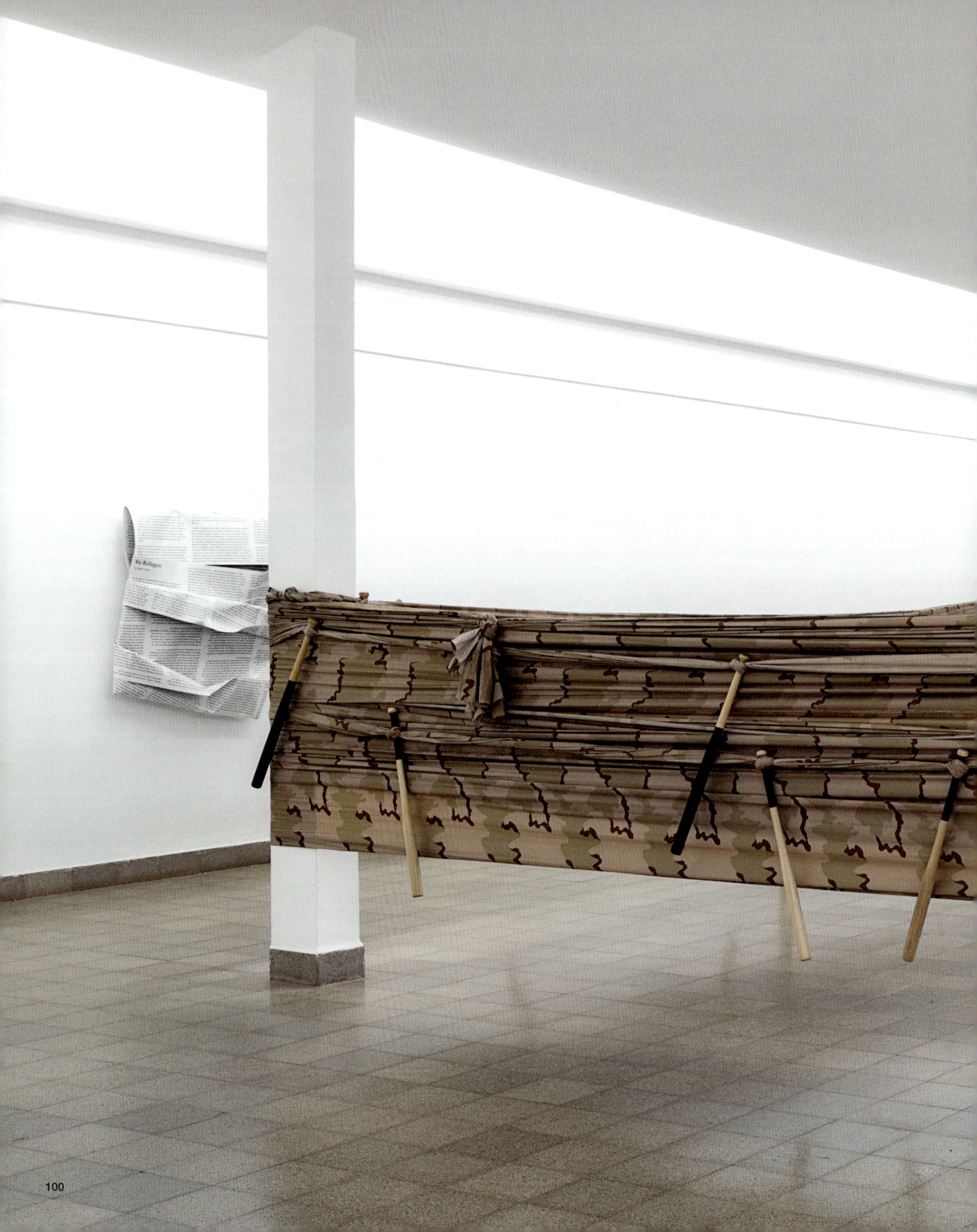
We Refugees

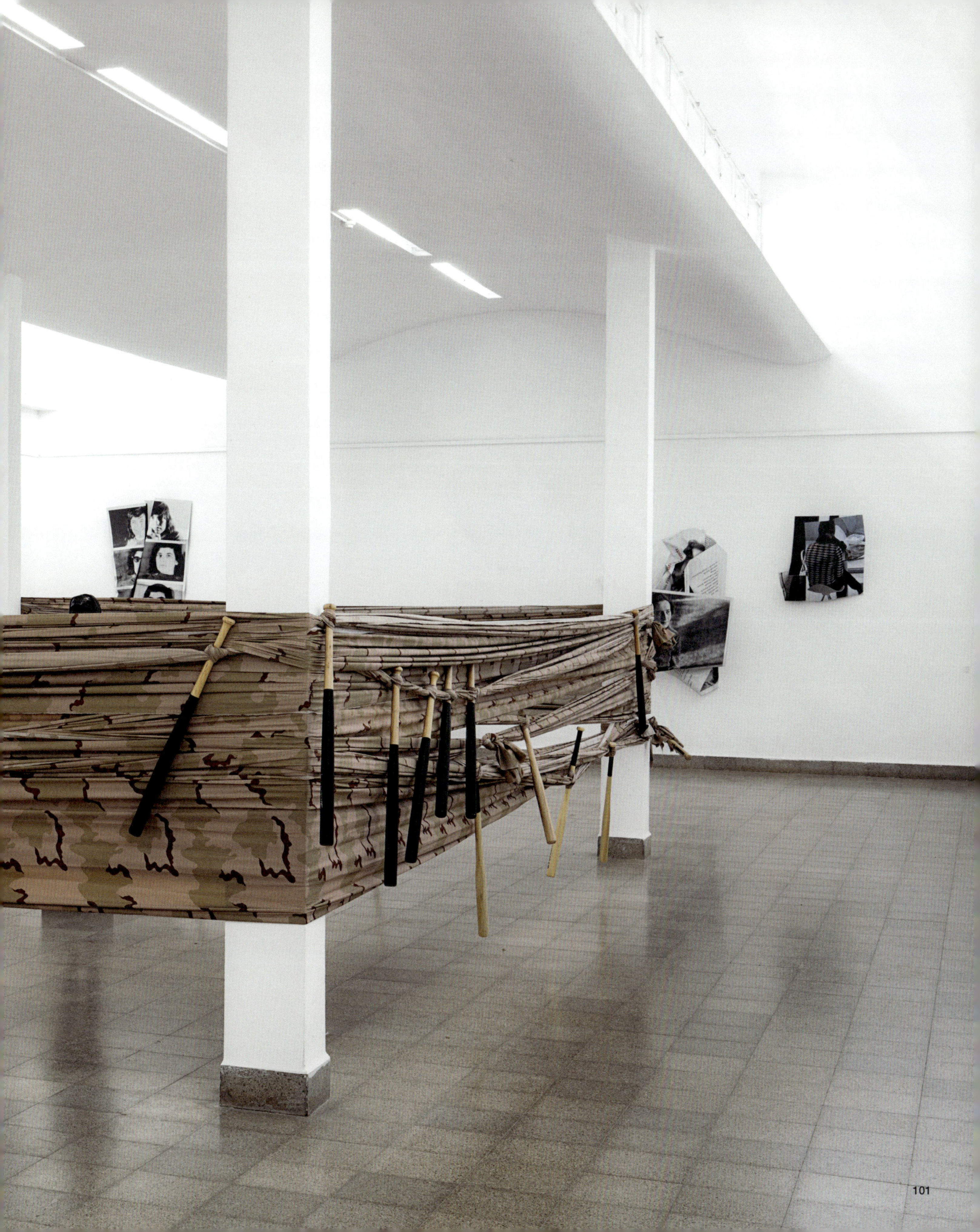

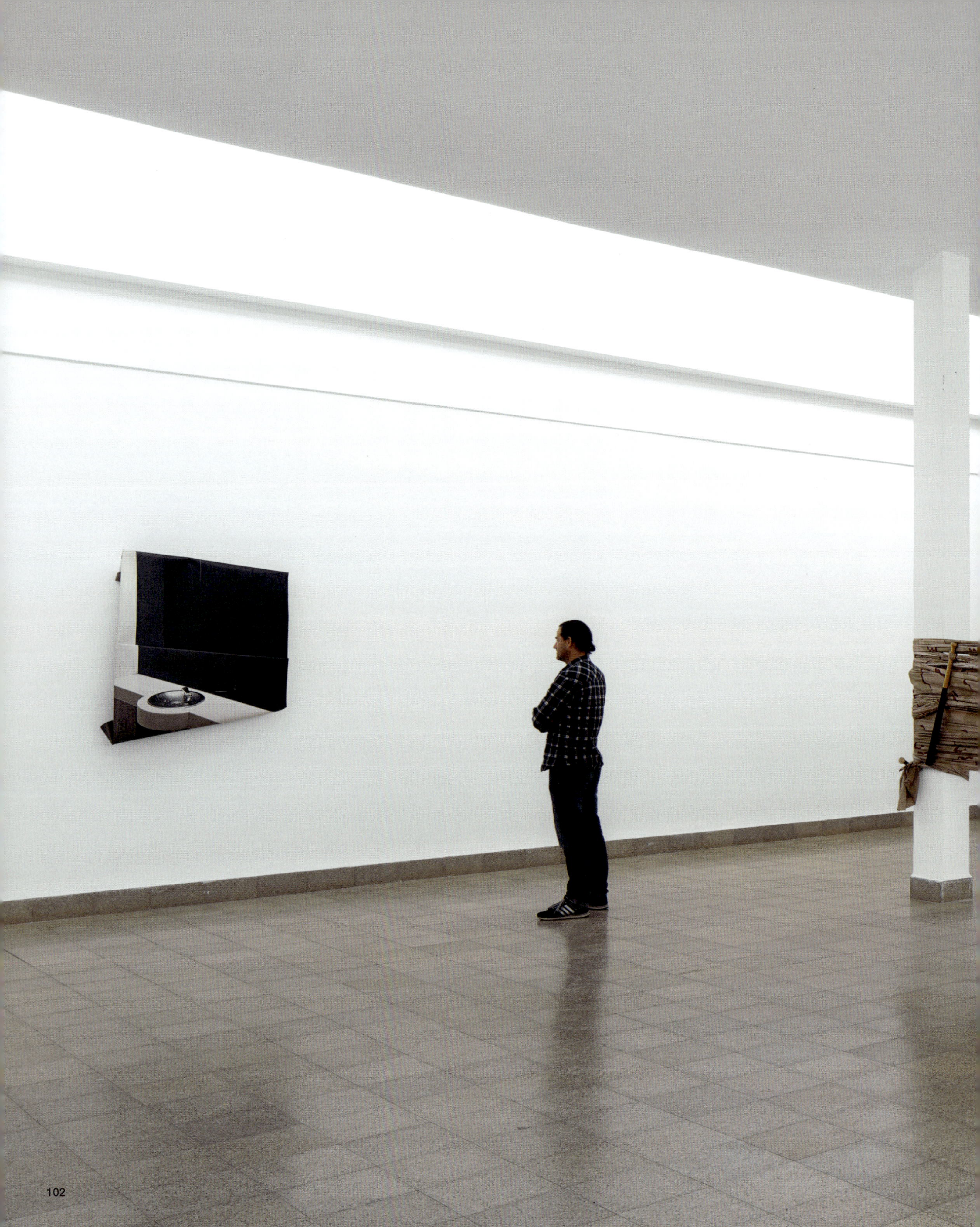

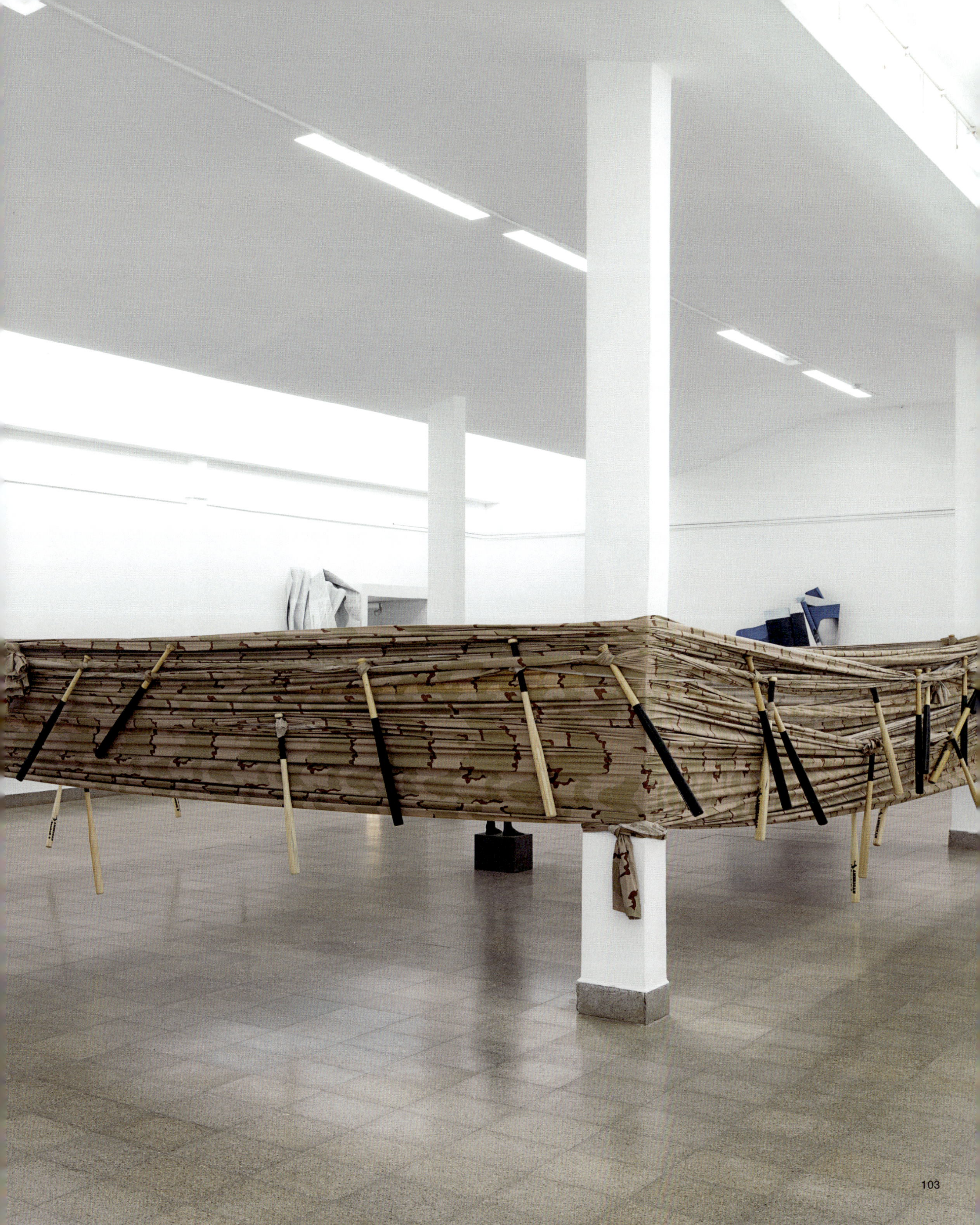

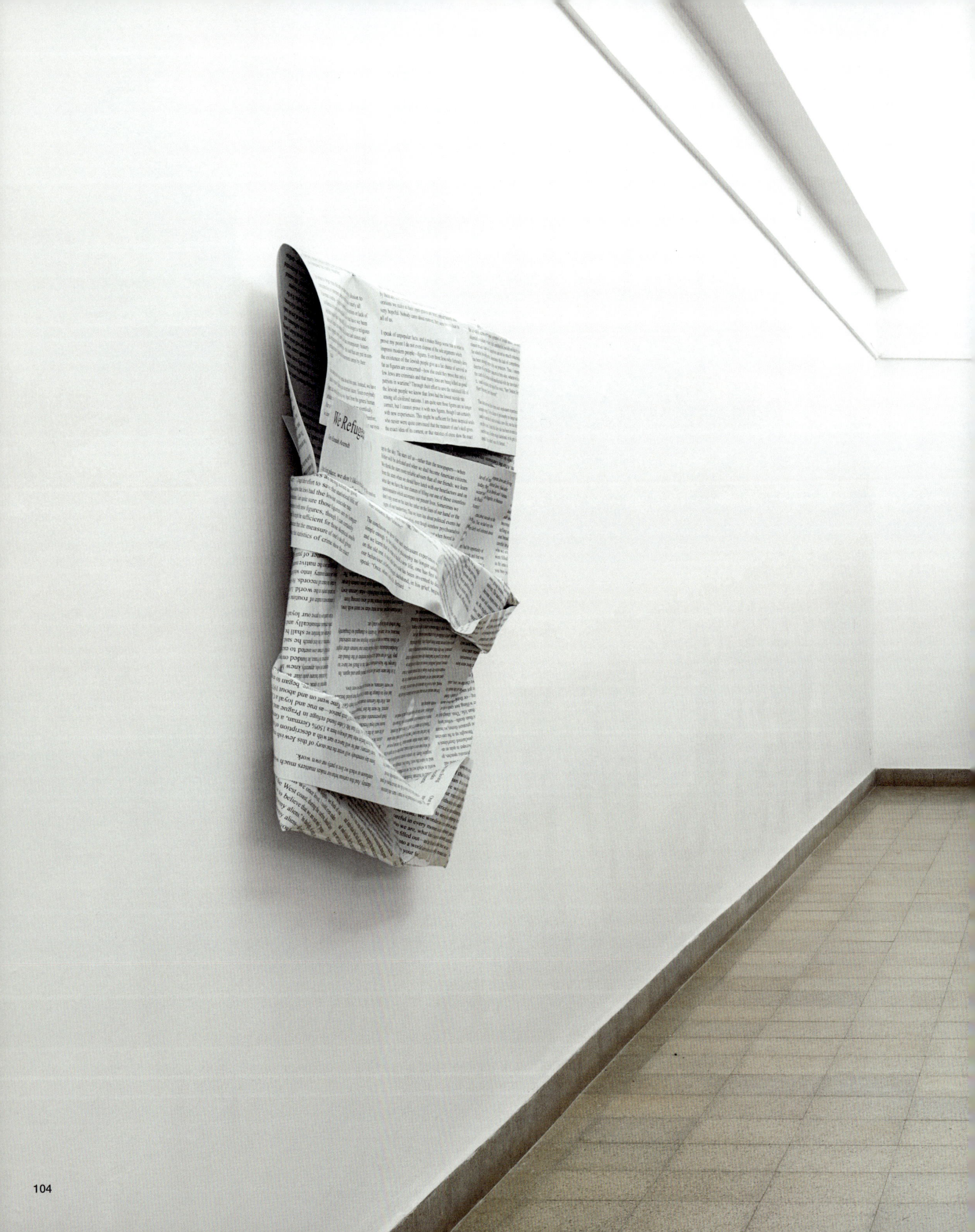

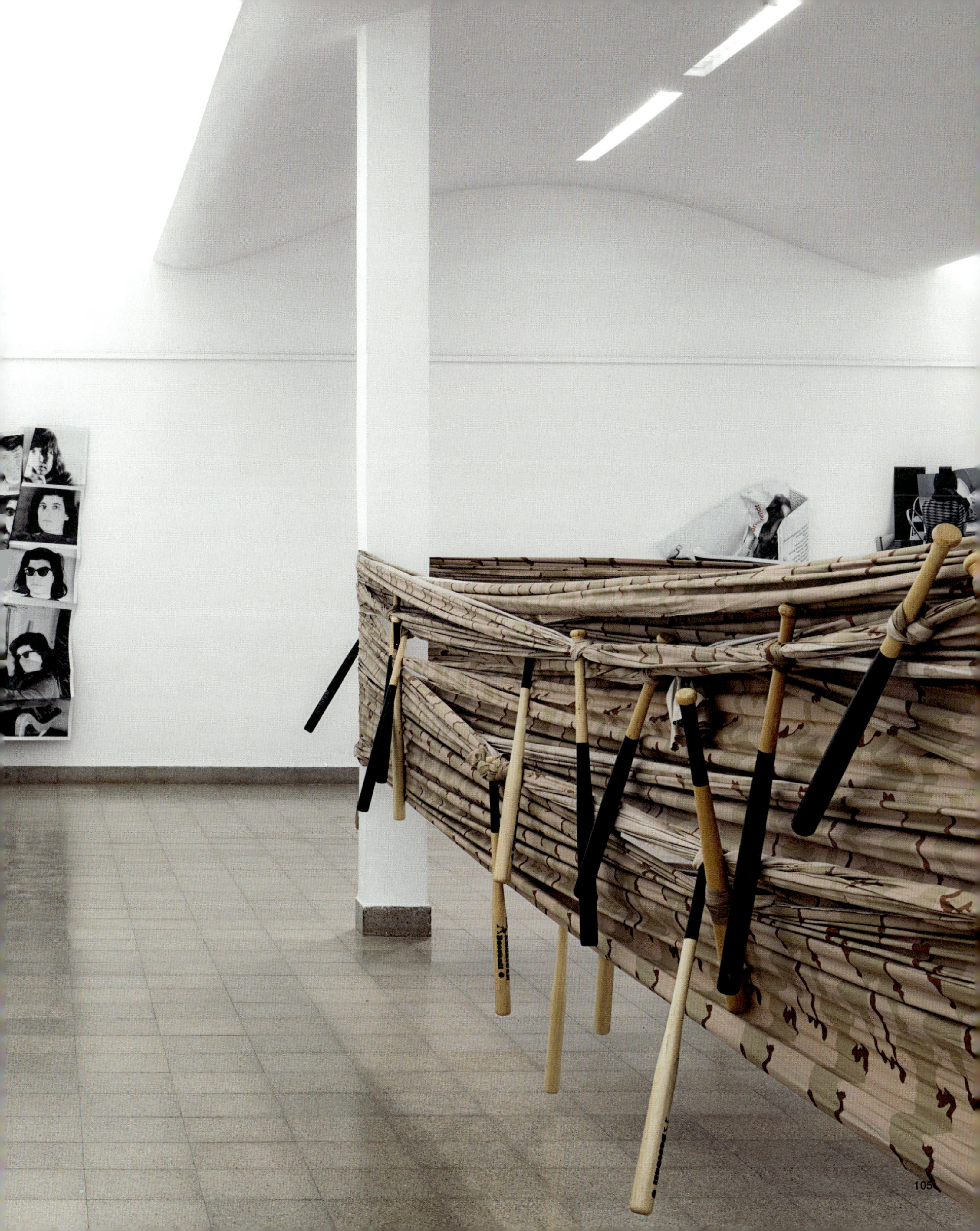

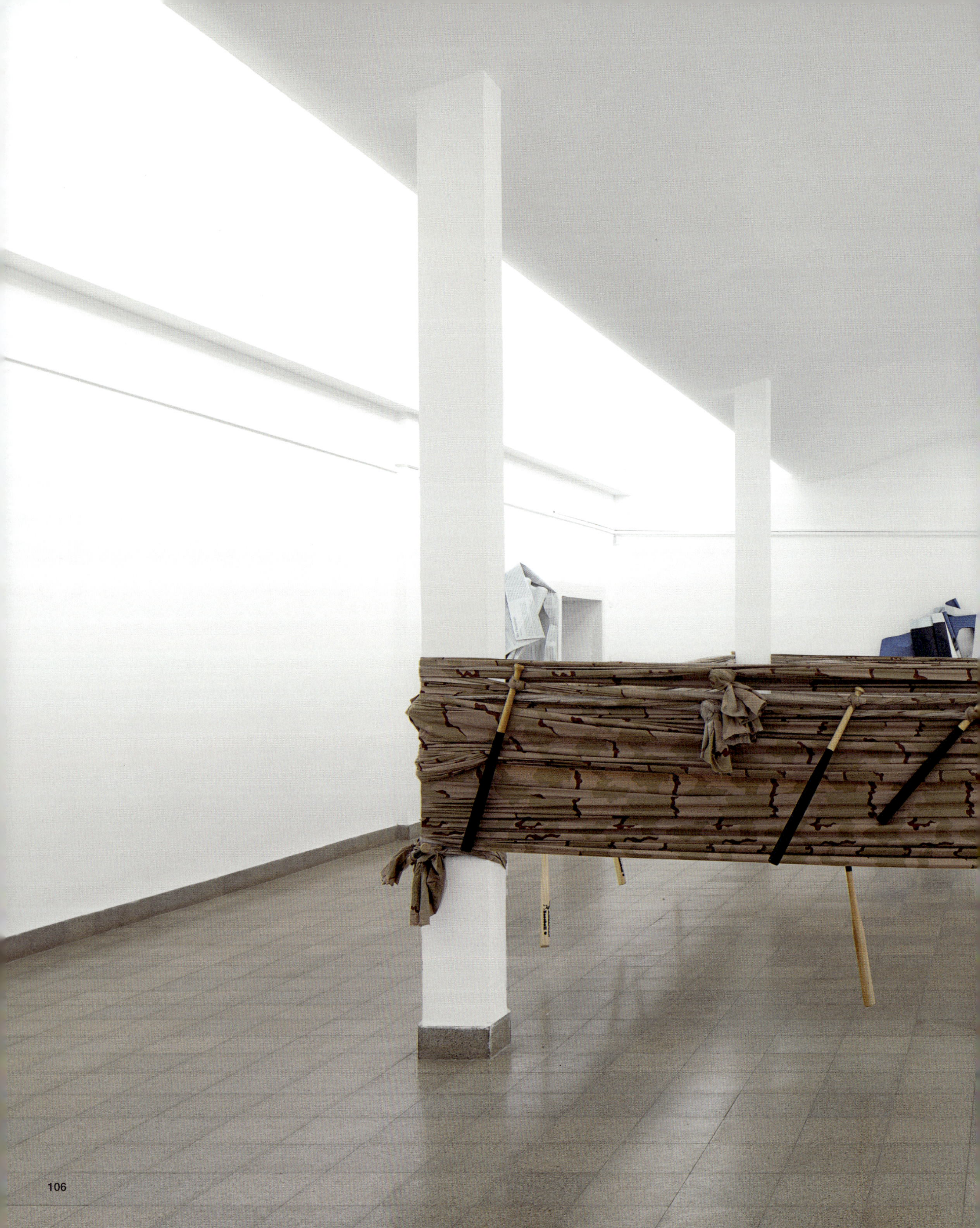

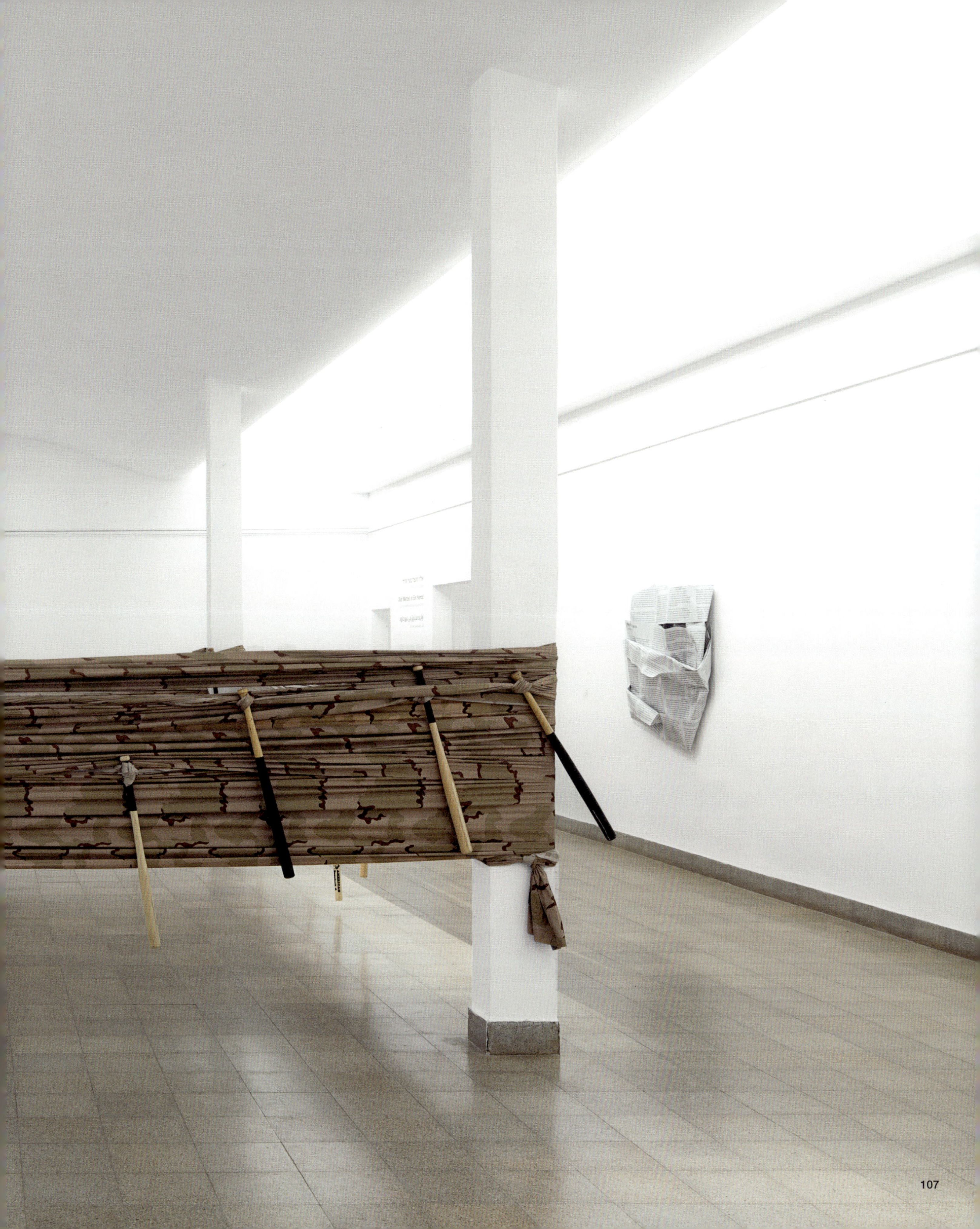

מעדן טורקי

המיצב "עוד שאלות?" שבו נפתח המאמר נגע כאמור ב"לא תקין" ככוח מניע, ועדיין לא נחשף לבו של הלא-תקין בתערוכה זו, הספון לו בתווך. כעת מותר לגלות שה"מסגרת" או החומה של המיצב הנושקת לקרקע מאפשרת הצצה פנימה: למרבה התדהמה, בלב המיצב של רשת ומחבטי בייסבול ניצב פסל אישה עירומה, אחת ויחידה, ולראשה כיסוי ראש כמקובל בטורקיה. "מעדן טורקי" מציינת הכותרת, ומכוונת לממתק מזרחי ספציפי, "רחת לוקום". אי-התקינות חוצה כבר כמה וכמה סימני עצור, כך נדמה, אבל מוטב להשתהות להתבוננות בפסל.

מידות הפסל משונות, קטנות מעט מהגודל הטבעי, ונראה שהוא נוצר במתודה אקדמית, כלומר, האלף-בית של מה שנלמד במשך מאות בשנים באקדמיות לאמנות יפה, שמסוגן האקדמיה בה מלמד האמן הפרופסור אולף מטצל במינכן זה קרוב לשלושים שנה. הבסיס הוא תרגול במיומנות הרישום, אינספור שעות של רישום עירום ממודל חי (בגרמנית Akt). מטצל עבד על הפסל במתודה קלאסית: הוא פיסל בחומר רך ועוד מוחש מגע היד בפסל. הוא העביר את הפסל שלבי יציקה וגימור כנהוג, אלא שה"קלאסי" המוטמע במתודה לא באמת כונן כאן הרמוניה. התנוחה שלו מסרבת לזו המקובלת ב-Nude הקלאסי. לא רק שנעדר ממנה ה"קונטרה פוסטו" - הגוף מוטה בסיבוב קטן על מרכז צירו כך שהוא מתקמר קמעה בצורת האות S ומושך כלפי מעלה כדי לייצג את "היפה" בה"א הידיעה - אלא שהגוף הזה מושך כלפי מטה. ה-Nude היה ל- Naked.

"היפה" הוא מעתה כולו שבירות אנושית הממוקדת בחוליה אחת בגוף, במותנית העומדת תחת לחץ. חומת הרשת המקיפה נדמית עתה פחות כקיר מגן ויותר כזר דפנה לדמות האישה הקורסת - ר' את "שטמהיים" (עמ...). מהדהד בו המרחב הציבורי האורבני שבו מוטבעים עקבות המקום המתערער ובו ניבט הסדר המופרע, ורעד המאמץ מייצר הגיון גופני אחר המפקיע את הכוח והסמכות ומאפשר לאנטגוניסטי לחלחל למרחב ציבורי. זר הדפנה והאשה העירומה במובן Naked אכן מרמזים למקומות הפרוצים והכותרת מאירה את הסטיגמות המובנות בתוך השפה המסגירה ביזוי והשפלה. חשיבה ביקורתית כבר זיהתה את המקומות האפלים של מושג ה- Nude , ה"נשגב" המושך כלפי מעלה ובעצם הוא משוקע ביחסי כוח ונקשר בין השאר למציצנות,[7] וגם במושג ה"אודליסק", על הדיכוי שבו בדגש על נשות המזרח. בדיוק במקום הזה, במרחב המגן-לא מגן של המוזיאון, פועל מטצל בלי הנחות ואינו מבאר, שמאל וימין, מזרח ומערב. ה"מעדן טורקי" שלו עומדת ערומה, יחפה על המרצפות החשופות, רעלה לראשה והיא מוקפת גדר. הגוף הערום, ה-naked בלא סימני שייכות (לבוש), חושף השפלה או לחילופין, העצמה נשית. הרעלה חושפת את הגוף הערום כ"זר". חנה ארנדט חשפה את דילמת הנראות והזהות של פליטות במאמרה המכונן "אנחנו פליטים" (ראו עמ..) דילמת נראות על שום מה? כי לפליטות אין מקום בעולם שבו דרכון חורץ זהות. הגוף של הזר, הגוף הנוכח במרחב ציבורי, מעצים תחושת אי-נוחות. גוף ה"זר" מזוהה כמפר סדר, מקור לזיהום, כפי שמאיר דיון עכשווי בפליטות.[8]

אולף מטצל מגיע לישראל בדיוק בזמן הזה - בימים רעים של גירוש פליטים. בביקורו הקודם פקד ערים וקיבוצים וחווה אדריכלות באוהאוס שיצרו כאן תנועות של מהגרים ועקורים. הוא חווה גם מוטציות שלה ושאריות מדורדרות של מיתוס הקדמה ויצר בהשראתן עבודות חדשות. הוא שב להציג במשכן לאמנות עין חרוד, מבנה שכל כולו חלל ואור, מרחב של פונקציונליות מיטיבה המאפשרת מרחב ספי. בחלל המוזאון הזה מעגן מטצל את המיצב "יש שאלות?" שבתווך שלו נוגע ביסוד הזמניות שבין הגופני לנפשי, נוגע ביסוד הנפיץ שאינו מנוסח בתקינות פוליטית - הוא נמנע מכל תוויות של מרחב מוגן ומרמז למקומות הפרוצים של מה שנדמה היה כנגעי עבר.

1
הוצגה לראשונה ב-1996.

2
תשתית ה"גריד" משמעותית בעבודתו של מטצל כפי שמעידים רישומיו בקטלוג זה. Paul Celan, Die Niemandsrose. Sprachgitter. Gedichte. S. Fischer: Frankfurt a. M, 1986.

3
פאול צלאן, סורג-שפה: שירים וקטעי פרוזה, תל אביב: הספריה החדשה לשירה, 1994. כאן נעשה שימוש במונח "גריד" בגלל קונוטציות שאינן מיתרגמות במונח "סורג".

4
תרגום של המחברת מאנגלית:
"O Little Root of a Dream" translated by Nikolai Popov and Heather McHugh
https://www.poets.org/poetsorg/poem/o-little-root-dream

5
בשיריו נודעת לעיניים גם קונוטציה של זמן, "עיני הזמן", ר': Shira Wolosky, pluto.huji.ac.il/~wolosky/CELANTR.doc

6
אנדרו בנג'מין חוקר אדריכלות ומרחב מנקודת מבט פילוסופית. שיח התלות באתר, שהיטה את הכף מאמנות-לשם-אמנות לאמנות תלוית הקשר, מהדהד בין השאר גם שינויי מגמה בפילוסופיה, מהתפיסה הפנומנולוגית (בדגש על חומריות והתנסות) של ראשית הדרך אל הפרדיגמה הדיסקורסיבית שהתנסחה בסוף המאה ה-20, ר' Miwon Kwon, One Place After Another: Site-Specific Art and Locational Identity. Cambridge: MIT Press, 2002.

7
Laura Mulvey, "Visual Pleasure and Narrative Cinema", Screen, vol. 16 (Autumn 1975), pp. 6-18.

8
Zygmunt Bauman, "Strangers" in Thinking Sociologically, Cambridge, Mass. Basil Blackwell, 1990, pp. 54-70; Sara Ahmed, Strange Encounters: Embodied Others in Postcoloniality, London and New York, Routledge, 2000.

אולף מטצל, תקינות פוליטית ומרחב ציבורי
גליה בר אור

עוד שאלות?

"עוד שאלות?" שתי מלים עם סימן שאלה הן לא פתיח שגרתי למאמר וגם לא כותרת שגורה לעבודת אמנות, בעיקר משום שמשתמעת מהן תחושה משונה של סוף בטרם התחלה וקונוטציה של יציאת ידי חובה של דובר משרד זה או אחר בנוגע לאירוע שכולו ממילא שאלה פעורה שאין עליה תשובה. אבל אותו חוסר שגרתיות מובלע, בעיקר כשהוא נקשר למרחב ציבורי, הוא כוח מניע בעבודתו של אולף מטצל, שבחר בכותרת "עוד שאלות?" לעבודת הצבה שלו המוצגת בגרסא חדשה במשכן לאמנות עין חרוד.[1]

חוסר השגרתיות או האי-נחת לא מתמצים בכותרת. העבודה הנכרכת כחומה או גדר סביב לארבעה עמודי תווך של אולם מרכזי ומואר חושפת הכלאה טורדת בין עולמות חוץ לעולמות פנים ומעצימה שאלות. מה פשרם, למשל, של חומה פנימית משונה בלב ארבעה קירות, קיר מגן בתוך קיר מגן של מוזיאון ובעיקר, האם ייתכן דיבור בין גריד של אמנות ומה שנראה כמו "גריד" מאולתר, תוצר של עימותי רחוב.[2] האם ייתכן דיבור כזה בין גריד ל"גריד"? נדמה שזו השאלה המכרעת בה עוסק מטצל כעניין קיומי בכל עבודתו: דיבור כהקשר חי ובועט, לא מנותק מהתרחשויות הזמן, לא עולם אסתטי לעצמו. כיצד מתאפשר הדיבור בין שפות שונות?

לשאלה זו מרמזת בהקשר שונה עבודתו "גריד-שפה" (או "סורג-שפה", עמ'..) שבה מסגרת תמונה שמצא באקראי שימשה נקודת מוצא לעבודת הצבה בבית כנסת בשטומלן. בהצבה זו, סבכת עץ מורכבת התעצמה למסגרת מונומנטלית המעוגנת בתקרה – מה היא ממסגרת? חלל של היעדר. אך הסבכה עצמה, יותר משהיא תוחמת הרי היא עצמה מרחב סף – מרחב על סף שפה, כי היא רצופה סימנים כחורים פעורים, אף שאפשר לראות בהם גם סמלים. בדומה לכך ניתן לראות גם את המסגרת התוחמת חלל שמקיפה ארבעה עמודים במיצב "עוד שאלות?" בעין חרוד.

"גריד-שפה", שהיה באחרונה למושג אינטרנטי, נקשר במקור למשורר איש הרוח פול צלאן, שבחר בכותרת זו לאחד משיריו וכן לספר שיריו שיצא לאור ב-1959.[3] בדומה לצלאן, עבודתו של מטצל נראית לכאורה אקראית ומחוסרת סדר מבני – שהרי לא אחת בהצבותיו נדמה שיד ענק השליכה הר קורס של שאריות וחלקי "רדי מיידס". יחד עם זאת, גם כאן ובדומה לצלאן, על אף הרושם של ארעיות, פועל מטצל על בסיס תכנון ותשתית מעמיקה. עבודותיו מדייקות מתח פנימי, וזאת בשפה שמשקעיה ופעריה מונשמים בזמניות, שפה הרוויה בהתנסות על קרעיה וחבלותיה ועל המחיקה הבלתי נמנעת של הזמן.

מומנט מונומנט

שורש קטן של חלום
[...]
שניתן יהיה דיבור, של אדמה
של להט, של
דברים עם עיניים, אפילו
כאן, היכן שאתה קורא אותי עיוור,

אפילו
כאן,
היכן שאתה
מפריך אותי,
לאות.[4]

"שניתן יהיה דיבור", מבקש צלאן, וגם "דברים עם עיניים", אולי של העצמי הנפרק במורד השיר כמו מיצב קורס ומקרטע בשורות שבורות שהן גם עיני הזמן, ההיסטוריה.[5] אפשר שהן ניבטות באורח דומה, בחומריות ובקריסה, ממיצב שהציב מטצל ב-1987 כפעולה תלוית-אתר (site specific), מיצב שכותרתו נושאת את תאריכו של מאורע שאירע שש שנים קודם להצבתו. ""13.4.1981, כותרת המסמנת נקודה ברצף זמן, יום פרוץ מהומות שסימנו תפנית במרחב הציבורי. אירע אז אירוע אלים שאלימותו לא התמקדה עוד בנציגי השלטון, אלא היתה זו מתקפת המון חסרת אבחנה של הכל בכל, פגיעה בחסרי בית ועובדי אורח ומרכזי קניות. הקיקלופ הקורס של מטצל, בעל עין אחת של עגלת קניות אחוזה במוט, ניצב על רגלי בריקדה ומחסומי משטרה ומסמן זמן ומקום: התנגשות בלתי נמנעת של כוחות העולים מלמטה וכוחות כופי סדר היורדים ורודים מלמעלה המהדהדת פרספקטיבות עבר ועתיד בהווה נמשך שבו המונומנט הוא מומנט מתריע.

הפסל שתואר כאן מהדהד זמניות, ארעיות ולא נצח, מסרב לגימור אסתטי המציע אחדות מרקם ונורמטיביות של שפה, מקעקע את מופרכות מושג המונומנט. הפסל הזה פועל כנגד סוג השיקום שמציע זיכרון ממלכתי בהתיימרו לגשר באחת על תהום שנפערה. מטצל מותיר זכר למה שעוות או נמעך ומדייק באיזון שביר על סף הקריסה – הוא מדייק ב"גריד-שפה", שפה המפריכה את עצמה כחלק בלתי נפרד מהקשרה החי שרק לו מחזירה ההיסטוריה מבט.

יצירתו של מטצל נוגעת בלב-לבה של אמנות עכשווית המתמודדת עם השאלה של עבודת אמנות תלוית-אתר ("סייט-ספסיפיק") – מושג הנקשר היסטורית למהלכי מפתח עקרוניים באמנות עכשווית. ההקשריות המובנית בספציפיות של מקום או אתר מחדדת שאלות של "חוץ" ו"פנים", שפת אמנות ועולם, יחסי תלות ובידול – מה שהוא חלק ממשהו, מהקשר, קונטקסט ספציפי, ונחלק ממנו בעת ובעונה אחת, במונחיו של אנדרו בנג'מין.[6]

הקונטקסטואליות הזו עברה בעשורים האחרונים תפנית חברתית, פדגוגית, וקהילתית . אלא שהעבודה של מטצל, אף שלא ניתן לומר כי איננה חברתית ופוליטית, אין בה דבר משיקוף מראה המציאות. היא נשמרת מהכשל הפדגוגי, היא לא מוסרנית, ובעיקר היא חפה מכל אידיאולוגיזם ותקינות פוליטית. עבודתו פועלת בנחישות בגריד השפה תוך שהיא מתהפכת במסורת האמנות היפה כחרב פיפיות של זמן הווה.

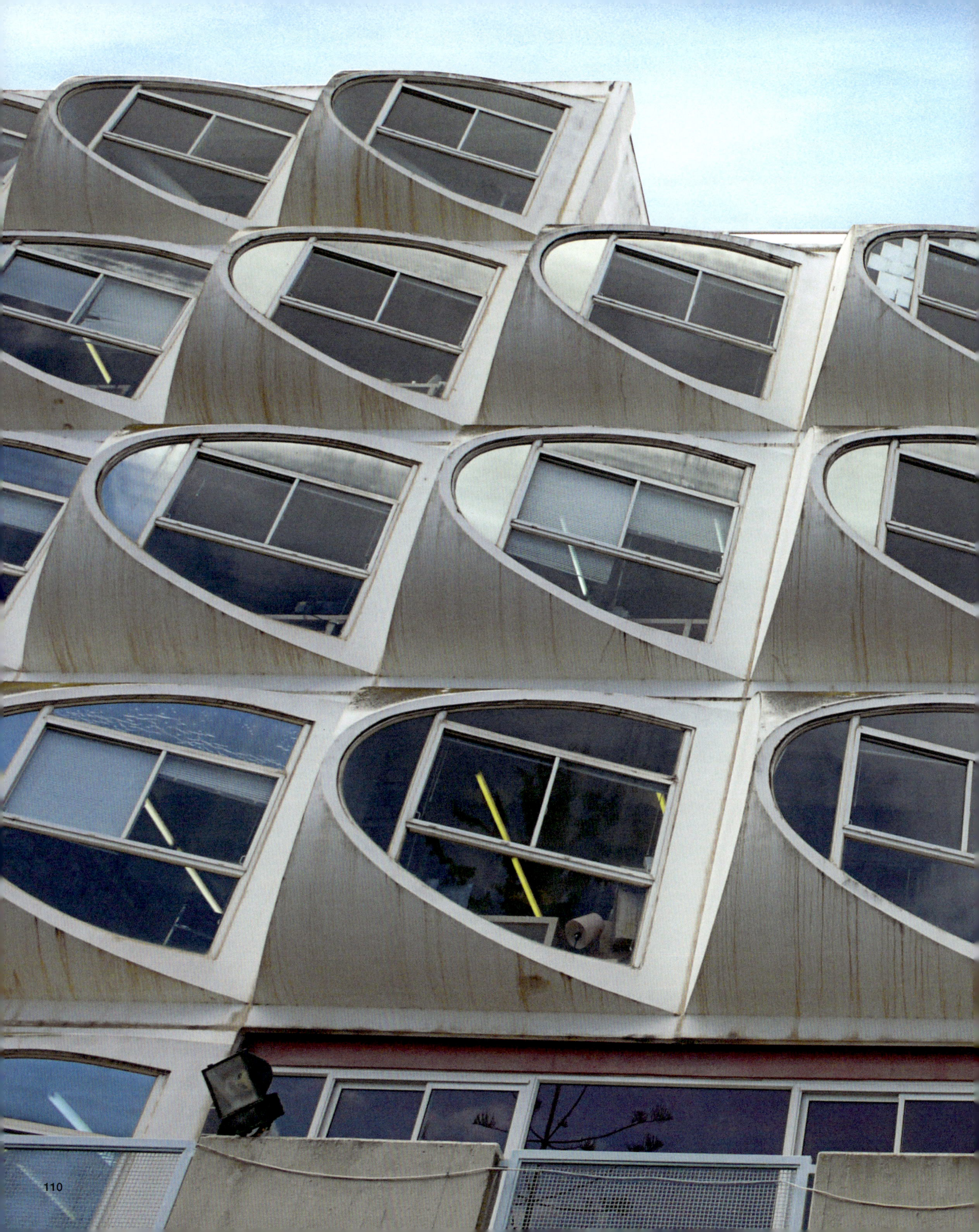

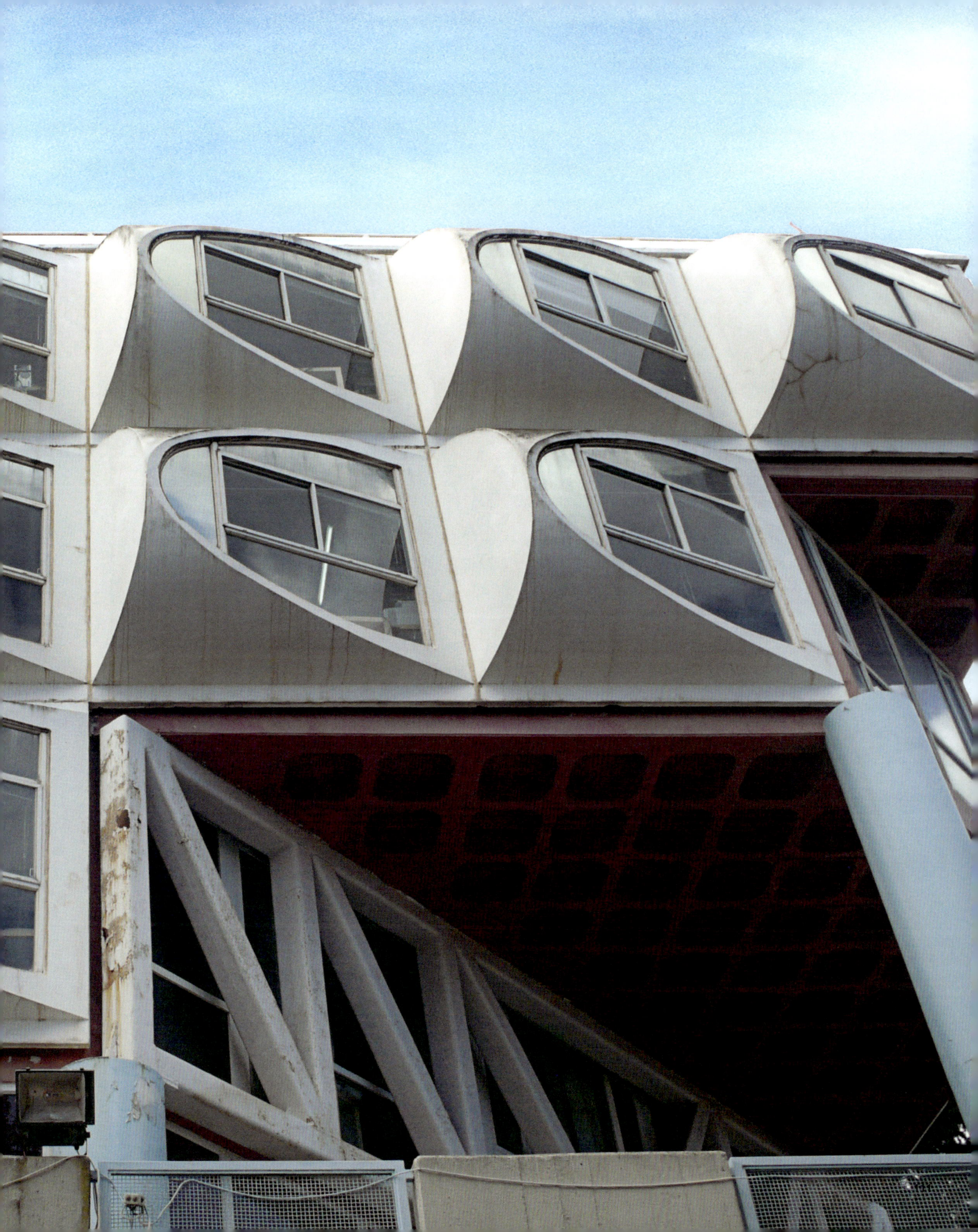

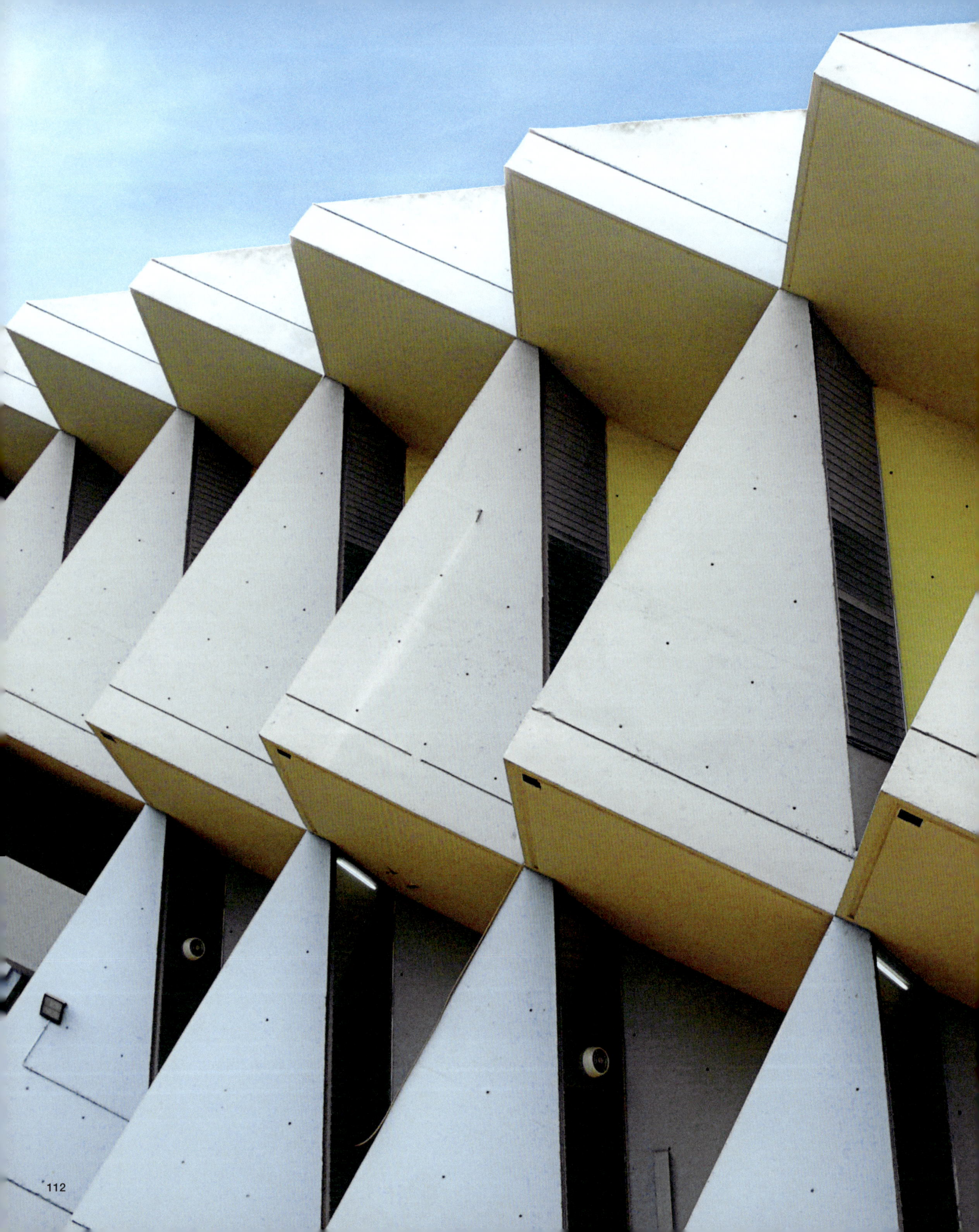

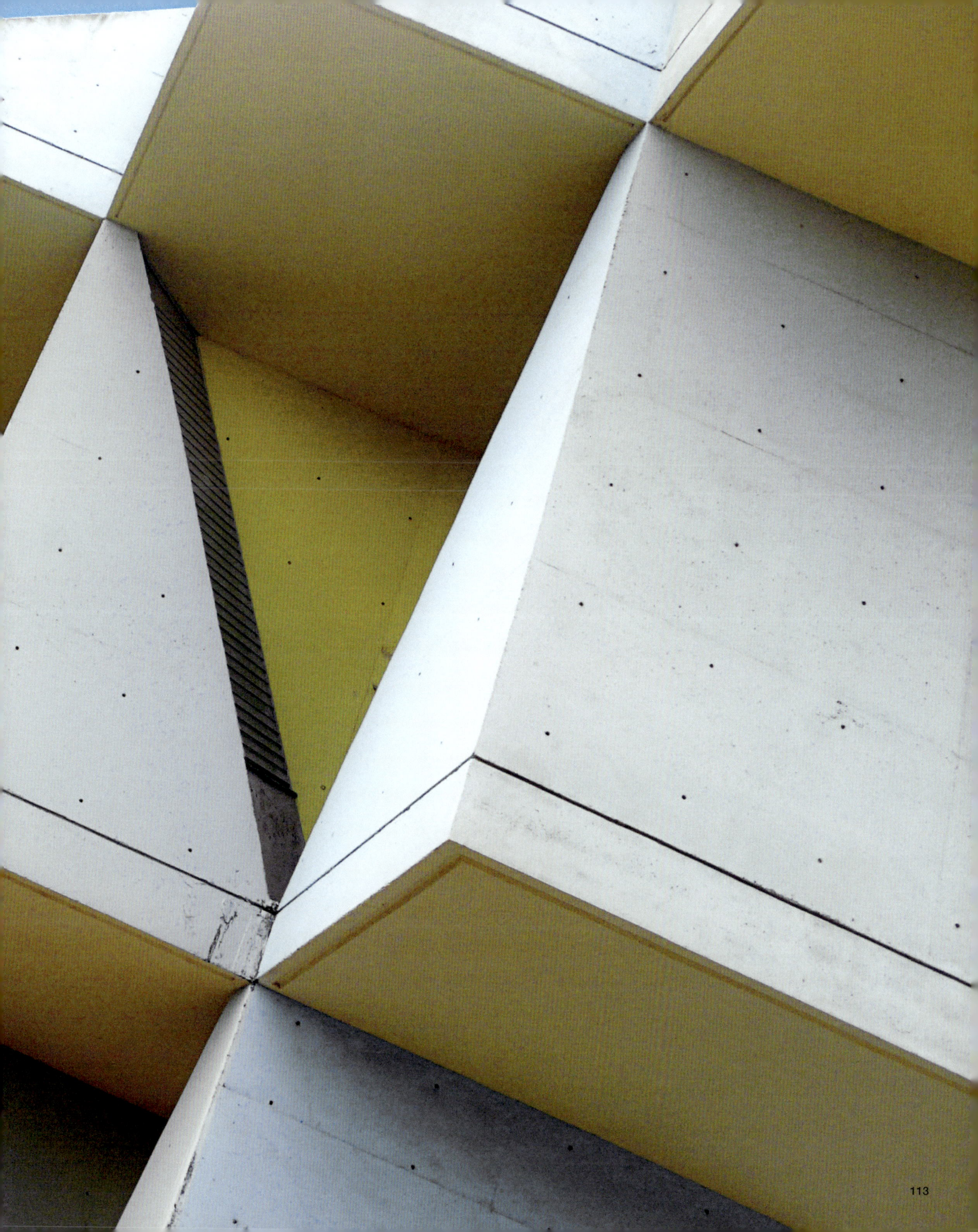

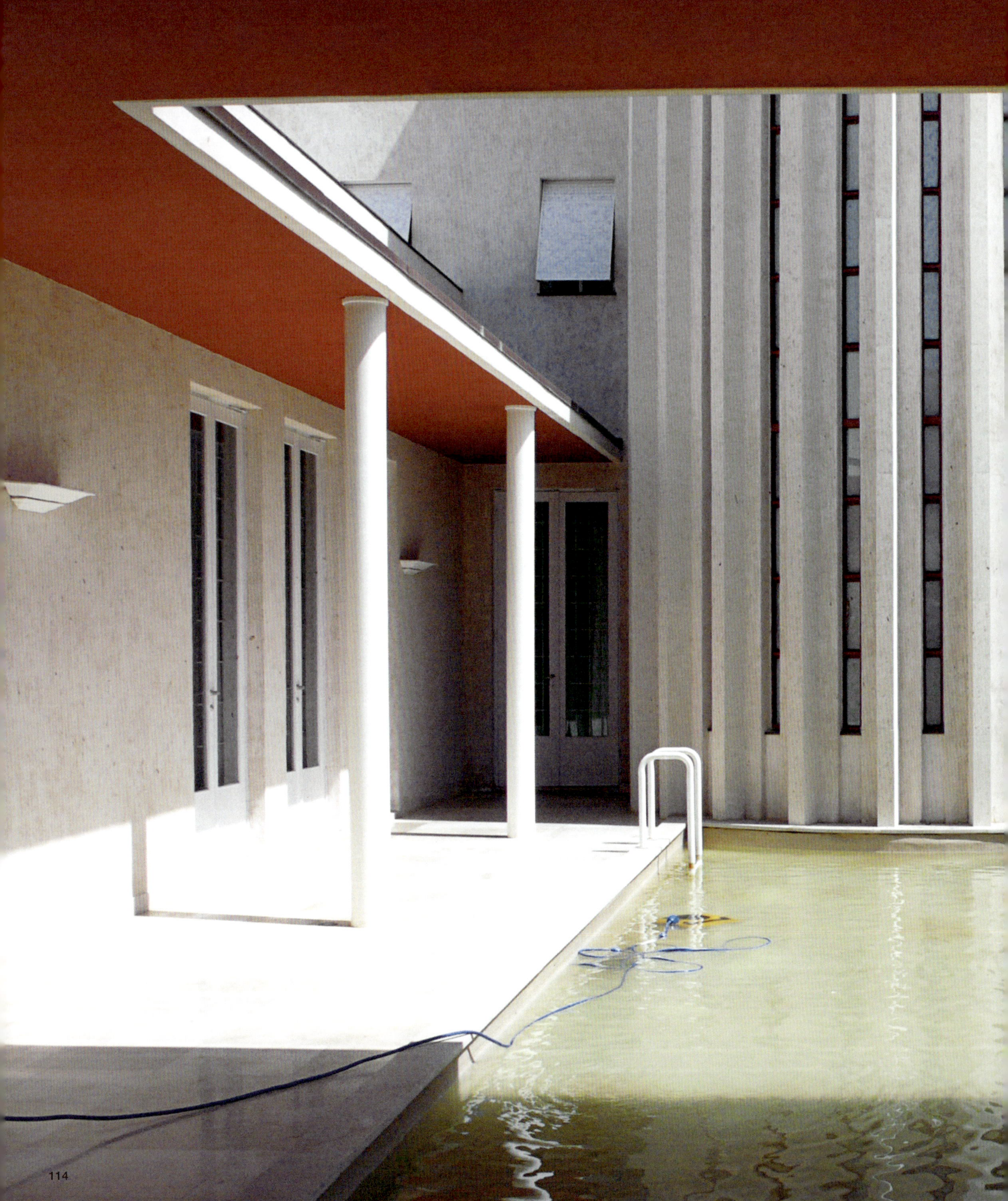

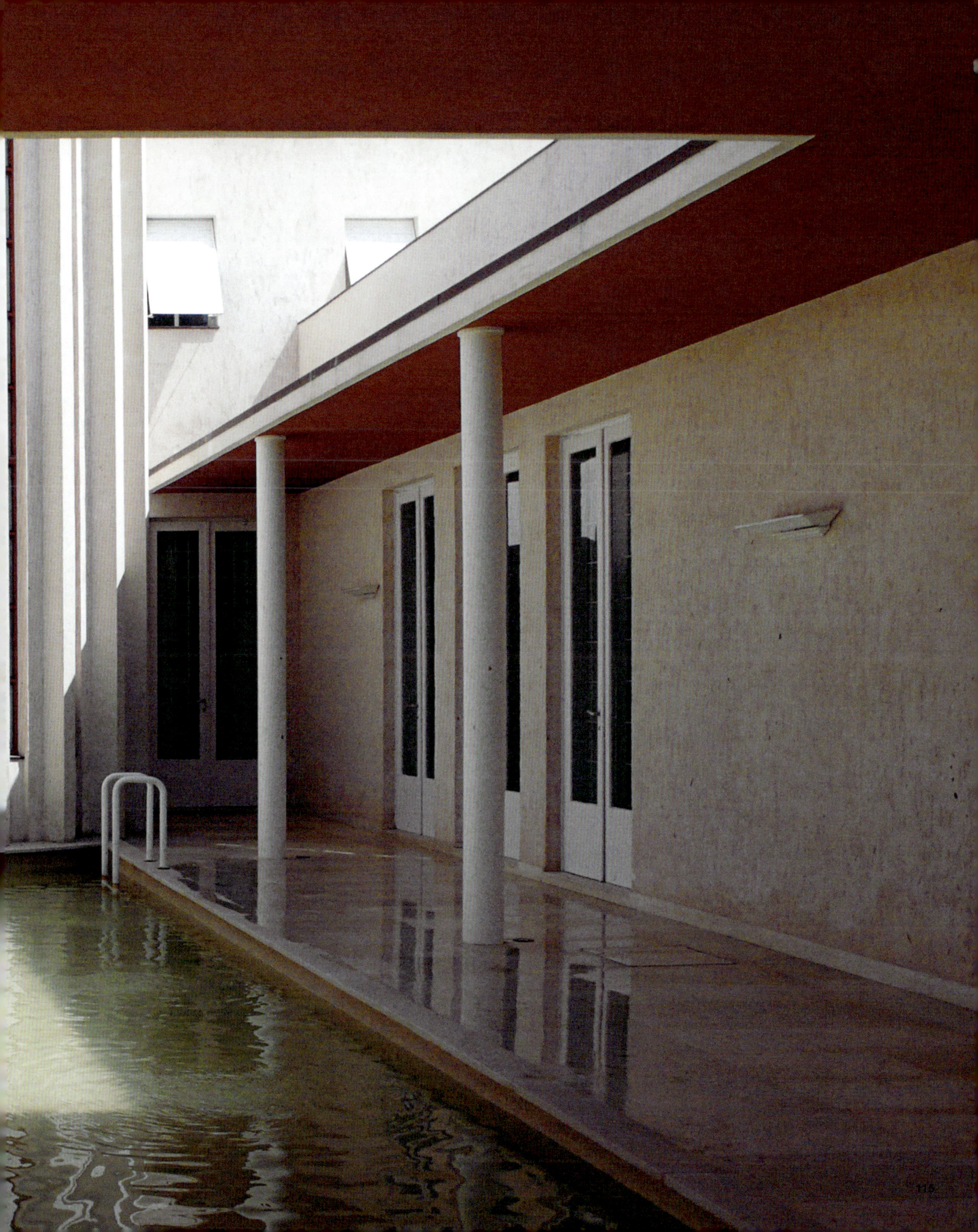

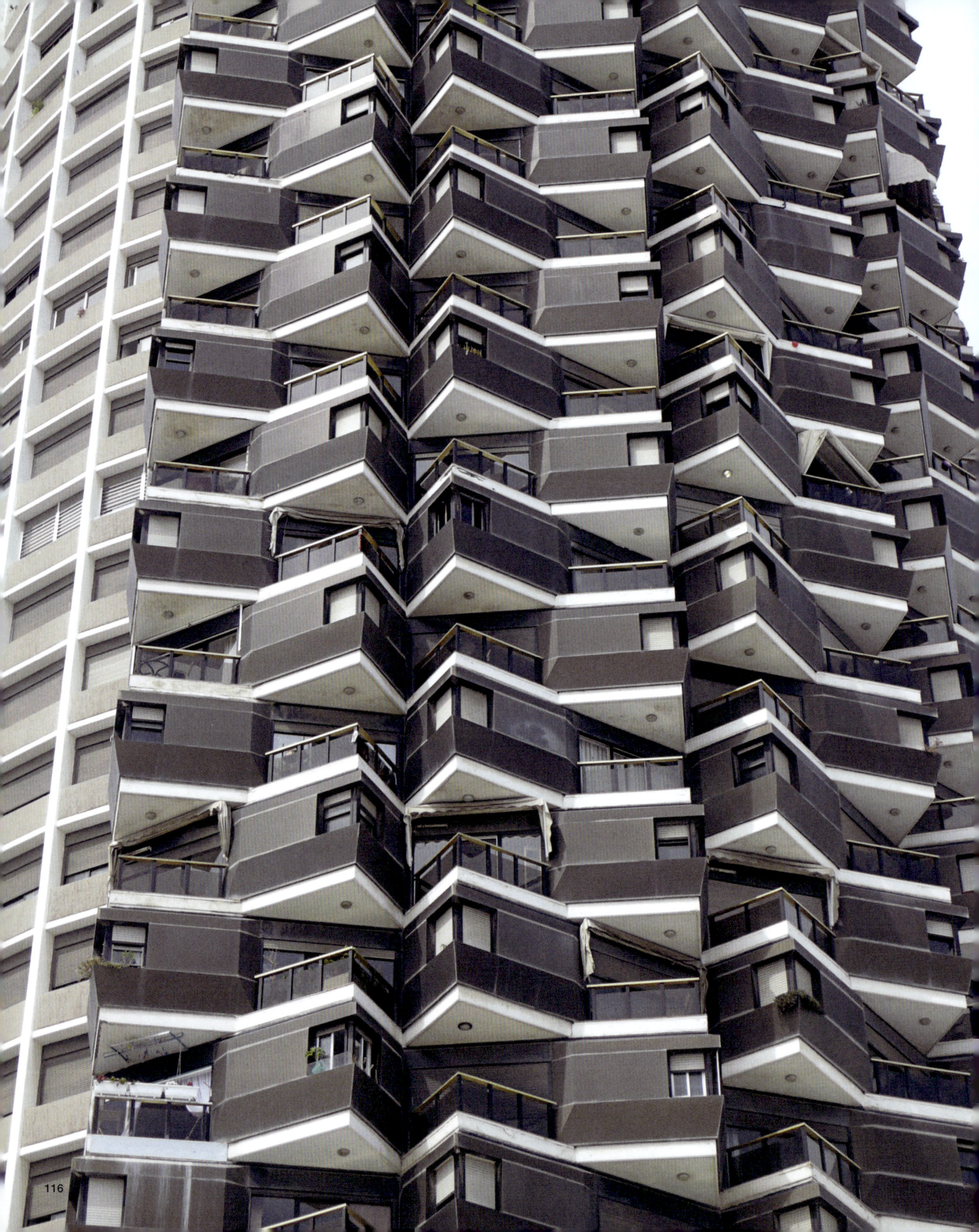

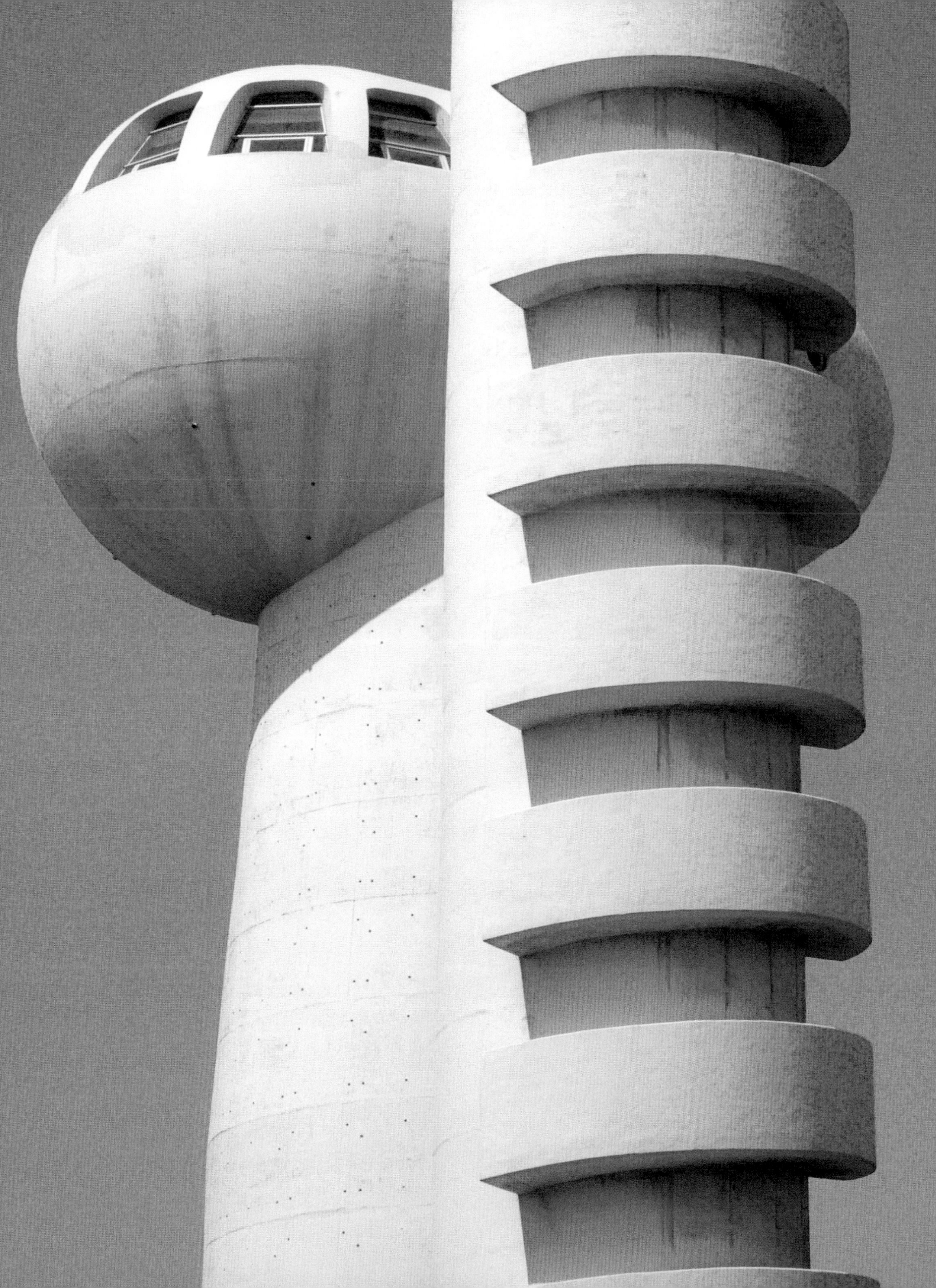

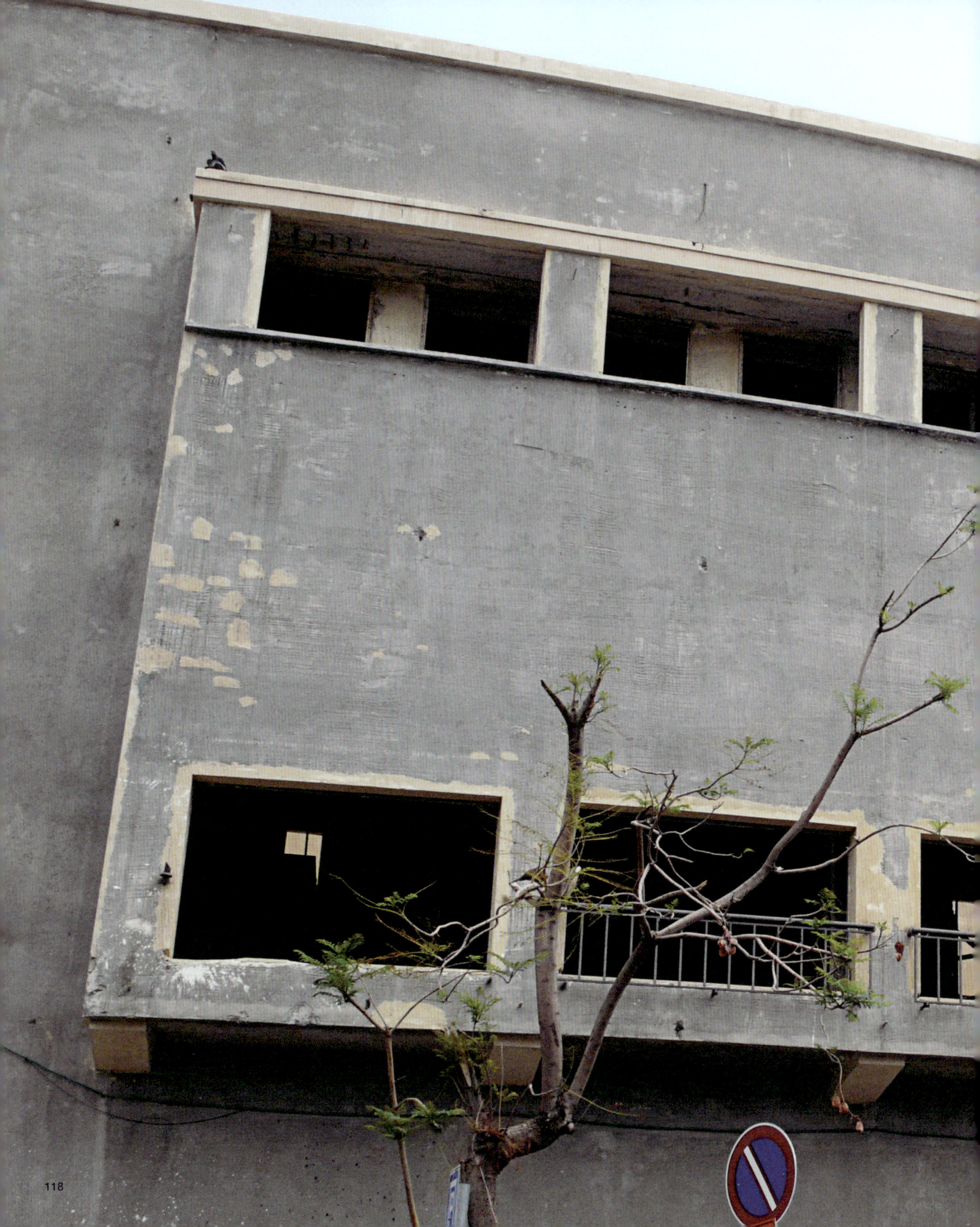

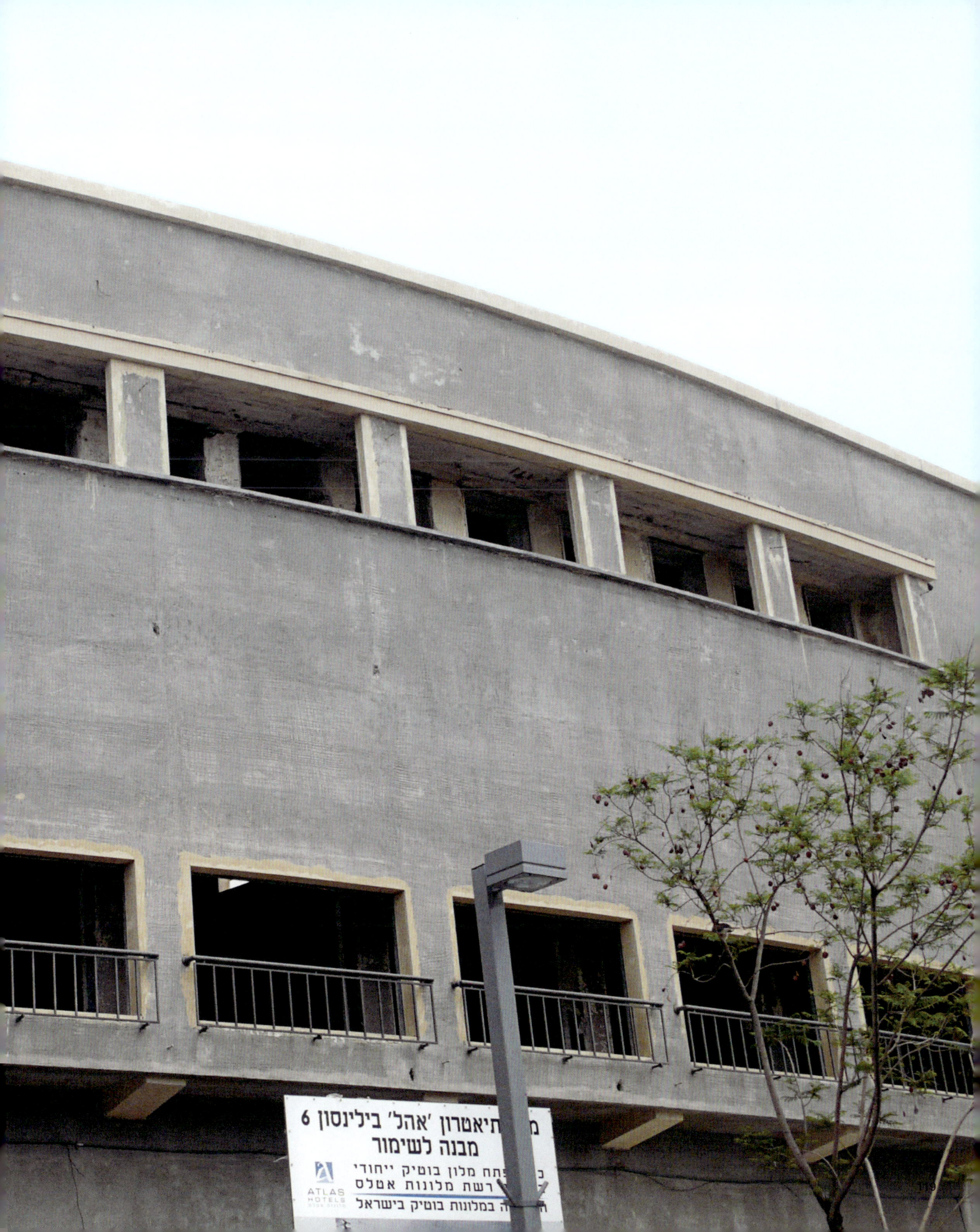
תיאטרון 'אהל' בילינסון 6
מבנה לשימור
פתח מלון בוטיק ייחודי
רשת מלונות אטלס
במלונות בוטיק בישראל
ATLAS
HOTELS

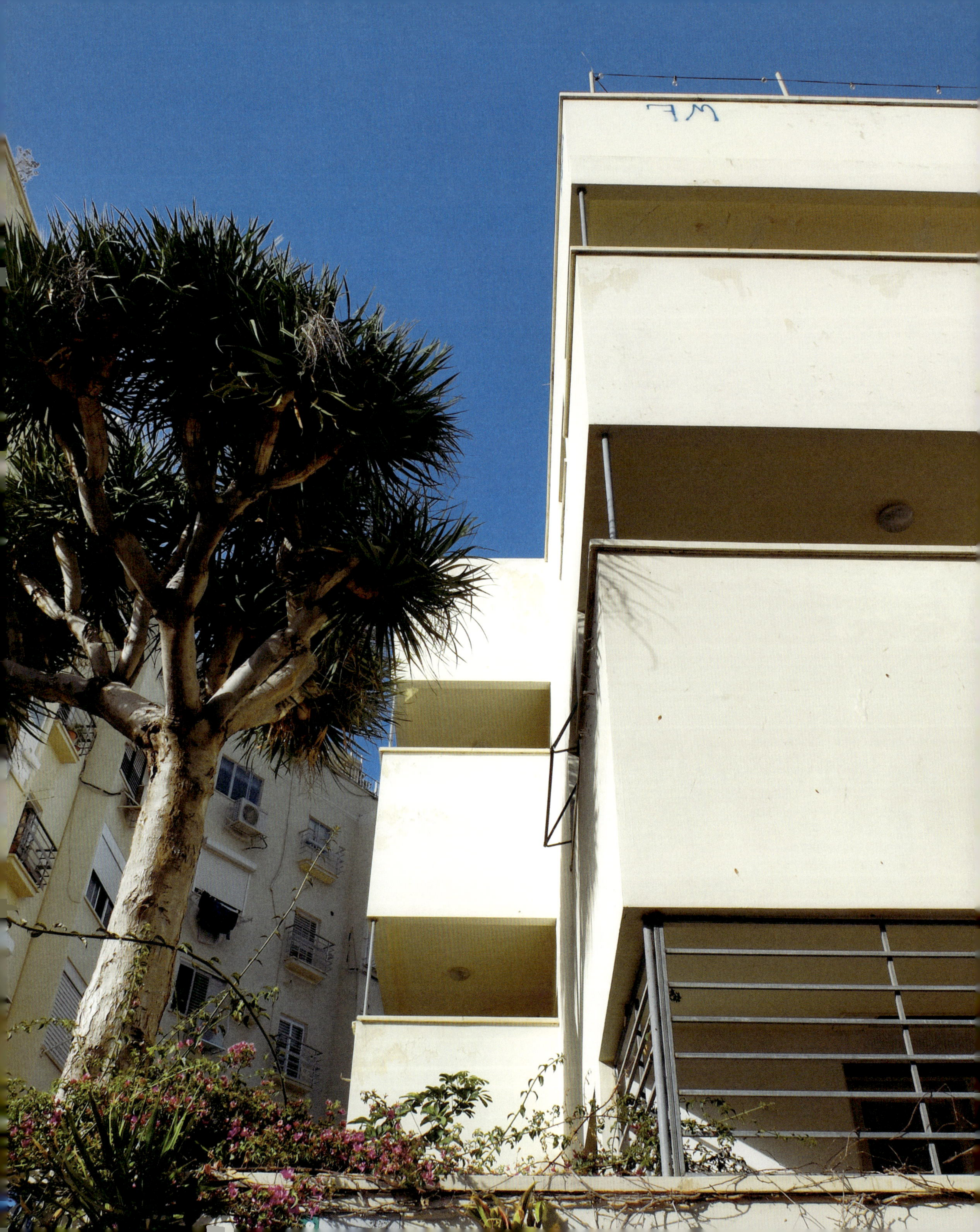

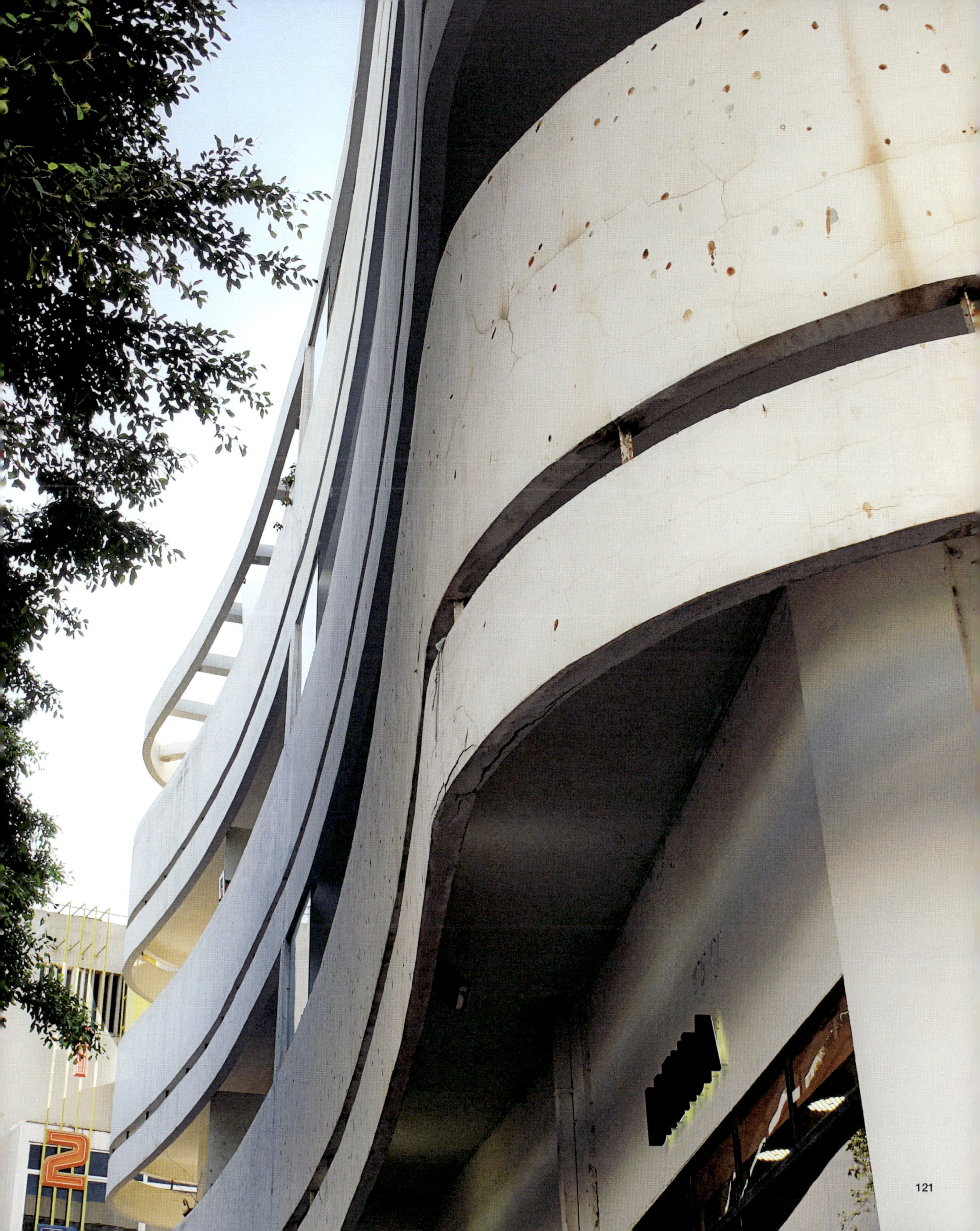

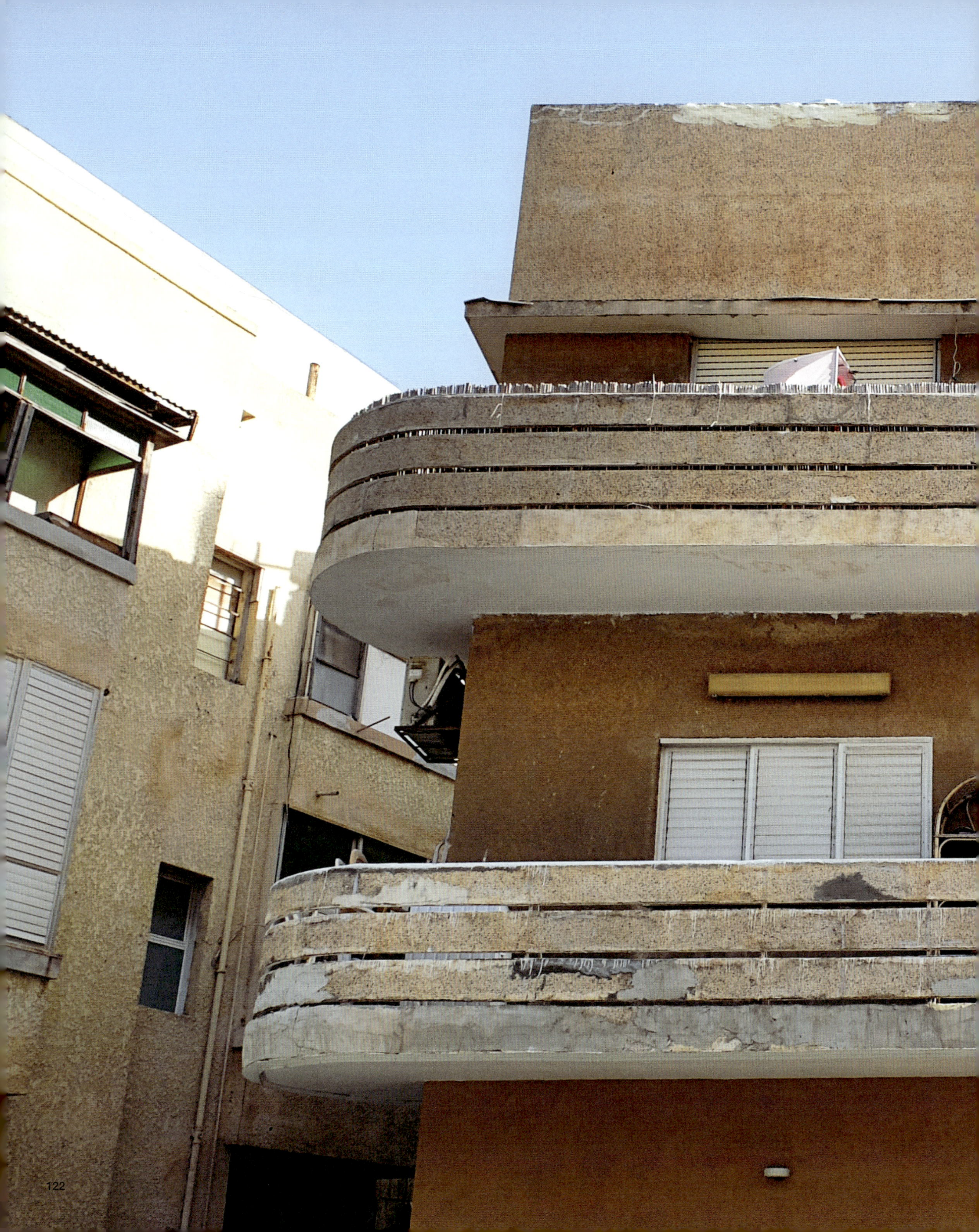

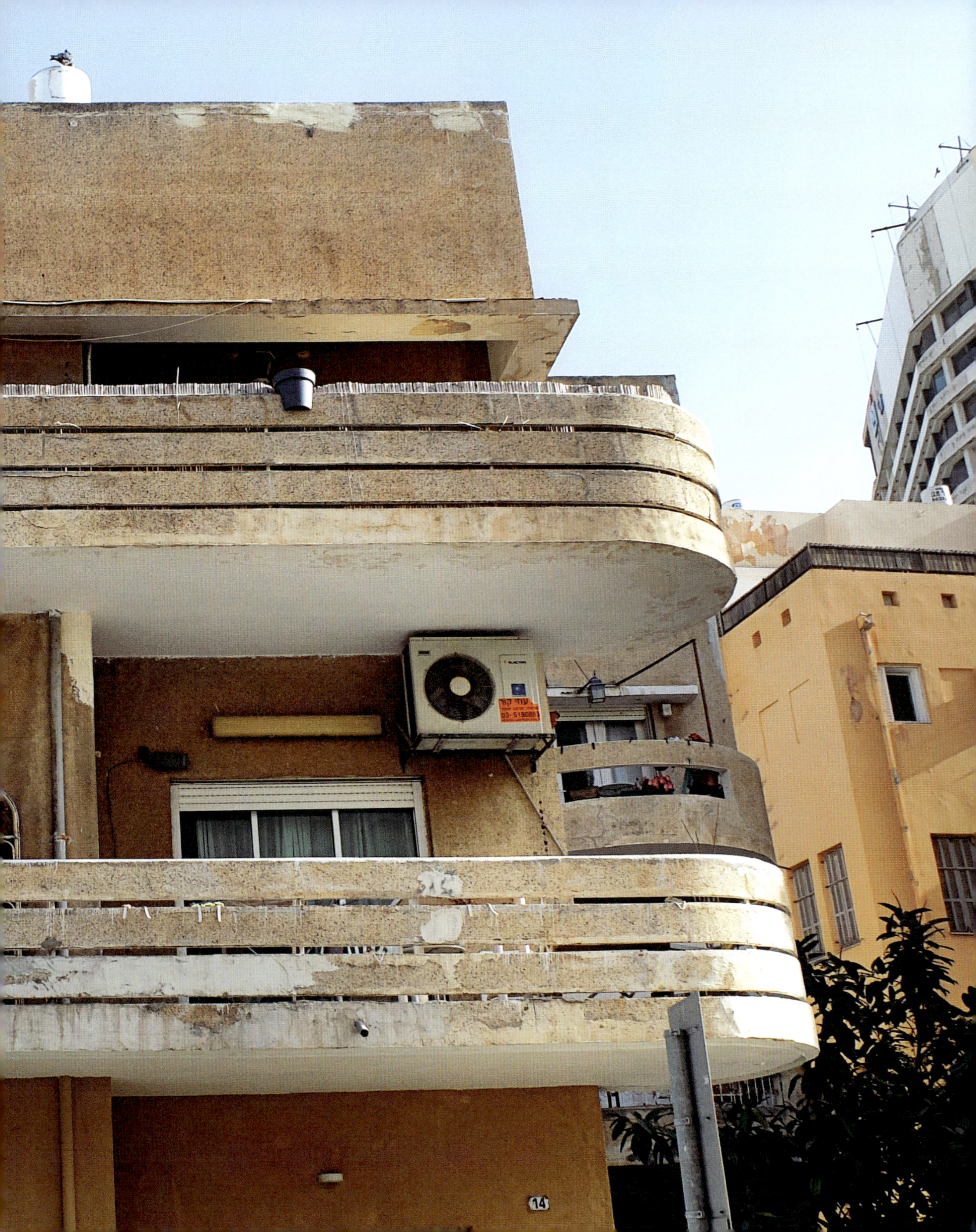
14

חללים מוארים באור טבעי עדין ולא פולשני. ספרים, עבודות אמנות, קריאה, התבוננות, הרהורים–הכול תחת אותו גג. זה סוג התרבות שאני אוהב. לא היתה לי דרך לצפות שלכך אגיע אחרי המסע הארוך. זה היה רושם עוצמתי מאד. הסגנון של הבניין לא מציף אותך, אלא מהווה מיזוג מדויק ופשוט של פנים וחוץ, שלווה ופתיחות.

וינצן:
לא תיארת לעצמך שתמצא בניין כזה בקיבוץ.

מטצל:
לא. למרות שהמוזיאון מתחבר איכשהו לנוף הארכאי שסובב את עין חרוד. אבל כמובן שאני זוכר גם את המחסום והשומרים בכניסה לקיבוץ, תזכורת מוזרה של מראות ילדות מברלין, קיר, גדר תיל, שומרים חמושים, וכו'. כברלינאי, חייתי מספיק זמן עם הדבר הזה: תראה תעודת זהות, בדיקה, הטרדה או העדר הטרדה, המחסום מורם. היה בזה משהו לא אמיתי להיזכר באופן כה בלתי צפוי בהתנהלות שנשכחה. בעיני המוזיאון של ביקלס מייצג את ערכי המודרניזם האותנטי. יכולת לראות בניינים כאלו בברלין ההרוסה והמחולקת של ילדותי. והיתה גם שגרת היומיום האפורה עם המחסומים והבדיקות. הפלשבק הכפול הזה כשהגעתי לעין חרוד העלה בי משהו דומה לחוויה של בעקבות הזמן האבוד.

וינצן:
כמו מרסל פרוסט ועוגיית המדלן שהחזירה אליו לפתע את זיכרונות ילדותו.

מטצל:
באופן שונה לגמרי כמובן. אבל הרשמים הראשונים האלו התחברו באופן משמעותי לזיכרונות ילדות ונעורים. הרגשתי שהמוזיאון והאווירה המסוימת שלו, המקום, סוג התרבות הזה–הבנתי הכול מיד, כאילו הכרתי אותו מזה זמן רב, למרות שזה עתה הגעתי לשם. כילד גידלה אותי לא רק אמי–שלמרבה הצער היתה חולה מאד–אלא גם חברתה הטובה ביותר, שכיהודיה עזבה לארה"ב, אבל חזרה לעזור לה.

וינצן:
מי שעזרה לגדל אותך הייתה אישה יהודייה שניצלה ממוות בברלין שני עשורים קודם לכן.

מטצל:
כן, אפשר לומר זאת כך. הדרך העדינה שבה ניסחה את הדברים, ההומור השקט שלה, המחשבות שלה על ישראל, שמעולם לא ביקרה בה, אני זוכר את כל זה. ואת הסיגריות הרבות שעישנה. רק מאוחר יותר הבנתי שאני פשוט מוכרח להגיע מתישהו לישראל ולהכיר את הארץ הזו. עבורי, עין חרוד הוא מקום מיוחד מאד.

משפיעה החברה בארץ המארחת על האמנות שלך? האם מדובר בסוג של תיבת תהודה, כמו זו של גיטרה, שעבודת האמנות משמשת לה כמיתר? בואו נראה כיצד הוא מהדהד!

מטצל:
כשאתה מגיע לארץ מסוימת כזר, אתה רואה את הדברים באופן שונה. אתה רוצה לצפות ולהבין ככל האפשר. לפני זמן רב הייתי מעורב בוויכוח עם הנס האקה (Haacke), שבמשך 40 שנה שימש כמצפון המוסרי-אמנותי של גרמניה ממקום מושבו בניו יורק. אמרתי לו: הנס, אתה לא יכול לשבת בניו יורק ולבחור לעבודות שלך נושאים מתוך העיתון הגרמני "דר שפיגל", ואז להציג את התוצאות בגרמניה. דפוסי ההתנהגות, המתחים, ההומור בארץ מסוימת הם משהו שצריך לחוות ברחוב, בפאב, בחיי היומיום. כיצד אנשים מתנהגים זה עם זה? מי שולט? כיצד נראות מודעות הפרסומת? מבלי שאתה מעורה בכל זה, כל מה שנוגע לאמנות הופך במהירות לסטרילי.
כשאני מתארח בארץ זרה אני אוהב לבוא במגע עם תולדות האמנות של אותו המקום. במוזיאון סדברק חנים באיסטנבול, לדוגמא, התבוננתי באריחים, בסירים, באגרטלים, בדוגמאות ובמבנים עותומאניים. לאחרונה, בנאפולי, עמדתי במשך שעה שלמה לפני ציור של קאראווג'ו (Caravaggio) והתבוננתי באופן שבו החדיר בציור שלו מתחים כמעט בלתי נראים, כיצד יצר עומק חלל כה מרשים בקלילות לכאורה, כשהוא מוסיף קצת אור כאן וקצת חושך שם. אי אפשר להבין דברים כאלו במהירות. בירושלים נדהמתי מהיכל הספר של פרדריק קיסלר וארמנד ברטוס. איך ניתן ליצור חיבור שכזה בין פיסול וארכיטקטורה?

וינצן:
בנסיעת ההכנה שלך לתערוכה בעין חרוד, ביקרת גם בעיר העתיקה בירושלים ובתל אביב.

מטצל: בתל אביב גיליתי שמודל הבאוהאוס של תכנון עירוני יושם בצורה גורפת יותר מאשר בכל מקום אחר. שדרות רוטשילד עם העצים במרכזן, החזיתות המודרניות הקלאסיות והמוזנחות במידה, עם ההוד המלנכולי שלהן, לצד בניינים משומרים היטב, החיים השוקקים, הקיוסקים-הכול יחד יוצר מטרופולין ים תיכוני, ותל אביב היא באמת עיר גדולה ותוססת. כשאתה יוצא לארוחה אתה נהיה מודע לתערובת-אוכל כשר, מזרח תיכוני, רוסי, אפילו גרמני. התרשמתי מאד מכך ששדרות רוטשילד הפכו לנקודת ההתחלה של כמה מעבודותיי החדשות.

וינצן:
האדריכלית ומתכננת הערים גניה אוורבוך (Averbuch) היתה אחת מאותן נשים חזקות שעיצבו את פני האזור המתהווה הזה בשנות ה-30 וה-40. אתה הקדשת את אחת מעבודותיך לאישה מפורסמת אחרת שהתעמתה עם האשמת הגרמנים ברצח עם כפי שבאה לידי ביטוי בבית המשפט המחוזי בירושלים בשנת 1961: חנה ארנדט.

מטצל:
גיליתי את חנה ארנדט דרך היידגר. לא התעניינתי ביחסיהם המיוחדים, אלא בטקסטים שלה. הכרך הצנום "אנו הפליטים" (We Refugees) עדיין רלוונטי ביותר. יש גם רעיון שלה עם גינתר גאוס (Gaus) ששודר בטלוויזיה הגרמנית בשנת 1964. אולי ראית אותו-שניהם כמעט מחקו אחד את השנייה עם עשן הסיגריות שלהם.

נקודת המוצא לעבודה, שהיא בת שלושה חלקים, היתה דיוקן צילומי של ארנדט. הוספתי לו צילומים שצילמתי בניו יורק. אישה יושבת וקוראת בבית קפה-עדיין ניתן לראות את כלי הפלסטיק המשומשים. לא ברור אם היא קוראת ספר או מגזין או מתעסקת עם האייפון שלה. משמאל מופיע מוטיב המראה מהשירותים במוזיאון גוגנהיים. היא שחורה והריבוע הופך לטרפז כתוצאה מהזווית הצדדית.

סוזן זונטג (Sontag) מרתקת באותה מידה כמו חנה ארנדט. המסות שלה על צילום הן קלאסיקות שנמשכים אליהן שוב ושוב. בעבר היו מכונות אוטומטיות, בדרך כלל בקרבת תחנות רכבת, שבהן יכולת להצטלם לתמונות פספורט ואנשים השתעשעו בהעוויות מצחיקות מאחורי הוילון. אז הייתה המכונה יורקת החוצה רצועת נייר צרה שעליה היו צילומי הפסורט, לעיתים בתוספת הפרצופים המצחיקים.

וינצן:
במהלך אותו ביקור גם הפכת למעורב בוויכוחים פוליטיים בקשר לאמנות בישראל.

מטצל: הוזמנתי להרצאות והדיונים שאחריהן היו תמיד סוערים. אהבתי את זה. ואז הסתכלתי על העיר העתיקה בירושלים, על הרובע הארמני, היהודי, המוסלמי, והנוצרי. הר הבית לא היה נגיש. המתח שם מעורר תחושה של דיכוי וקשה מאד להבין למה זה עבד פעם בעבר וכבר לא עובד היום.

וינצן:
נולדת בברלין, כך שאתה מכיר היטב את החוויה של חיים יומיומיים לצד קווים שתוחמים את המרחב.

מטצל:
עיר שחולקה פעם אחת ואז חולקה שוב. חומת ברלין חתכה את העיר. הייתי ילד כשהיא נבנתה-בן כמה הייתי, תשע? ומגרש המשחקים-באותם ימים הוא נקרא גן החלוצים-היה במזרח, היכן שרבים מחבריי גרו. יכולתי לראות את החומה שנבנתה בן לילה מחלון המטבח שלנו, אבל לא יכולתי להבין את זה בכלל. החבר שלי גר מעברו השני של הרחוב. הוא היה במזרח. מעולם לא ראיתי אותו שוב.

וינצן:
זו היתה בוודאי חוויה מטלטלת...

מטצל:
...זה משהו שאי אפשר לשכוח בחיים. ואז, אחרי עשורים שלמים, כשהחומה נעלמה, הכול נפתח שוב-זה היה באמת משהו. באותו זמן הייתי בקנדה והצגתי תערוכה בתחנת הכוח בטורונטו. לפני הפתיחה חזרתי למלון להחליף בגדים והטלוויזיה הייתה דלוקה. חשבתי: ואוו, לא הייתי מאמין שהוליווד יכולה לעשות את זה בצורה כל כך משכנעת. הייתי בדרכים במשך זמן ממושך ולא ממש עקבתי אחרי הסיפור של איחוד גרמניה. כשאתה צופה בטלוויזיה בארה"ב, פרסומות, סרטים וחדשות מתמזגים זה בזה. אבל באותו הערב, במהלך הפתיחה, כולם שאלו: שמעת? והאמת שראיתי, אבל לא האמנתי!

וינצן:
מה היה הרושם הראשון שלך כשהגעת לעין חרוד?

מטצל:
הגעתי במכונית משדה התעופה ולפתע מצאתי את עצמי מול המוזיאון, אותו בניין נפלא של שמואל ביקלס. התרשמתי כל כך מהסמכות השלווה ומהאלגנטיות של הבניין. הוא היה נגיש, פרקטי-מודרניזם טהור שלא יופה במשך הזמן באמצעות שיפוצים מוזרים. ספריה, קפה, מוזיאון,

וינצן:
מה לדעתך האלמנט המרכזי ביצירת עבודות העיתון? האם זהו תהליך קימוט הנייר, העיוות שלו, או אפקט הכוח, הרגע שבו הוא נהרס? או שאולי זה האופן שבו העבודה מוצבת, או הקומפוזיציה? לעיתים קרובות העבודות המנותצות מאופיינות במקצב ובאיכות אלגנטית ייחודית להן.

מטצל:
חשוב לציין שאני לא משתמש רק בעיתונים, אלא גם בצילומים וקולאז'ים. צריך לחשוב על כך כעל יומן ויזואלי. בנוגע לשאלה שלך, הרעיון הוא לא לעבוד סביב הפיסות היפות ביותר, אלא לנתץ אותן ראשונות–זו הדרך היחידה להתקדם. הרגע שבו זה נראה מוגמר הוא הרגע שבו אני באמת מתחיל. אני מתעניין באפשרויות שגלומות בפיסול. פיסול מבחינתי הוא המדיום שמאפשר לי ליצור את הרושם החזק ביותר באמצעות הנוכחות שלו בחלל, בניגוד לציור. כשמשהו מכופף או נחתך, הוא מתייחס לאגרסיה ולכוח, אפילו אם מדובר רק בטיפול הטכני בחומר. החומריות הופכת להיות ברורה יותר, כמו למשל כשאני מכופף פיסת אלומיניום שהיא כבר מקופלת. אם היא מקופלת כמו פיסת נייר, צריך לעשות זאת פעמיים. בפעם השלישית היא כבר נהיית מוצקה וחזקה יותר. אם אחר כך אתה הופך אותה, היא נהיית ממש כבדה וגם קשה. אפשר לעשות את זה רק ידנית, לא עם מכונה. וכמובן שבאופן אוטומטי אתה מפתח מיומנות מוטורית שונה. המוטיב מתעוות או נעלם, או שלפתע מראה של אחורי לוח אלומיניום מודפס נחשף ומשחק תפקיד. העבודה הטכנית עם החפץ יוצרת לפתע קומפוזיציה חדשה. לפעמים, אבל לפעמים גם לא.

וינצן:
אם אתה מכופף את החומר פעם אחת יותר מדי, האם אתה זורק אותו?

מטצל:
לאחת העבודות שלי קוראים רק "פח הזבל נזרק" (Only the Waste Bin is thrown away). כשמשהו לא עובד, הוא רודף אותך. אני חייב להמשיך לנסות, לסובב אותו בכיוונים שונים, לכופף או לעקם אותו, או פשוט לנתץ אותו. בניו יורק צילמתי פח אשפה בצד הכביש שהציצו ממנו כמה פיסות של נייר עיתון מקומט, ואז השתמשתי בצילום כנקודת המוצא לעבודה: עיתונים מקומטים כדימוי המורכב מלוחות אלומיניום מודפסים שנראים כמו ניירות עיתון מקומטים. מהו אמיתי ומהי אשליה? היו כאלו שחשבו שצילמתי עבודה שלי ואז יצרתי ממנה את העבודה הבאה. למעשה במבט ראשון פח האשפה הזה בניו יורק היה נראה כאילו מישהו העתיק בכישרון רב עבודה שלי תוך שימוש בנייר עיתון אמיתי. אולי זו הסיבה ששמתי לב אליו מלכתחילה. במקרים כאלה, השאלה שמתעוררת כבר בשלב מוקדם היא, האם מדובר בפריט "אמיתי" או "מזויף", כמו העובדות או הידיעות הכוזבות בעולם התקשורת.

וינצן:
אתה נחשב לאמן פוליטי. האם אתה חושב שההגדרה הזו מתארת אותך במדויק?

מטצל:
לא. אני עייף כבר מלשמוע על הניצול של אמנות למטרות מוסריות, על הגישה הפטרונית הזו, שבה נעשה שימוש באמנות לצרכים פוליטיים. כשאני נשאל לגבי הממד הפוליטי של העבודות שלי, כל מה שאני יכול לעשות הוא לשאול בתשובה: מה זה "אמנות פוליטית" לעזאזל? אני מעדיף את הריבוע השחור על פני הדגל האדום.

וינצן:
אז אין בכלל התייחסויות לנושאים חברתיים בעבודותיו של אולף מטצל?

מטצל:
ההיפך הוא הנכון, יש הרבה התייחסויות כאלו, אבל לא מדובר בהנחיות של תקינות פוליטית הניתנות לצופה. עבודת אמנות חייבת תמיד להרחיק מעבר לחוויה האישית של היחיד: מצד אחד יש את חוויית הצופה העומד בפני עבודה רב-משמעית ורב-ממדית המאתגרת אותו לחשוב בעצמו, ומצד שני ישנן החוויות שלי בחברה שבה אני חי. חלק מהמבקרים שכתבו על עבודותיי מהתקופה האחרונה האמינו שהתבליטים הגדולים של נייר עיתון מקומט הופיעו בדיוק באותה נקודה בזמן שחדשות הכלכלה נדדו לאינטרנט. האירוניה היא שלא ניתן היה ליצור את העבודות האלו ללא שימוש בטכנולוגיה דיגיטלית.

וינצן:
המהירות הגוברת של האינטרנט יוצרת לחץ מתמיד שמאתגר את יכולת האדם להבחין בדברים. הלחץ הזה גובר בגלל הדימויים המלווים את החדשות או המידע ושמוחלפים ללא הרף בדימויים חדשים, או שמופיעים מלכתחילה כסרטונים. לפני זמן מה עוד קראנו לזה "מבול של דימויים", אבל הביטוי הזה נשמע לי כיום כמעט בלתי מזיק לנוכח עומס היתר המנטאלי התמידי הזה.

מטצל:
אני חווה את השיטפון היומי של חדשות ודימויים כאילו שאני נוסע ברכבת. המהירות שלה הולכת וגוברת עד שברגע נתון אני מרגיש צורך להפעיל את בלם החרום. ואז זה מתחיל שוב. אבל מה שבאמת מעניין אותי הוא הרגע שבו הכול נעצר, כמו בדימוי סטיל. ודימוי סטיל שאמן יצר בשנת 1984 שונה מדימוי סטיל שנוצר ב-1994, 2004, או 2018.

וינצן:
אז עבודה שלך, כלומר עבודת אמנות ייחודית, היא "סטיל"?

מטצל:
כן, רגע קפוא בזמן. אני מנסה לתפוס את הרגע הזה. והוא מכיל את כל הרקע, את האווירה של תקופה מסוימת, בעיות חברתיות מסוימות, כמו בעבודות "מעדן טורקי" (Turkish Delight) או "שאלות נוספות?" (Noch Fragen?) החברתי והפוליטי נרמזים, אבל מבחינתי הביצוע של הפסל או המיצב הוא תמיד בקדמת הבמה. אני שמח אם זה עדיין עובד ומעניין אנשים כעבור 30 שנה. זה התבהר לי שוב לאחרונה כשהצגתי את "112:104", מגרש הכדורסל המנותץ. זה לא ממש מגרש כדורסל. זהו פסל טהור, תמצית המלאכותיות של האמנות. יצרתי רצפה חדשה לאולם ספורט ואז חתכתי אותה בהתאם לתכנית מדויקת, תוך שינוי ועיוות המידות. מדובר בקרשים כבדים שארבעה אנשים יכולים בקושי להרים יחד. מיותר לומר שהמבנה אינו יכול לקרוס, גם אם נראה שהוא עומד לקרוס. מצד אחד, חשבתי על הציור "תקווה מנותצת" (Failed Hope) של קספר דוד פרידריך במוזיאון האמנות של המבורג, ומצד שני על המצב במהלך המשחק, האגרסיה כששתי קבוצות, ולא שני שדות קרח, מתנגשים. האמביוולנטיות המוזרה הזו כאשר שתי קבוצות מדורבנות על ידי האוהדים שלהן ותוקפות זו את זו באופן פיזי, והאלימות שלעיתים קרובות עדיין נמצאת באוויר גם אחרי סיום המשחק.

וינצן:
הצגת רבות ברחבי העולם ולעיתים קרובות אתה מפתח את העבודות בארצות שבהן תוצבנה–בצרפת, באוסטריה, או בטורקיה. בשנת 1995 באיסטנבול, עבדת יחד עם מועדון הכדורגל בשיקטש על מיצב. עד כמה

די, תשאיר את זה כך!
שיחה בין אולף מטצל ומתיאס וינצן

ראיון:
מתיאס וינצן: האם אתה נהנה להיות פרובוקטיבי?

אולף מטצל:
לא, למה? האם אני אמור ליהנות מכך? מי שמרגיש שמדובר בפרובוקציה לא הבין או שאינו רוצה להבין. בנוסף, לא ניתן לתכנן משהו כזה. בזמן שאני עובד, אני לא עסוק כל הזמן בשאלה את מי אני עומד לעצבן. אני מנסה לחדד נושאים ומתוך כך לפתח עבודות שעבורי הן חדשות ושונות. אם אתה עובד כך בהתמדה, התוצאה נתפסת תכופות כרדיקלית או פרובוקטיבית.

וינצן:
יחד עם זאת, פסל הברונזה שלך "מעדן טורקי" (Turkish Delight), לדוגמא, מציג אישה ערומה החובשת על ראשה כיסוי ראש. כשהוצב בקרלספלאץ בווינה בשנת 2007, היו אנשים שכעסו כל כך עד שלילה אחד הם הפילו את הפסל. לאירוע היו אפילו השלכות שליליות על יחסי טורקיה-אוסטריה. אני מניח שזו לא הייתה הפתעה עבורך, נכון?

מטצל:
עדיין הופתעתי. אנחנו חשבנו מראש על ההשלכות וארגנו דיון בנושא בווינה. בפסל הזה אני התייחסתי למחלוקת ההיסטורית ולייצוג של נשים בציורים כמו של דלקרואה (Delacroix) או כמו ציורו הידוע של אנגר (Ingres) מרחץ טורקי (Turkish Bath). במאה ה-19, האופנות האקזוטיות האלו גבלו לפעמים בוולגריות. חיברתי את הממד ההיסטורי הזה למה שניתן לראות בהווה בחיי היומיום. יש נשים שחובשות כיסוי ראש שנאלצות לפסוע מספר צעדים מאחורי הבעלים שלהן, ואינן יכולות להביע את עצמן במרחב הציבורי. בעבר, כאשר נשים בשכונת קרויצברג בברלין חבשו כיסויי ראש, זה היה בגלל שהשיער שלהן היה רטוב אחרי שחייה בבריכה. מעבר לכך, אני נמשך למוטיב הפיסולי הקלאסי של אישה ערומה עומדת. ניסיתי לדחוס את כל זה אל תוך דימוי אחד. נשים חושבות שהעבודה מצוינת, רק המצ'ואים המוכרים לנו מתלוננים.

וינצן:
עבדת על הפסל בסטודיו שלך, עם מודל, בתהליך קלאסי למדי, אבל התוצאה היא אישה צעירה עם מראה טבעי ולא נשגב.

מטצל:
כשאתה עובד עם מודל חי אתה שם לב שכעבור זמן מה, הדוגמנית משנה את צורת עמידתה ומבטה נהיה מרוחק מאד. בכדי שהאפקט לא יהיה מונומנטלי, הדמות צריכה להיות קטנה ממימדיה האמיתיים ויש להימנע מאידיאליזציה. כתוצאה מכך, הרושם אינו של שלמות-הלניסטית, קלסית, קלסיציסטית, או אחרת-אלא של משהו יומיומי. בנוסף ערכתי מחקר שלם בנוגע לכיסויי ראש: ישנם סוגים רבים של כיסויי ראש שניתן לחבוש בדרכים שונות מאד.

וינצן:
מהי דרך העבודה הקלה ביותר עבורך? כיפוף מתכות או חומרים אחרים, יצירת דיוקנאות בחמר, או רישום? יצרת קבוצות גדולות של עבודות בכל הטכניקות האלו.

מטצל:
שום דבר לא קורה אצלי בקלות. בהתחלה אתה מזיז את העבודה בעיני רוחך ימינה ושמאלה, קדימה ואחורה, ואז אתה מתעצבן כשזה לא עובד. למרות שאני עוסק בכך במשך מספר עשורים, כל פעם מדובר בהתחלה חדשה. כמובן שיש לי אסיסטנטים, אבל חשוב לי להיות מעורב בכל באופן פעיל. לא משנה באיזה מדיום מדובר-עץ, פלדה, בטון, אלומיניום, או טכניקות דיגיטליות-אני בוחר את החומר שמתאים ביותר לנושא. זה למעשה הכול. אני תמיד מקווה שבסוף זה ייראה לצופה כאילו זה קרה בקלות.

וינצן:
כשאתה אומר שמשהו לא עובד, על אילו קריטריונים אתה מסתמך?

מטצל:
כשאתה מעורב בפרויקט חדש, מדובר תמיד במסע אל הלא-נודע. אתה נקרע בין שאיפות לבין האפשרות להוציא אותן לפועל. בדרך כלל הדברים יוצאים אחרת ממה שתכננת. מה שמרגש ביצירת העבודה בפועל הוא שאינך יודע לאן השביל מוביל והיכן הוא ייגמר.

וינצן:
ובמהלך תהליך העבודה הזה, מהו הקריטריון שלפיו אתה שופט אם זה "מעניין" או, חשוב מכך, "לא מוצלח"? כלומר, איך אתה מחליט אם קל מדי לזהות את הדברים, או אם הכוונה האמנותית ברורה מדי?

מטצל:
כאן נכנס הרישום לתמונה. אני מתחיל ברישום. אני מנסה לחוג סביב הנושא באופן אסוציאטיבי, לאחוז באיזשהו רעיון, בפתרון צורני. אני עושה זאת גם כדי לא לאבד את הקשר עם הפרויקט ולהגיע למבוי סתום.

וינצן:
אבל מה בדיוק הקריטריון שלך, או מה שיכול לגרום לך להתחיל מחדש?

מטצל:
כשזה נראה פשוט איום ונורא. זה קשור לחוויות שהיו לך בעבר ושחוזרות בהווה. באותו הרגע, אני מנסה להבחין מייד במה שעובד ובמה שלא עובד. לפעמים, כשאתה עובד עם צורות או שילובים מסוימים, אתה מרגיש משהו שאתה בעצמך עדיין לא יכול לשים עליו את האצבע. ואז אתה אומר לעצמך, טוב, בוא נניח את זה באיזו פינה מרוחקת ונכסה את זה. אחרי שישה חודשים אתה מוציא את זה שוב ופתאום מבין איך אפשר להמשיך עם זה, ואולי אתה מצרף את העבודה הגמורה למחצה לעבודה אחרת שגם איתה לא התקדמת. בהרבה מקרים, אחד ועוד אחד שווה שלוש. ואז אתה מגיע למקום שלא האמנת שאי פעם תגיע אליו.

וינצן:
העבודות שלך נראות לעיתים קרובות כאילו הניחו אותן שם במקרה, או כאילו מישהו שבר אותן או הפך אותן במקרה. במבט שני, נראה שהקומפוזיציה מתוכננת בדייקנות וניתן לשים לב לקנה המידה. "עבודות העיתון" מאופיינות לעיתים קרובות בקומפוזיציות שהתנועתיות שלהן מאזכרת ציורי בארוק איטלקיים. ואילו האלכסונים בעבודה 112:104 מאזכרים את ציורו של קספר דויד פרידריך "תקווה מנותצת" מנותצת (Failed Hope).

מטצל:
להגיע לעבודה שהיא מדויקת לגמרי, ושיוצרת רושם עז מבלי להיראות מחושבת ומכוונת מידי, זה משהו שאפשר להצליח בו רק כשאתה אומר ברגע הנכון, "די, תשאיר את זה כך!". במקרה שלי, צורת העבודה הזו דומה לביקור בארמון איטלקי שבו אתה הולך מחדר לחדר, הדלתות הכפולות נפתחות, ואז זוג הדלתות הבא, ולפתע הכול חשוך. אולי יש עוד דלת ואולי לא. וברגע מסוים אתה עובר דרך הדלת האחרונה, והעבודה באה על סיומה. האסיסטנטים שלי יודעים את זה. מתי הוא יעצור? איך ואיפה הוא יעצור? או שאולי הוא ימשיך? כמובן שתמיד אפשר להמשיך ולהפוך את הכול-גם זה קורה.

List of Works

Cover / pp. 008–009 / 010 / 051
Hannah Arendt
2017
Aluminum, stainless steel, digital print
165 × 128 × 40 cm

Frontispiece / 011 / 050
Susan Sontag
2017
Aluminum, stainless steel, digital print
250 × 145 × 35 cm

013 / 051 / 131
Die Lesende (Reading Woman)
2017
Aluminum, stainless steel, digital print
95 × 80 × 25 cm

014–015 / 099
Wir Flüchtlinge (We Refugees)
2018
Aluminum, stainless steel, digital print
135 × 100 × 87 cm

016 / 017, 134–135
Rothschild Blvd (2)
2016
Aluminum, stainless steel, digital print
133 × 140 × 39 cm

142 / 143
Shrine of the Book (Frederick Kiesler)
2017
Aluminum, stainless steel, digital print
165 × 145 × 35 cm

044–047 / 049 / 052 / 100–107 / 132–133 / 144
Noch Fragen? (Any More Questions?)
1998
Fabric, baseball bats
Variable sizes

018–019 / 048–049 / 144
Turkish Delight
2006
Bronze, diabase
171 × 44 × 30 cm

012 / 137
Mirror
2017
Aluminum, stainless steel, digital print
118 × 103 × 17 cm

Back Cover, 139, 140–141
We Refugees
2018
Aluminum, stainless steel, digital print
127 × 145 × 25 cm

020 / 136
Minima Moralia (Theodor Adorno)
2017
Aluminum, stainless steel, digital print
128 × 150 x 42 cm
(not in the exhibition)

148
Rothschild Blvd
2016
Marble, aluminum, stainless steel, digital print
133 x 140 x 39 cm
(not in the exhibition)

רשימת עבודות

כריכה / עמ' 009–008 / 010 / 051
חנה ארנדט
2017
אלומיניום, פלדת אלחלד, הדפסה דיגיטלית
165 × 128 × 40 ס"מ

איור שער / 011 / 050
סוזן זונטג
2017
אלומיניום, פלדת אלחלד, הדפסה דיגיטלית
250× 145 × 35 ס"מ

013 / 051 / 131
אשה קוראת
2017
אלומיניום, פלדת אלחלד, הדפסה דיגיטלית
95 × 80 × 25 ס"מ

015–014 / 099
אנו הפליטים
2018
אלומיניום, פלדת אלחלד, הדפסה דיגיטלית
135 × 100 × 87 ס"מ

016 / 017 / 134–135
שד' רוטשילד 2
2016
אלומיניום, פלדת אלחלד, הדפסה דיגיטלית
133 × 140 × 39 ס"מ

142 / 143
היכל הספר (פרדריק קיסלר וארמן ברטוס)
2017
אלומיניום, פלדת אלחלד, הדפסה דיגיטלית
165 × 145 × 35 ס"מ

044–047 / 049 / 052 / 100–107 / 132–133/ 144
יש עוד שאלות?
1998
בד, מחבטי בייסבול
ממדים משתנים

018–019 / 048–049 / 144
מעדן טורקי
2006
ברונזה, סלע דיאבז
171 × 44 × 30 ס"מ

012 / 137
מראה
2017
אלומיניום, פלדת אלחלד, הדפסה דיגיטלית
118 × 103 × 17 ס"מ

כריכה אחורית / 139 / 140–141
אנו הפליטים
2018
אלומיניום, פלדת אלחלד, הדפסה דיגיטלית
127 × 145 × 25 ס"מ

020 / 136
מינימה מורליה (תיאודור אדורנו)
2017
אלומיניום, פלדת אלחלד, הדפסה דיגיטלית
128 × 150 × 42 ס"מ
(לא מוצגת בתערוכה)

148
שד' רוטשילד
2016
שיש, אלומיניום, פלדת אל-חלד, הדפס דיגיטלי
133 × 140 × 39 ס"מ

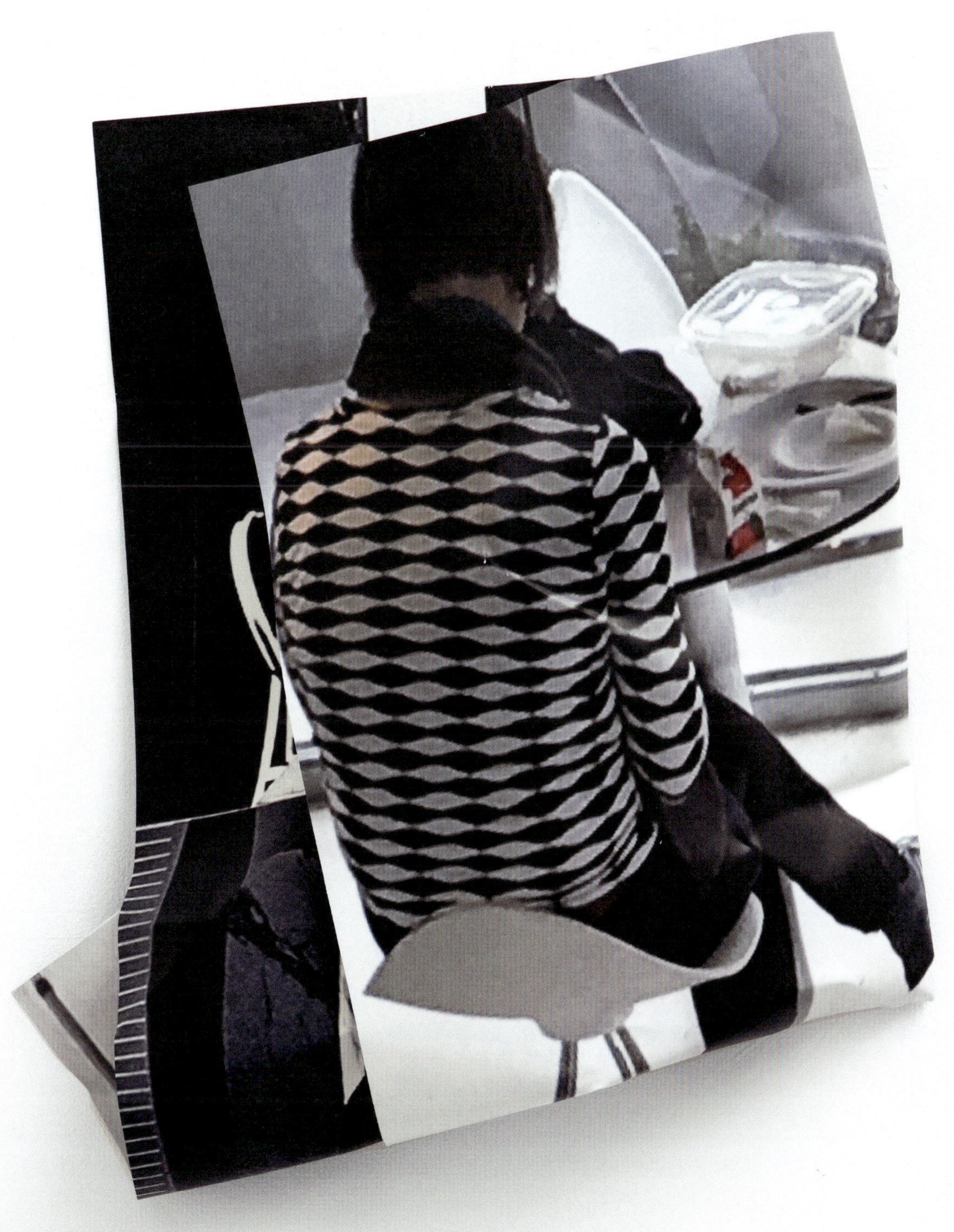

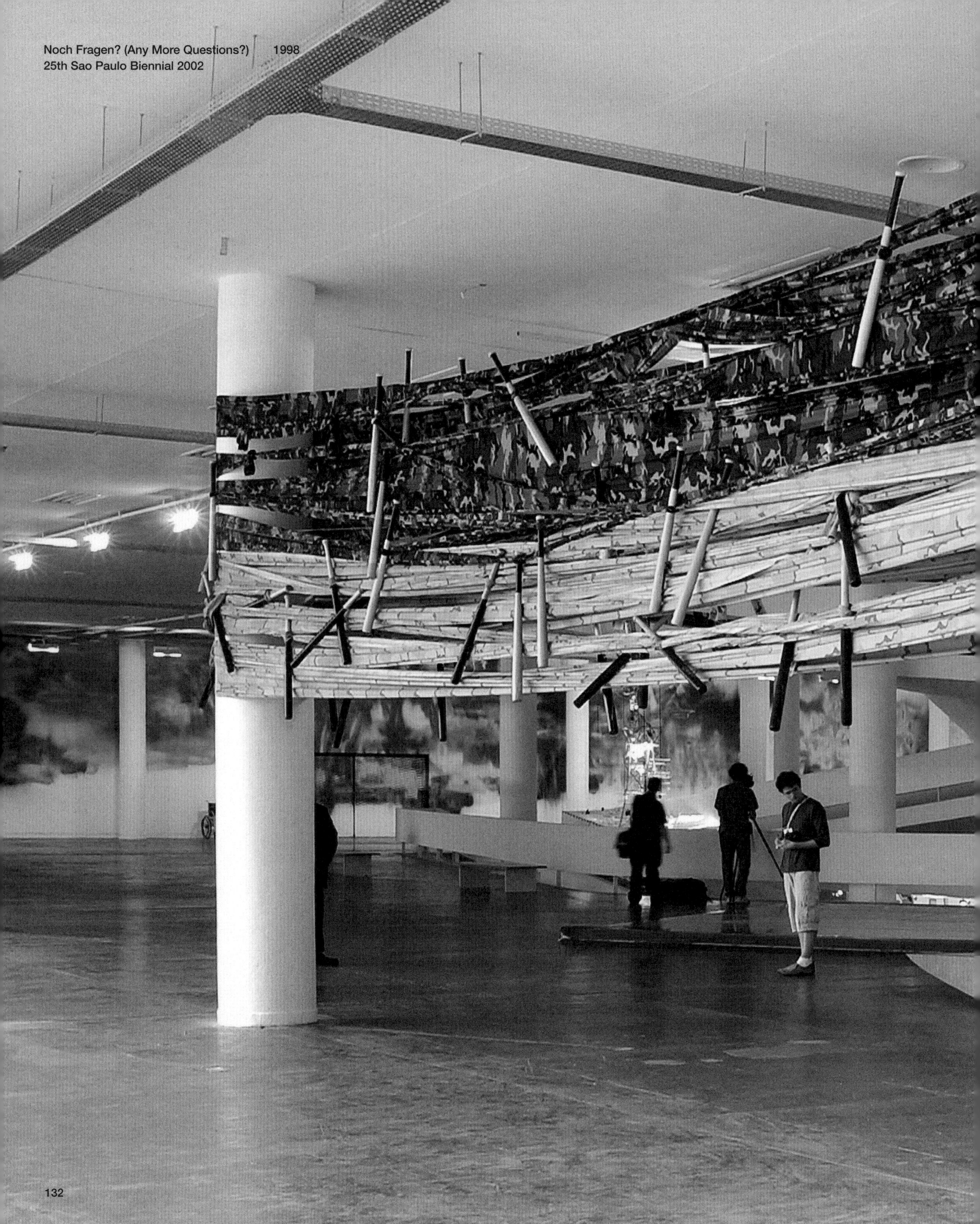

Noch Fragen? (Any More Questions?) 1998
25th Sao Paulo Biennial 2002

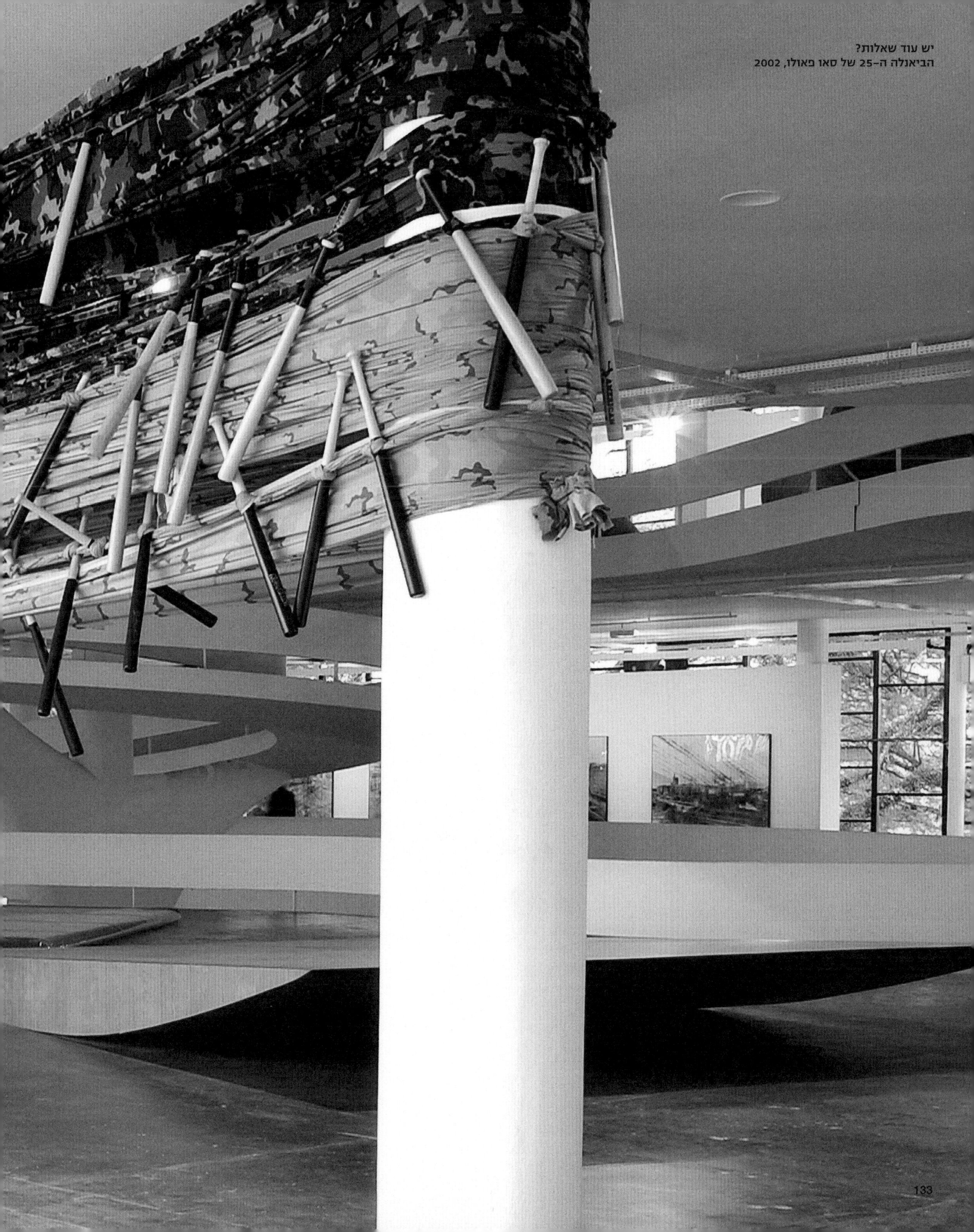

יש עוד שאלות?
הביאנלה ה–25 של סאו פאולו, 2002

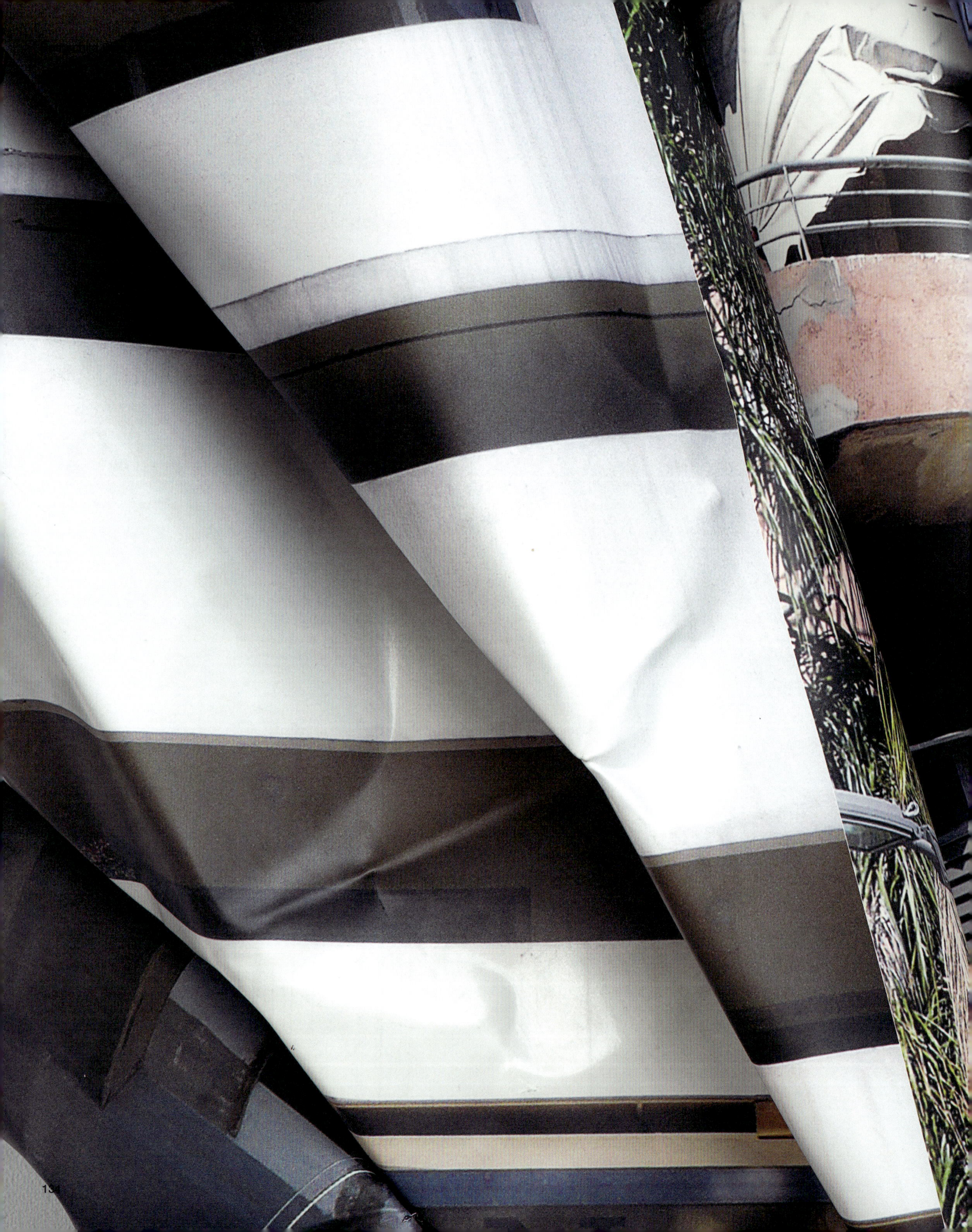

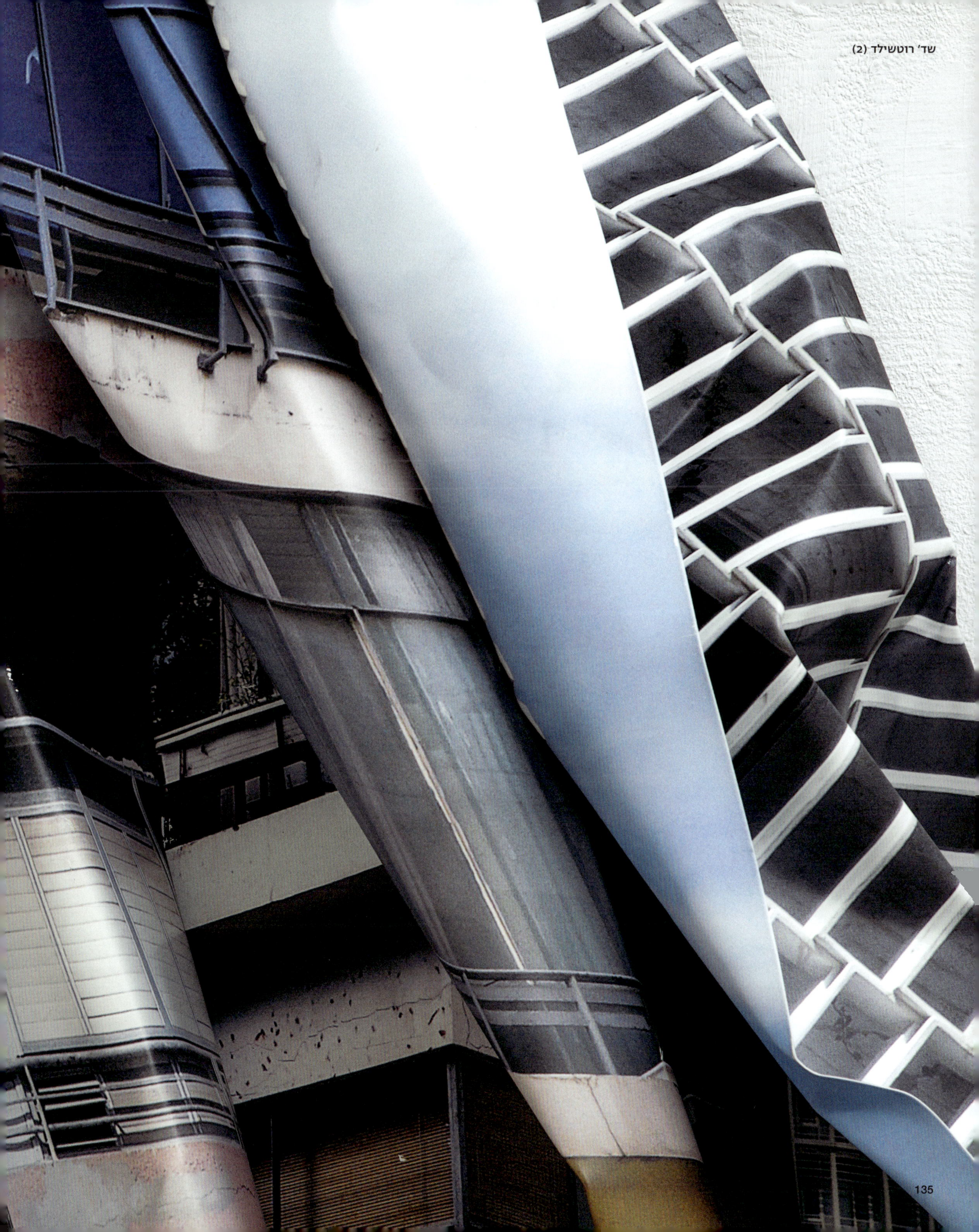

שד' רוטשילד (2)

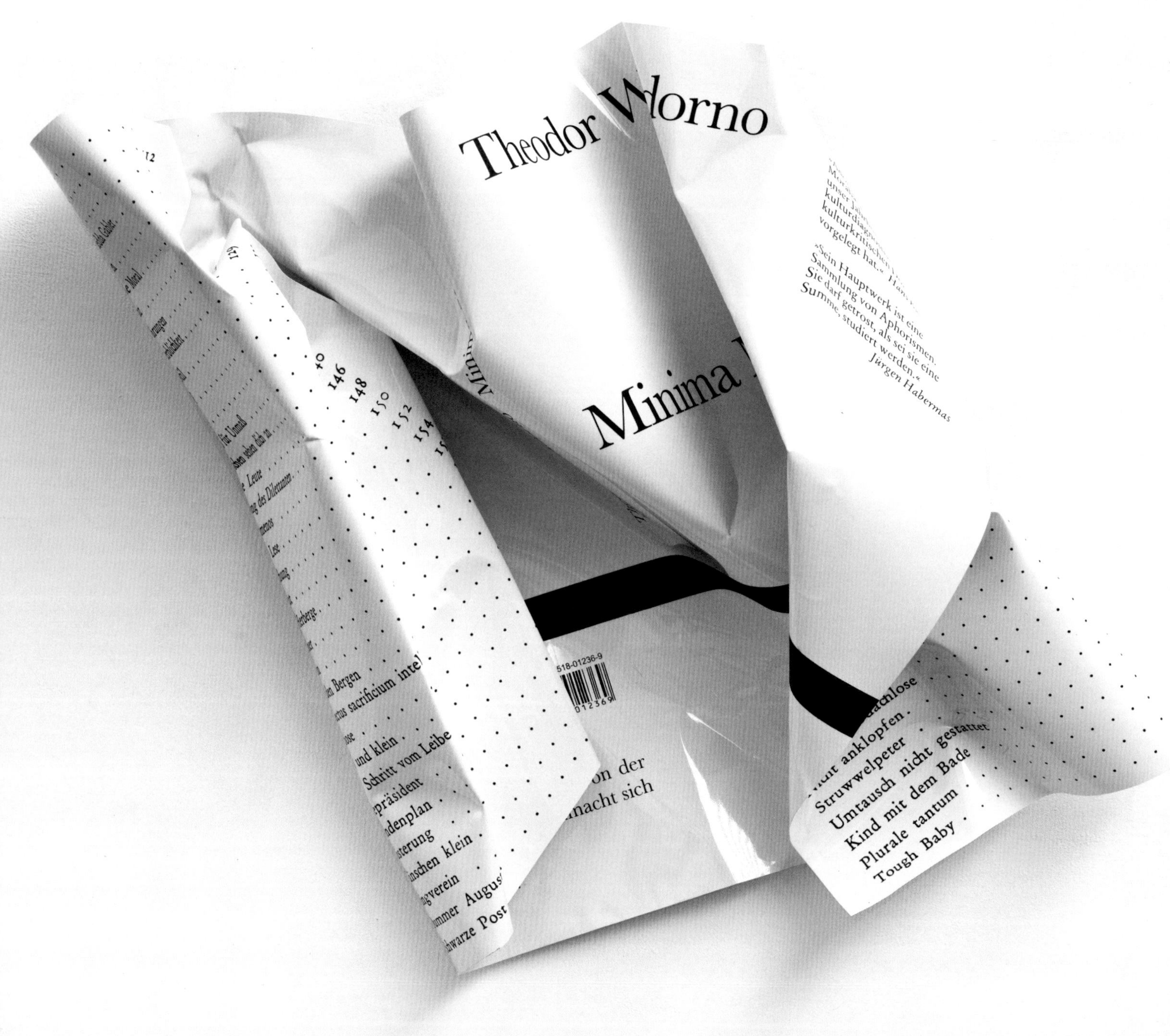
Theodor
orno
Minima
»Sein Hauptwerk ist eine
Sammlung von Aphorismen.
Sie darf getrost, als sei sie eine
Summe, studiert werden.«
Jürgen Habermas
Struwwelpeter
Umtausch nicht gestattet
Kind mit dem Bade
Plurale tantum
Tough Baby
Schritt vom Leibe
und klein
schwarze Post

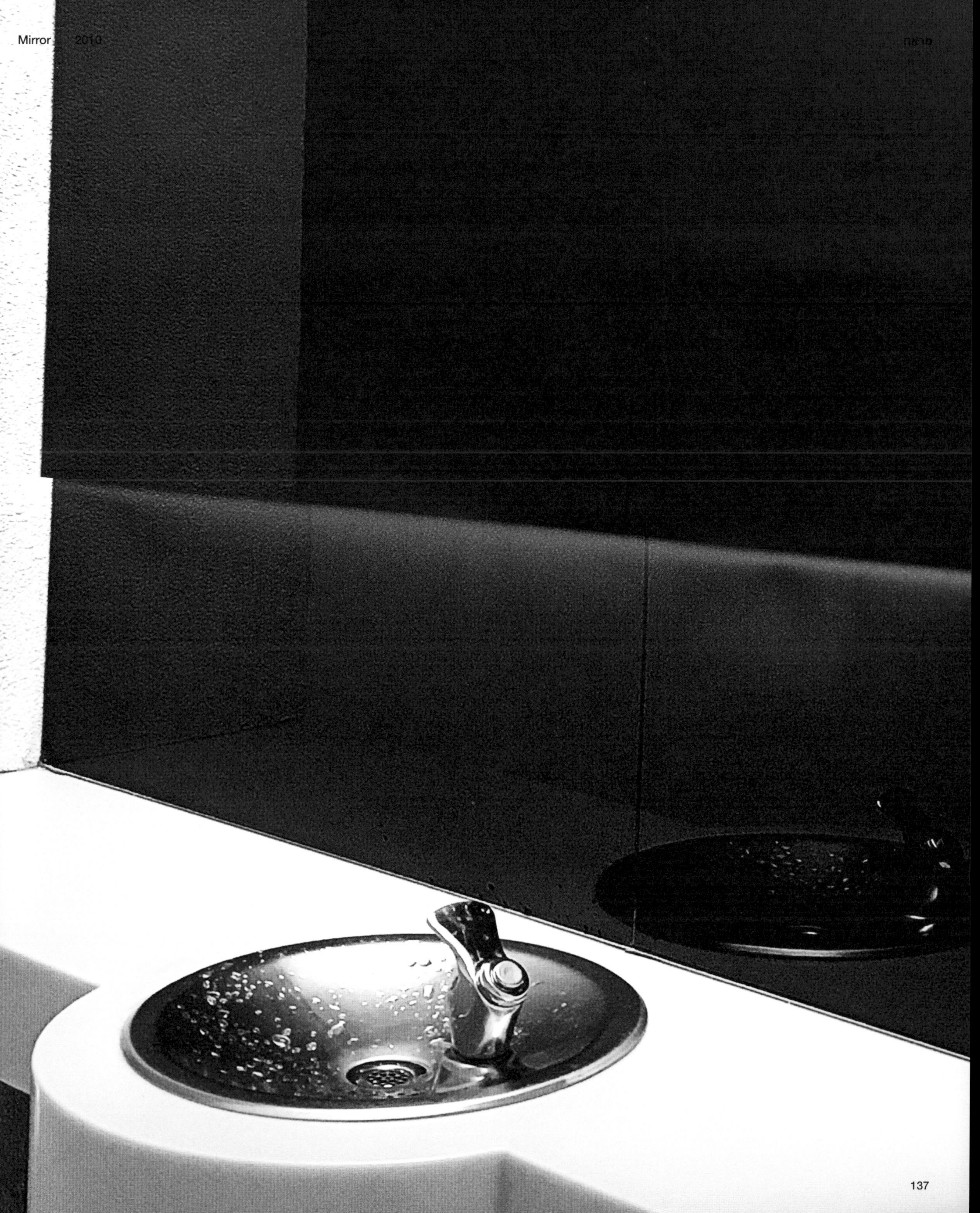

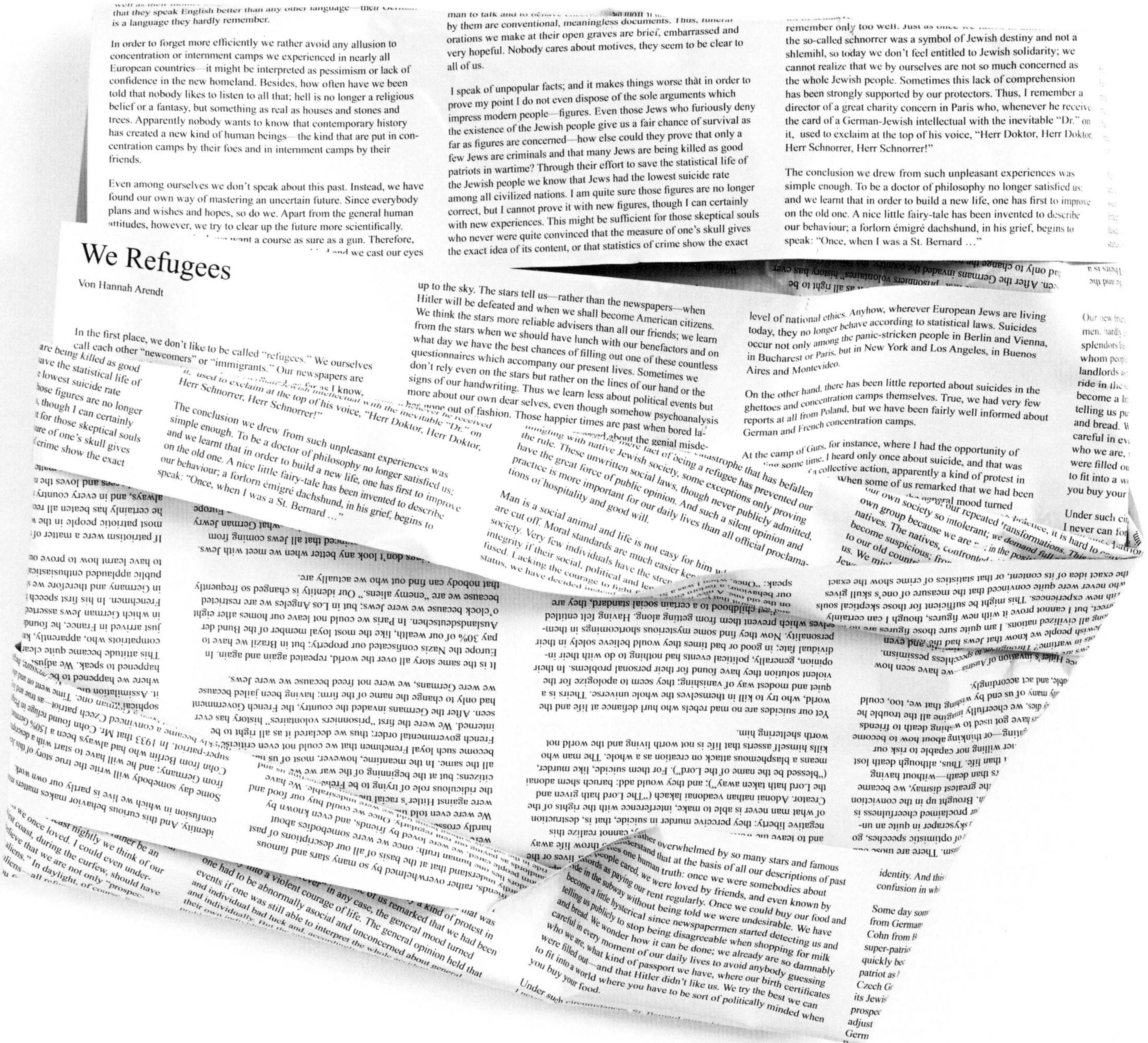

that they speak English better than any other language—their German is a language they hardly remember.

In order to forget more efficiently we rather avoid any allusion to concentration or internment camps we experienced in nearly all European countries—it might be interpreted as pessimism or lack of confidence in the new homeland. Besides, how often have we been told that nobody likes to listen to all that; hell is no longer a religious belief or a fantasy, but something as real as houses and stones and trees. Apparently nobody wants to know that contemporary history has created a new kind of human beings—the kind that are put in concentration camps by their foes and in internment camps by their friends.

Even among ourselves we don't speak about this past. Instead, we have found our own way of mastering an uncertain future. Since everybody plans and wishes and hopes, so do we. Apart from the general human attitudes, however, we try to clear up the future more scientifically. … want a course as sure as a gun. Therefore, … and we cast our eyes

by them are conventional, meaningless documents. Thus, funeral orations we make at their open graves are brief, embarrassed and very hopeful. Nobody cares about motives, they seem to be clear to all of us.

I speak of unpopular facts; and it makes things worse that in order to prove my point I do not even dispose of the sole arguments which impress modern people—figures. Even those Jews who furiously deny the existence of the Jewish people give us a fair chance of survival as far as figures are concerned—how else could they prove that only a few Jews are criminals and that many Jews are being killed as good patriots in wartime? Through their effort to save the statistical life of the Jewish people we know that Jews had the lowest suicide rate among all civilized nations. I am quite sure those figures are no longer correct, but I cannot prove it with new figures, though I can certainly with new experiences. This might be sufficient for those skeptical souls who never were quite convinced that the measure of one's skull gives the exact idea of its content, or that statistics of crime show the exact

remember only too well. Just as once … the so-called schnorrer was a symbol of Jewish destiny and not a shlemihl, so today we don't feel entitled to Jewish solidarity; we cannot realize that we by ourselves are not so much concerned as the whole Jewish people. Sometimes this lack of comprehension has been strongly supported by our protectors. Thus, I remember a director of a great charity concern in Paris who, whenever he receive[d] the card of a German-Jewish intellectual with the inevitable "Dr." on it, used to exclaim at the top of his voice, "Herr Doktor, Herr Doktor, Herr Schnorrer, Herr Schnorrer!"

The conclusion we drew from such unpleasant experiences was simple enough. To be a doctor of philosophy no longer satisfied us; and we learnt that in order to build a new life, one has first to improve on the old one. A nice little fairy-tale has been invented to describe our behaviour; a forlorn émigré dachshund, in his grief, begins to speak: "Once, when I was a St. Bernard …"

We Refugees

Von Hannah Arendt

In the first place, we don't like to be called "refugees." We ourselves call each other "newcomers" or "immigrants." Our newspapers are …

up to the sky. The stars tell us—rather than the newspapers—when Hitler will be defeated and when we shall become American citizens. We think the stars more reliable advisers than all our friends; we learn from the stars when we should have lunch with our benefactors and on what day we have the best chances of filling out one of these countless questionnaires which accompany our present lives. Sometimes we don't rely even on the stars but rather on the lines of our hand or the signs of our handwriting. Thus we learn less about political events but more about our own dear selves, even though somehow psychoanalysis has gone out of fashion. Those happier times are past when bored la…

level of national ethics. Anyhow, wherever European Jews are living today, they no longer behave according to statistical laws. Suicides occur not only among the panic-stricken people in Berlin and Vienna, in Bucharest or Paris, but in New York and Los Angeles, in Buenos Aires and Montevideo.

On the other hand, there has been little reported about suicides in the ghettoes and concentration camps themselves. True, we had very few reports at all from Poland, but we have been fairly well informed about German and French concentration camps.

At the camp of Gurs, for instance, where I had the opportunity of spending some time, I heard only once about suicide, and that was … collective action, apparently a kind of protest in … When some of us remarked that we had been …

The conclusion we drew from such unpleasant experiences was simple enough. To be a doctor of philosophy no longer satisfied us; and we learnt that in order to build a new life, one has first to improve on the old one. A nice little fairy-tale has been invented to describe our behaviour; a forlorn émigré dachshund, in his grief, begins to speak: "Once, when I was a St. Bernard …"

… the rule. These unwritten social laws, though never publicly admitted, have the great force of public opinion. And such a silent opinion and practice is more important for our daily lives than all official proclamations or hospitality and good will.

Man is a social animal and life is not easy for him w… are cut off. Moral standards are much easier ke…

… overwhelmed by so many stars and famous … understand that at the basis of all our descriptions of past … one human truth: once we were somebodies about … people cared, we were loved by friends, and even known by landlords as paying our rent regularly. Once we could buy our food and ride in the subway without being told we were undesirable. We have become a little hysterical since newspapermen started detecting us and telling us publicly to stop being disagreeable when shopping for milk and bread. We wonder how it can be done; we already are so damnably careful in every moment of our daily lives to avoid anybody guessing who we are, what kind of passport we have, where our birth certificates were filled out—and that Hitler didn't like us. We try the best we can to fit into a world where you have to be sort of politically minded when you buy your food.

Under such circumstances …

has created a new kind of human beings—the kind that are put in concentration camps by their foes and in internment camps by their friends.

Even among ourselves we don't speak about this past. Instead, we have found our own way of mastering an uncertain future. Since everybody plans and wishes and hopes, so do we. Apart from the general human attitudes, however, we try to clear up the future more scientifically.

... want a course as sure as a gun. Therefore, ... and we cast our eyes

the existence of the Je... far as figures are conc... few Jews are criminal... patriots in wartime? T... the Jewish people we... among all civilized na... correct, but I cannot p... with new experiences... who never were quite... the exact idea of its c...

We Refugees

Von Hannah Arendt

up to the sky. The stars tell u... Hitler will be defeated and w... We think the stars more relia... from the stars when we shou... what day we have the best ch... questionnaires which accomp... don't rely even on the stars b... signs of our handwriting. Thu... more about our own dear selv... has gone out of fashion. Those...

In the first place, we don't like to be called "refugees." We ourselves call each other "newcomers" or "immigrants." Our newspapers are

are being killed as good ... ave the statistical life of ... e lowest suicide rate ... hose figures are no longer ... though I can certainly ... t for those skeptical souls ... ure of one's skull gives ... f crime show the exact

... it, used to exclaim at the top of his voice, "Herr Doktor, Herr Doktor, Herr Schnorrer, Herr Schnorrer!"

The conclusion we drew from such unpleasant experiences was simple enough. To be a doctor of philosophy no longer satisfied us; and we learnt that in order to build a new life, one has first to improve on the old one. A nice little fairy-tale has been invented to describe our behaviour; a forlorn émigré dachshund, in his grief, begins to speak: "Once, when I was a St. Bernard ..."

... the r... have ... practic... tions o...

Man is a ... are cut off... society. Ver... integrity if th... fused. Lackin... status, we hav...

how else could they prove that only a
at many Jews are being killed as good
their effort to save the statistical life of
at Jews had the lowest suicide rate
am quite sure those figures are no longer
with new figures, though I can certainly
ight be sufficient for those skeptical souls
ced that the measure of one's skull gives
r that statistics of crime show the exact

it, used to exclaim at the top of his voice, "Herr Doktor, Herr Doktor, Herr Schnorrer, Herr Schnorrer!"

אנו הפליטים

The conclusion we drew from such unpleasant experiences was simple enough. To be a doctor of philosophy no longer satisfied us; and we learnt that in order to build a new life, one has first to improve on the old one. A nice little fairy-tale has been invented to describe our behaviour; a forlorn émigré dachshund, in his grief, begins to speak: "Once, when I was a St. Bernard …"

er than the newspapers—when
shall become American citizens.
sers than all our friends; we learn
unch with our benefactors and on
f filling out one of these countless
present lives. Sometimes we
on the lines of our hand or the
rn less about political events but
though somehow psychoanalysis
times are past when bored la-
versed about the genial misde-

level of national ethics. Anyhow, wherever European Jews are living today, they no longer behave according to statistical laws. Suicides occur not only among the panic-stricken people in Berlin and Vienna, in Bucharest or Paris, but in New York and Los Angeles, in Buenos Aires and Montevideo.

On the other hand, there has been little reported about suicides in the ghettoes and concentration camps themselves. True, we had very few reports at all from Poland, but we have been fairly well informed about German and French concentration camps.

At the camp of Gurs, for instance, where I had the opportunity of … some time, I heard only once about suicide, and that was … a collective action, apparently a kind of protest in … When some of us remarked that we had been … the general mood turned

Our new
men, ha
splendo
whom
landlor
ride in
become
telling u
and brea
careful i
who we
were fille
to fit into
you buy

… the mere fact of being a refugee has prevented our
… catastrophe that has befallen
th native Jewish society, some exceptions only proving
se unwritten social laws, though never publicly admitted,
force of public opinion. And such a silent opinion and
e important for our daily lives than all official proclama-
ity and good will.

imal and life is not easy for him wh
tandards are much easier kept
lividuals have the streng
l, political and leg
urage to fight f

our own society so intolerant; we demand full …
own group because we are not in the posit…
natives. The natives, confronted …
become suspicious; from …
to our old countri…
us. We migh…
Jews

Under suc
I never can

of what man never is able to make, interference with the ri… Creator. Adonai nathan veadonai lakach ("The Lord hath g… the Lord hath taken away"); and they would add: baruch sh… ("blessed be the name of the Lord"). For them suicide, like … means a blasphemous attack on creation as a whole. The m… kills himself asserts that life is not worth living and the wor… worth sheltering him.

Yet our suicides are no mad rebels who hurl defiance at life … world, who try to kill in themselves the whole universe. Th… quiet and modest way of vanishing; they seem to apologize … violent solution they have found for their personal problem… opinion, generally, political events had nothing to do with t… dividual fate; in good or bad times they would believe solel… personality. Now they find some mysterious shortcomings i… …lves which prevent them from getting along. Having felt e… …childhood to a certain social standard the

…ur proclaimed cheerfulness is
…h. Brought up in the conviction
…the greatest dismay, we became
…s than death—without having
… than life. Thus, although death lost
…er willing nor capable to risk our
…ting—or thinking about how to become
…s have got used to wishing death to friends
…y dies, we cheerfully imagine all the trouble he
…lly many of us end by wishing that we, too, could
…uble, and act accordingly.

…ce Hitler's invasion of Austria—we have seen how
… to speechless pessimism.
…ots in wartime? …
…Jewish people we know that Jews had the … and even
…ong all civilized nations. I am quite sure those figures are …
…rect, but I cannot prove it with new figures, though I can certainly
…h new experiences. This might be sufficient for those skeptical souls
… never were quite convinced that the measure of one's skull gives
…xact idea of its content, or that statistics of crime show the exact

…seen. After the Germans invaded the country, the French …
…had only to change the … "prisonniers volontaires" history has ever … it as all right to be

With us from …

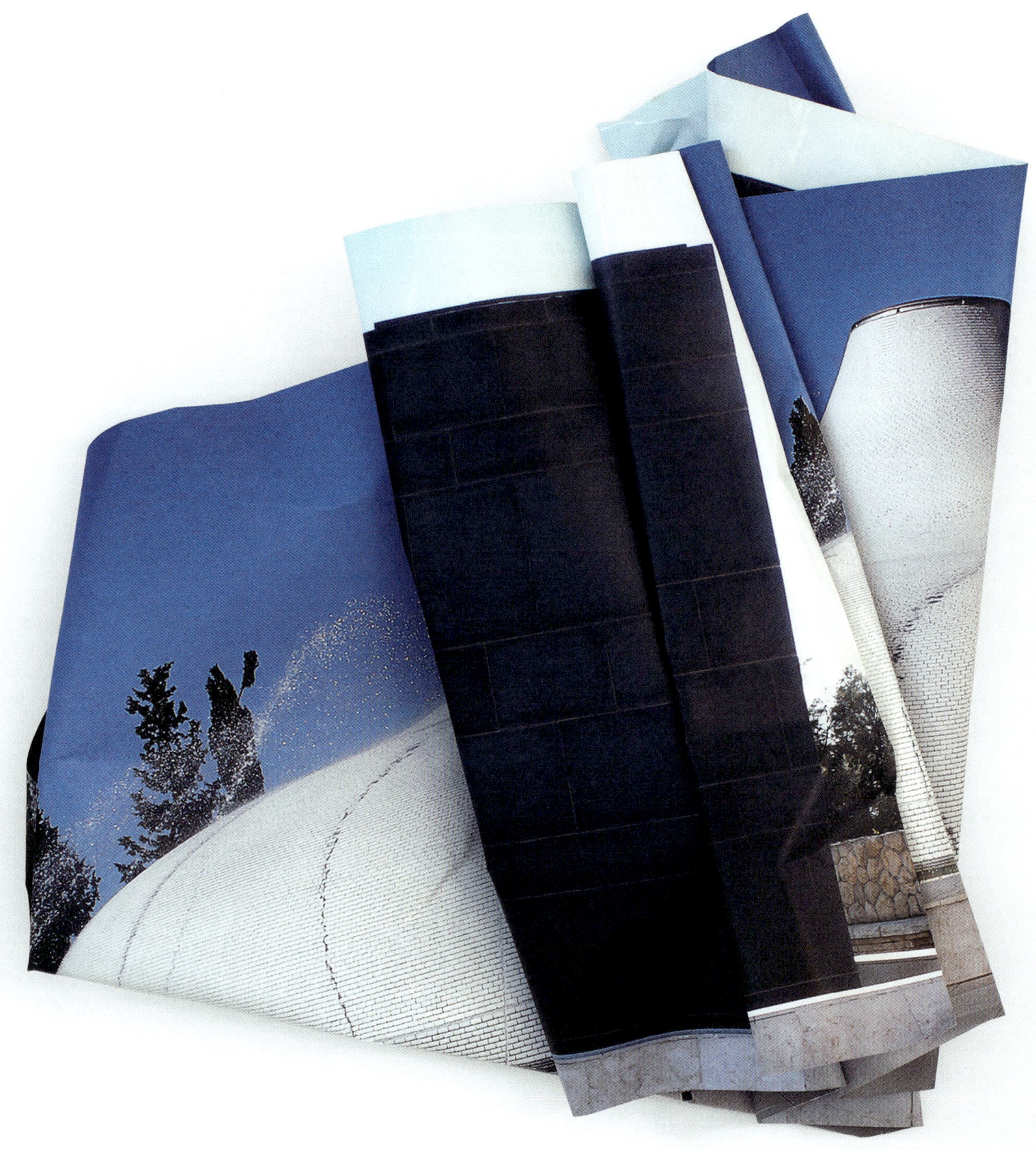

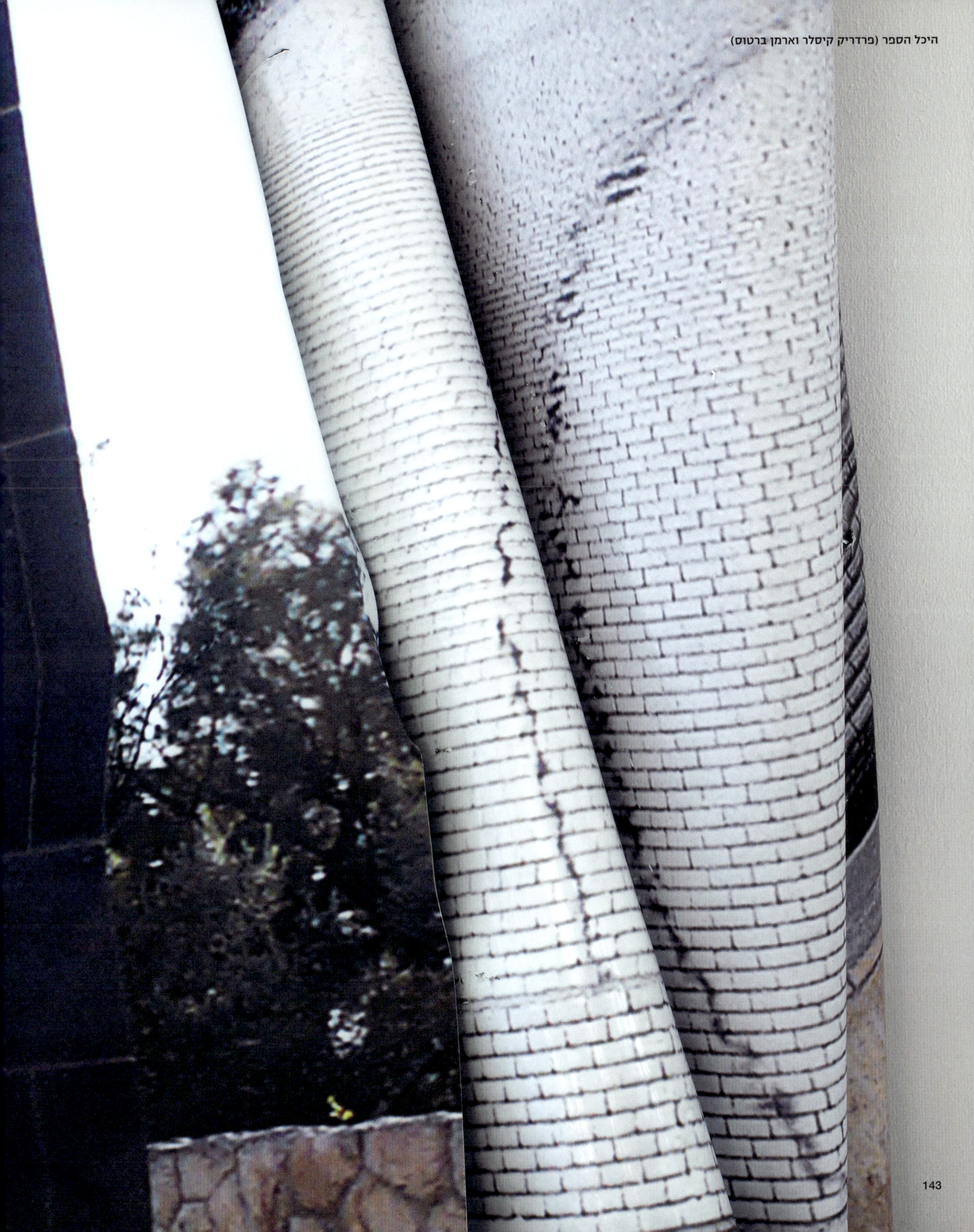
היכל הספר (פרדריק קיסלר וארמן ברטוס)

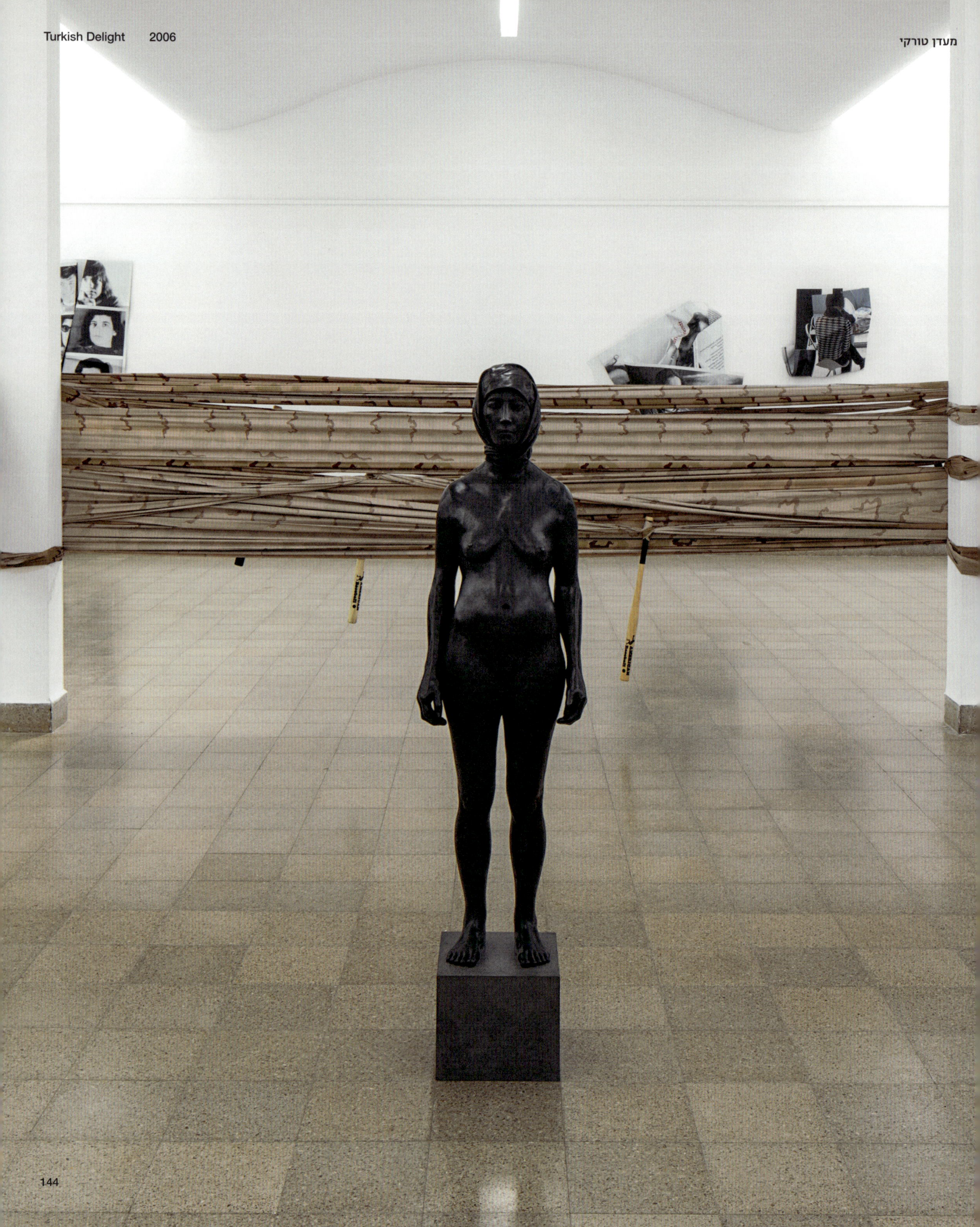

פתח דבר
יניב שפירא

התערוכה 'אולף מטצל בעין חרוד' והקטלוג המלווה אותה מאפשרים לקהל הישראלי להתוודע מקרוב להיקף ולתכני יצירתו של אולף מטצל, הנמנה על הבולטים באמניה העכשוויים של גרמניה. עבודותיו כוללות הצבות פיסוליות גדולות במרחב הציבורי העירוני, תבליטים העשויים מהדפסי משי על יריעות דקות של מתכת ורישומים עזי מבע שעוצבו במידה רבה בנסיבות של ביוגרפיה אישית ולאומית.

מטצל נולד במזרח ברלין של ראשית שנות ה-50 וכילד בן 9 חווה את הקמתה של חומת ברלין שחצתה בין לילה את זיכרונות הילדות שלו לשניים: בין חברי ילדות, בין מזרח למערב, בין מותר לאסור. חוויה מעצבת זו היא המכתיבה את עיסוקו החוזר ונשנה במוטיבים של גדרות וחסמים, בשיח חברתי ופוליטי, בסוגיות של זהויות לאומיות וב"תרבויות מקבילות", כפי שביטא בספרו 'השכן הטוב' שקטע ממנו מובא בקטלוג זה:

> היה משהו מובן מאליו באופן שבו הסתדרנו עם בני ובנות המהגרים, שהיה קשור גם לסודות הטיפוסיים שחלקנו. יחד עם זאת, איש לא הזמין אותך לביתו – אנשים נטו להסתגר בדלת אמות. [...] למרות הליברליות שאפיינה את יחסינו, היה בהם משהו הרמטי, שכיום היה זוכה להגדרה 'תרבויות מקבילות. מכאן גם לא מפתיע שמרכיב מהותי בעבודותיו של מטצל הוא ביצירת גשרים חברתיים ותרבותיים, ממש כשם שהן נובעות מתוך הבנת כוחו של הדימוי האמנותי ויכולתו לפעול על רוח האדם.

תערוכה זו המוצגת במשכן לאמנות בעין חרוד מכנסת עבודות מוכרות לצד כאלה שנעשו במיוחד עבורה, תולדה של ביקורו של מטצל בישראל בסתיו 2016. הוא שוטט ברחובות תל אביב וירושלים, ביקר והציג בעין חרוד (בתערוכה "אמנות עכשווית מגרמניה") וקיבץ דימויים מהמרחב הציבורי הישראלי, בהם משדרות רוטשילד ומהיכל הספר. הללו מצטרפים לעיסוק בדמותן והגותן של חנה ארנדט וסוזן זונטג, למיצב 'עוד שאלות?' שהותאם למידותיו של האולם המרכזי במוזאון ולעבודה 'מעדן טורקי', המקבלת יתר תוקף בהקשר הנוכחי.

הספציפיות של תערוכה זו נובעת גם מתחושות הקרבה של מטצל למשכן לאמנות, עין חרוד כמייצג של ערכים אנושיים ואוניברסליים הנקשרים אצלו עם זיכרונות ילדות. בביקורו הראשון במקום העיד כי חש שהמוזיאון והאווירה המסוימת שהוא משרה חופפים לקוד פנימי ותרבותי עמוק ובר זיהוי, "הבנתי הכול מיד, כאילו הכרתי אותו מזה זמן רב, למרות שזה עתה הגעתי לשם".

אני מבקש להודות מקרב לב לאולף מטצל על שיתוף הפעולה הפורה, על השיחה הפתוחה ועל התערוכה רבת ההשראה והמשמעויות שהציב. תודה גדולה ומיוחדת למתיאס וינצן, אוצר התערוכה ומי שרקם את רעיון הצגתה מתחילתו וכן על השיחה מאירת העניים שקיים עם מטצל והמופיעה בקטלוג, צרור תודות לגליה בר אור, על האוצרות ועל רשימתה המאירה את יצירתו של מטצל בהקשר מקומי ועכשווי. תודה לכותבים האחרים, כריסטוף היינריך והנס בלטינג שתרמו להרחבת המבט הפרשני ביצירתו של מטצל. תודה לפטרה ליר על עיצוב הקטלוג הנאה, לפולין קאמברס ושרה טרנקר על התרגום והעריכה האנגלית, לטליה הלקין ועמי אשר על התרגום והעריכה העברית. תודות ליובל בראל ולזהר דורון על העזרה בהתקנת התערוכה. לבסוף תודה מעומק הלב לשותפיי לצוות המשכן לאמנות, שהקדישו ממרצם ומאהבתם לאמנות להקמתה של תערוכה חשובה זו.

מוקדש לאליזבת הנזל

הקטלוג הזה יוצא לאור לרגל התערוכה
משכן לאמנות, עין חרוד
24 בינואר עד 14 ביולי, 2018

אוצרים: מתיאס וינצן וגליה בר אור

עורך: מתיאס וינצן
עבודת עריכה: נינה הולם
עריכה בעברית: עמי אשר
תרגום לעברית: טליה הלקין
תרגום לאנגלית: פאולין קאמברס
עריכה באנגלית: שרה טרנקר
עיצוב גרפי: WIGEL, פטרה ליר
ליתוגרפיה: Reproline Genceller, מינכן
הדפסה וכריכה: Druckerei Vogl, מינכן
הודפס בגרמניה

כריכה
חנה ארנדט, 2017 (פרט)
אנו הפליטים, 2018 (פרט)

מידע ביבליוגרפי פורסם על ידי הספריה הלאומית של גרמניה
הספריה הלאומית של גרמניה רושמת את הפרסום הזה
בביבליוגרפיה הלאומית של גרמניה; נתונים ביבליוגרפיים מפורטים
מופיעים ב: http://www.dnb.de
ISBN: 978-3-95476-244-6

הודפס בגרמניה
מופץ ע״י הוצאה לאור
DISTANZ
www.distanz.de

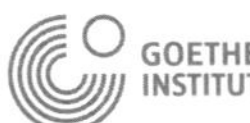

משכן לאמנות עין חרוד, ע״ש חיים אתר בע״מ (חל״צ)
Mishkan Museum of Art, Ein Harod

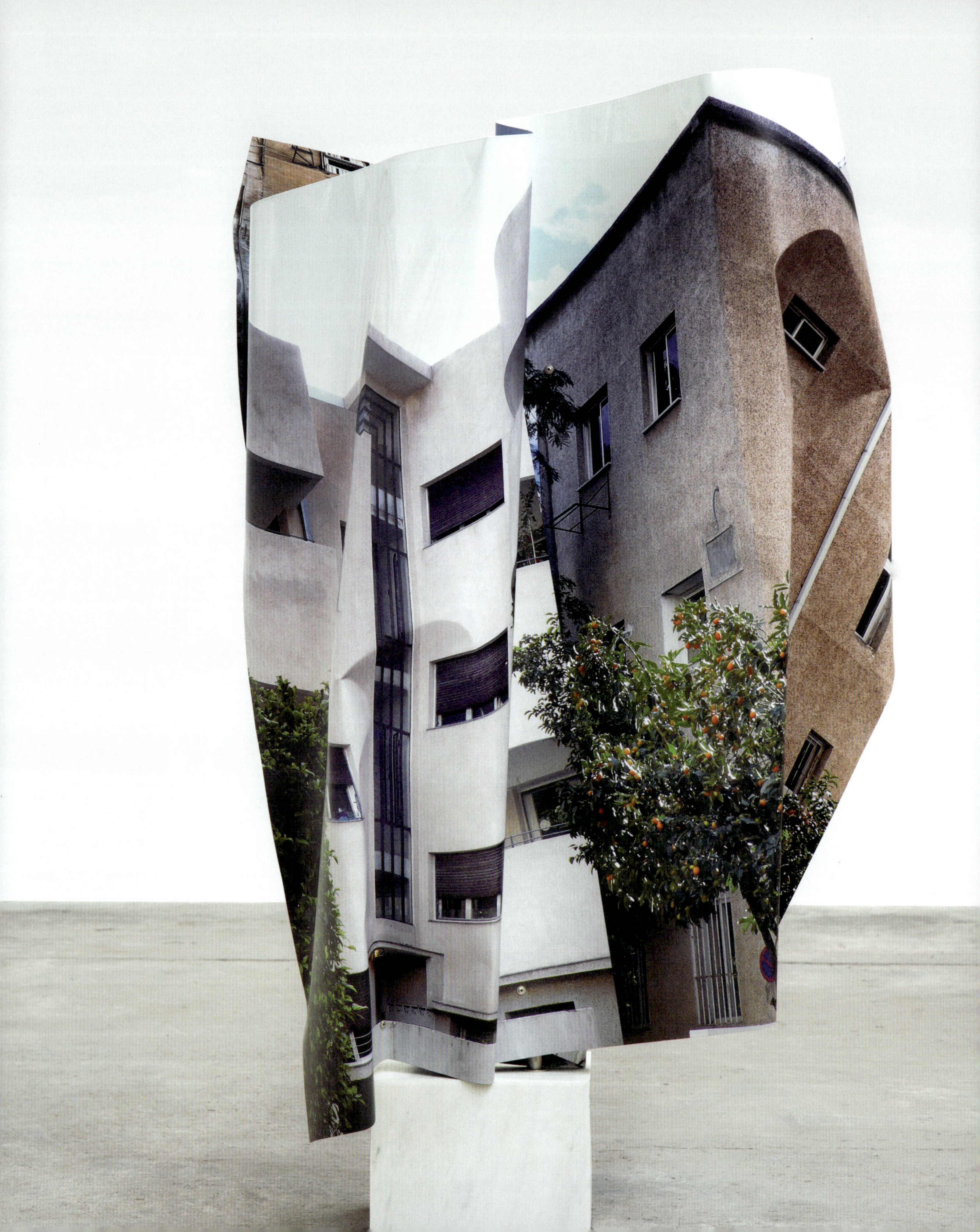

אולף מטצל בעין חרוד

24 בינואר עד 14 ביולי, 2018

משכן לאמנות עין חרוד, ע"ש חיים אתר בע"מ (חל"צ)
Mishkan Museum of Art, Ein Harod

אולף מטצל בעין חרוד